Fashioned from Nature

Fashioned from Nature

Edited by Edwina Ehrman
V&A Publishing

Published to accompany the exhibition *Fashioned from Nature* at the
Victoria and Albert Museum, London, from 21 April 2018 to 27 January 2019.

Supported by:

First published by V&A Publishing, 2018
Victoria and Albert Museum
South Kensington
London SW7 2RL
www.vandapublishing.com

Distributed in North America by Abrams, an imprint of ABRAMS

ISBN 9781 85177 945 1

10 9 8 7 6 5 4 3 2 1
2022 2021 2020 2019 2018

Cover and flaps: William Kilburn (1745–1818), designs for printed cotton (detail, see
pl. 38). Watercolour on paper. Britain, c.1788–92. Purchased from the funds of the
H.B. Murray Bequest, V&A: E.894:49/1&2–1978
p. 2: detail of pl. 6

Designer: Charlotte Heal Design
Copy-editor: Linda Schofield
Origination: Altaimage
Index: Hilary Bird

New photography by Robert Auton, V&A Photographic Studio

Printed by Printer Trento, Italy, using vegetable-based inks

V&A Publishing
Supporting the world's leading
museum of art and design,
the Victoria and Albert
Museum, London

Forewords   6
Introduction   10

Chapter 1:   18

1600–1800

From Cocoon to Court: 46
An Eighteenth-Century Mantua

Drawn from Nature: 1600–1800   54

Chapter 2:   62

1800–1900

Walking in Flora and Fauna: 94
A Nineteenth-Century Dress and Hat

Engaging with Nature: The Fern Craze   100

Chapter 3:   106

1900–1990

Cellulose in Couture: An Evening Coat   136

Imagining Nature: 1952–2010   142

Chapter 4:   148

1990–Present

Traceability and Responsibility: 174
A Twenty-First Century T-Shirt

Endnotes   180
Bibliography   183
Glossary   187
Contributors   188
Acknowledgements   188
Picture Credits   188
Index   189

Foreword

BY

Emma Watson

Over the past decade, I've become fastened to sustainability, transparency and my responsibility to question and influence how the fashion industry is evolving. At a time when fashion is the second most polluting industry and fast fashion is the norm, it is imperative that we collectively address our influence as consumers and the impact of the industry in its current wasteful state. Now is the time for thoughtful fashion.

At 18, I wrote my A-Level geography coursework on the topic of sustainable fashion and interviewed Fair Trade expert Alex Nichols at Saïd Business School in Oxford. The more I learned, the more I realized how much I did not know and how much I needed to learn. In my early twenties, I travelled to Bangladesh and saw Rana Plaza garment factory a few years before it collapsed. I met a girl my age, working for Fair Trade company People Tree, living a very different life from my own: she was exhausted from trying to get an education at the same time as doing a full-time job. This encounter expanded my understanding of what having a job and fair pay meant. While she was working unbelievably hard, she was also proud of her work and deeply grateful to be receiving an education. This was what a fair working wage could mean to another woman.

After returning home and reignited again, I started to reexamine my participation in fashion and the urgency of a healthier, more responsible system. Utilizing the red carpet, I pledged to wear sustainable designs by creatives embracing concepts and materials that could reshape the future of fashion. This challenge spread into my daily wardrobe. I find peace of mind knowing what I'm wearing is either vintage and reused, or carefully sourced and produced in a way that strives to improve the working lives of the makers. I don't get it right all the time, but if I start by asking questions then I'm conscious of making a better choice.

Highlighted in the exhibition is a particular dress of mine, which I wore to the Met Gala in 2016 (pl. 1). In collaboration with Calvin Klein, every part of the gown was produced with sustainability in mind – from the use of Newlife (a yarn made from post-consumer plastic bottles) to the zippers fashioned from recycled materials. The threads of this dress were woven in a reinvented tale of our consumption. We even designed different layers so that separate components could be worn again in different ways. I am proud of this dress.

Clothes are something that touch our lives every day, and I admire the Victoria and Albert Museum for creating this exhibition and book to highlight the importance of questioning where, how and by whom our clothes are made. Regardless of social or economic status, we can all dress and shop more mindfully and sustainably. It is so important and timely that we now re-conceptualize what it means to wear and consume, and what is fashionable.

1 / RIGHT Calvin Klein dress for the Green Carpet Challenge, worn by Emma Watson to the Met Gala, 2016

7

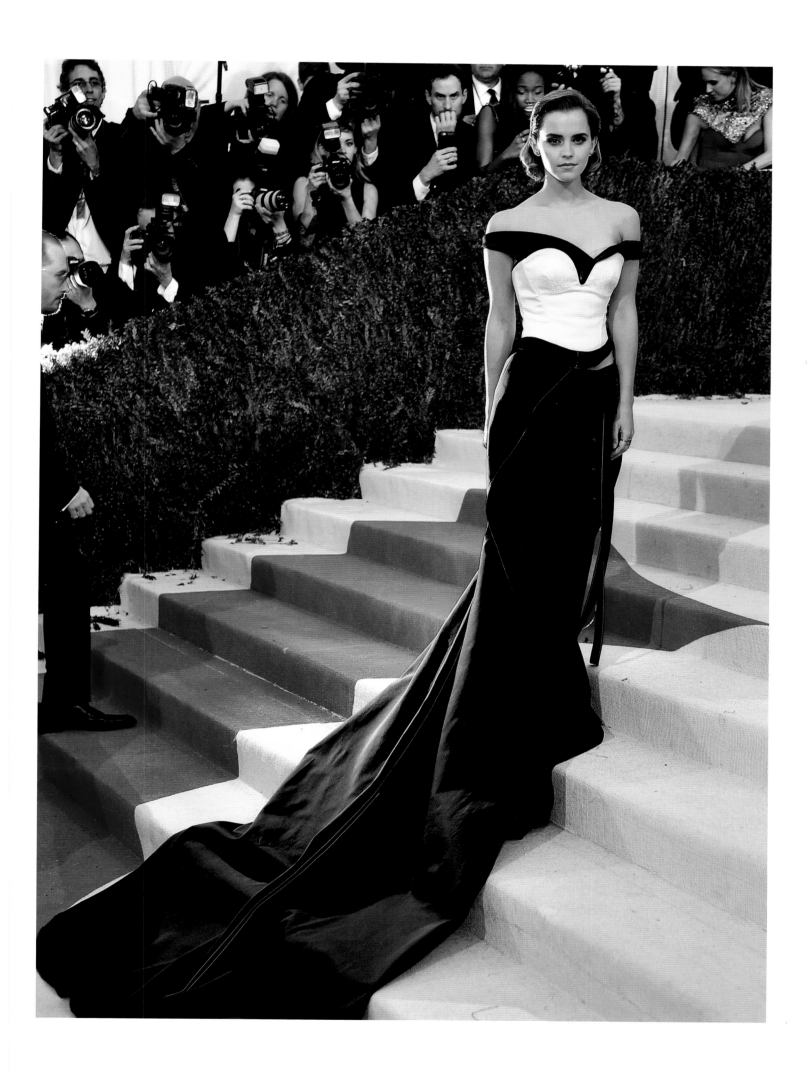

Sponsor's Foreword

BY

Marie-Emmanuelle Belzung
European Confederation of Flax and Hemp — CELC

In a world of fast fashion, flax stands out as a fibre of substance. It has been used for millennia and, as this book shows, its properties and versatility have given it an important place in the fashionable wardrobe. Today, more than ever, we appreciate its creative potential and inherent sustainability.

This blue-flowering plant is known as flax in its fibre form, and as linen when spun into yarn, knitted or woven to create a fabric. The expertise of the people who work in the flax industry – whether farmer, scutcher, spinner, weaver or knitter – is at the heart of a unique production process. Although it represents less than 1% of the world's natural fibres, flax enjoys a reputation far greater than that statistic suggests. Its success lies in how it feels. Linen has a special handle and can be both dense and fluid, heavy or airy, refined or rustic. Above all it provides pleasure and comfort.

Flax's environmental footprint is reassuringly light: it requires no irrigation, only rainfall; there is no waste and every part of the plant can be used; grown in rotation it benefits the soil and no GMOs are used in its cultivation. It is sustainable and traceable through two labels certified by the European Confederation of Flax and Hemp (CELC): European Flax®, which guarantees flax fibre of European origin; and Masters of Linen®, which guarantees 100% traceability within Europe, from fibre to finished product.

The European Confederation of Flax and Hemp, through the I Love Linen campaign, is pleased to sponsor *Fashioned from Nature*, an exhibition that connects field to fibre, fabric to fashion – past, present and future.

Director's Foreword

BY

Tristram Hunt

Fashioned from Nature celebrates the myriad ways that nature's immense beauty and power have inspired fashion: from embroidered motifs to exotic fabrics and fantastical prints. Spanning 400 years, this exhibition explores garments and accessories from the V&A's remarkable collection of textiles and fashion that have been influenced by this perennially rewarding resource.

However, at a time when we are increasingly scrutinizing fashion's material impact on the natural world, *Fashioned from Nature* also provides an opportune moment to investigate the often-devastating effects of fashion production on the earth's flora, fauna and environment. The exhibition examines the impact at every stage, from the materials and the global networks that supplied them, to their manufacture, production and use.

Fashioned from Nature asks what we can learn from the past in order to design a better fashion industry for the future. It challenges designers to create clothes that are both beautiful and responsible, but also encourages us all to consider our own choices more carefully. The V&A is proud to provide a forum for discussion through this thought-provoking exhibition and publication.

The research for the exhibition has benefited greatly from the generosity and expertise of colleagues in many other institutions including the Natural History Museum, Science Museum, Museum of Economic Botany at Kew and Chelsea College of Arts. It demonstrates the strength of shared knowledge and the power of partnerships across disciplines to explore new narratives and find contemporary relevance in objects from the past. We are also extremely grateful to the European Confederation of Flax and Hemp (CELC) for its generosity, enthusiasm and support.

The Centre for Sustainable Fashion (CSF) at the London College of Fashion (LCF) has played a key role, acting as special advisor to the exhibition. Our collaboration with CSF has highlighted the innovative research taking place to resolve the challenges raised in the exhibition. These high- and low-tech solutions express the industry's determination to create a more sustainable future.

Fashioned from Nature is not just a tribute to the versatility and enduring influence of the natural world, but also a crucial and timely reminder for us all to reconsider the contents of our wardrobes.

Introduction

BY

Edwina Ehrman

This book and the associated exhibition at the V&A explore the complex relationship between fashion and nature from 1600 to the present day. Everything we wear, from clothes and accessories to jewellery, is 'fashioned' from matter found in the world around us, in the raw materials of which they are made, in the energy used to produce and transport them and often in their design inspiration. We express ourselves through our appearance and enjoy fashion for its novelty, variety and creativity. Yet, fashion's demands threaten the environment and endanger flora, fauna and human communities, an issue of considerable concern in the twenty-first century as the industry has become increasingly global. The challenge of reducing fashion's consumption of the earth's natural resources is at the heart of this book. *Fashioned from Nature* examines how we have arrived at this point and introduces some of the solutions being developed today to minimize fashion's impact. It also draws attention to the consumer's role in the fashion cycle and the part that we can all play in developing systems and strategies that respect and protect the natural world upon which all the earth's inhabitants depend.

The narrative of *Fashioned from Nature* was prompted by today's widespread concerns about environmental damage and also by the V&A's collection of fashion and textiles, which includes many objects acquired because they exemplify particular materials and techniques, and which often stimulate new questions when viewed through the lens of present-day environmental preoccupations. Very few clothes dating from before 1600 survive and so both the book and exhibition start in the seventeenth century. The book is divided into four chronological chapters, which follow the sections of the exhibition. The first chapter covers 200 years in the course of which the principal inventions that paved the way for the mechanization of the textile industry in the nineteenth century were conceived. This was a time when clothing and textiles were made by hand, and during which raw materials and man-made products from Asia, Africa and the Americas reached Europe in increasing quantities as international trading routes spread. By the end of the period more people than ever before in Europe could afford small fashionable luxuries. The second chapter focuses on 1800–1900, introducing a new phase in the evolution of the

ready-to-wear industry whose expansion was underpinned by mechanization and other innovative technologies, such as the development of chemical dyes and the vulcanization of rubber. The third chapter begins in 1900 with the commercial development of viscose. The man-made fibre industry revolutionized textiles, creating a whole new range of fibres of varying qualities, textures and attributes that complement and are often combined with the traditional fibres derived from plants and animals. The chapter ends in 1990 when the fashion industry was becoming increasingly global in its scale and individuals such as Katharine Hamnett had begun to campaign for more responsible practices.

Each chapter describes the organization of the fashion industry, its broadening consumer base and its growth in scale due to the adoption of new technologies, and is complemented by case studies of objects in the V&A collection that reveal key issues. The first three chapters focus on fashions made and worn in Britain while acknowledging the leadership of France for much of the period under review, and intimate how Britain's textile and fashion industry had impacts far beyond its borders. They also reflect on consumers, considering why particular materials were especially valued. The text then examines the production and processing of raw materials into fashion before addressing the effect they had on the environment and the earth's flora and fauna. The composition of the V&A's collection, the prevalence of clusters of similar garments in other British collections and descriptions of fashionable dress found in writings of the time have informed the choice of the fashions and materials selected for discussion. The book takes its lead from fashion trends. The range of materials available to satiate these trends has increased substantially between 1600 and now, so not all materials are covered in every chapter, although cotton remains a constant throughout. The status of materials also changed over time, with some raw materials becoming controversial or their use regarded as unethical, such as fur and ivory. Understanding the past – what sparked debates and changed attitudes – puts today's laws and campaigns into context.

The length of the book necessarily limits its scope. It focuses on the environmental impacts of fashion. It does not analyse the social effects of abhorrent labour practices such as the use of sweated labour or of slavery, which have been

2 / LEFT Mantua and petticoat (detail). Brocaded silk. Britain, 1730s. Given by Gladys Windsor Fry, V&A: T.324&A–1985

FRENCH CASHMERE.
ILKY LAMBS' WOOL OF GRAUX DE MAUCHAMP.
(PRESENTED BY HER MAJESTY THE QUEEN.)

IN THE GREASE.   WASHED OR   CARDED   SPUN
RAW STATE.   SCOURED WOOL.   WOOL.   WOOL.

H. R. H. PRINCE ALBERT
the projector of the grand Exhibition of all nations. 1851.

NOTTINGHAM
MACHINE MADE LACE.

White
Cream
Tuscan
Malta
Heliotrope
Beige
Serpent
Slate
Dk. Grey
Lt. Grey
Pink
Sky
Coquelicot
Grenat
Coral
Navy
Gold
Lt. Brown
Mid Brown
Dk. Brown

condemned since the eighteenth century. Indeed, in 1850, an anti-slavery pamphlet insisted that it was a moral duty to avoid slave-made products, yet acknowledged that in an increasingly global world it was almost impossible to trace the origins of everyday commodities unless one chose to 'live in the woods on roots and berries'.[1] Despite reforms to improve working conditions and outlaw slavery, these lamentable practices are still prevalent today. In terms of uncovering fashion's environmental impact, the story presented here is uneven. Statistics on various aspects of environmental damage are available for the late twentieth and twenty-first centuries, but there is nothing readily comparable for earlier periods, and historians do not seem to have delved into the primary sources that might reveal underlying similarities and differences. This book flags these issues in order to encourage further in-depth research.

The final chapter, which addresses the globalization of the fashion industry from 1990 to the present day, adopts a different approach but with the same aims. It explores the damage caused by the fashion system, the challenges the industry faces and the approaches being taken to meet them. Globally the human population has increased from 1 billion in 1800 to 7.6 billion in 2017, and the United Nations has predicted that it will reach 8.6 billion by 2030 and 9.8 billion by 2050.[2] Although many of the world's inhabitants live in appalling poverty, more people are more affluent than ever before and their consumption of commodities has risen accordingly. This is particularly true of their consumption of fashion and clothing, the production and use of which draw heavily on natural resources such as water and fossil fuels while generating significant levels of pollution, carbon dioxide emissions and waste. Since the 1980s a growing realization of the extent of the industry's negative impact has led campaigners and industry leaders to encourage their peers and consumers to rethink and change their practices to protect the natural world and the human populations affected by the industry.

One of the initial triggers for investigating fashion's relationship with nature came from the V&A's Collection of Animal Products. Only about 800 objects from this collection survive today but the majority fall into the category of textiles and dress. The collection, which originated from exhibits at the Great Exhibition of 1851 (pl. 3), was overtly educational and focused on the economic purposes to which animals and animal parts could be put.[3] Echoing the spirit of the exhibition it encompassed an astonishingly diverse range of objects from around the globe chosen to show the 'productions, industrial resources, manufactures and commerce of all countries' from raw material to the finished product. Its acquisition was driven by the Museum's early focus on developing scientific reference collections that could potentially provide practical examples for Britain's manufacturing and mercantile classes and encourage innovation.

The collection was exhibited at the Bethnal Green Branch of the South Kensington Museum (as the V&A was known until 1901). The Bethnal Green Museum (1872, now the Museum of Childhood) was located in London's impoverished, overcrowded and dirty East End. The area was home to artisans and labourers working in local industries and London's dockyards where huge quantities of raw materials arrived from the British Empire and elsewhere to be unloaded, stored in bonded warehouses and sold on. Although its inhabitants were poor, the economic activity that they supported was valuable.[4] In 1875 the Collection of Animal Products was joined by another group of objects with a similarly didactic purpose acquired to illustrate 'the Utilization of Waste Products'.[5] They included examples of recent discoveries such as dyes derived from coal tar, which was a byproduct of the gas industry (p. 76). Samples of both were displayed side by side. The exhibits showed that profits could be made from recycling waste but industrialists and scientists were also aware of its environmental benefits. Pollution from liquid and solid industrial and domestic waste was a significant problem that affected human health, the environment, flora and fauna. Waste remains a significant concern today and the challenge of recycling the waste products generated during the manufacture of textiles (pre-consumer waste) and cast-off clothes (post-consumer waste) is an important area of research.

Framing nature as a material and aesthetic source for human use (pl. 4) is crude and reflects an anthropocentric world view that has dominated the human relationship with nature for centuries. In cultures where Christianity was the dominant religion it was justified by biblical teaching, particularly Genesis I, verse 26, where God granted man 'dominion over the fish of the

3 / PREVIOUS PAGE Textile samples from the V&A's Collection of Animal Products, c.1850, V&A: AP.357:1, AP.356:2, AP.358:4, T.2–1959, AP.402:10, AP.402:12, AP.405:4/A, AP.406:14, AP.409:17, AP.120–1862, T.145–1972, MISC.26–1923, T.31–1959, T.29–1947, T.310–1967, AP.358:1, AP.119–1862

4 / RIGHT Benjamin Waterhouse
Hawkins (1807–1894), 'The
Cochineal and Lac Insects', from
Graphic Illustrations of Animals
(printed by J. Graf, published
by Thomas Varty, London).
Coloured lithograph on paper.
Britain, mid-19th century.
V&A: E.307–1901

5 / BELOW Imperial Federation
World Map, *The Graphic*,
London (24 July 1886), vol. 34,
no. 869. V&A: National Art Library

6 / LEFT Waistcoat embroidered with a design of macaque monkeys after Georges-Louis Leclerc (1707–1788), Comte de Buffon, *Histoire Naturelle, générale et particulière*, 2nd edition (London 1785). Silk and linen. France, 1780–9. V&A: T.49-1948

sea, and over the fowl of the air, and over the cattle, and over all the earth, and over every creeping thing that creepeth upon the earth'. This belief in man's God-given mastery over the environment and the moral obligation to make good use of it dovetailed nicely with an economy based on producing industrial and manufactured goods from raw materials supplied by the rest of the world (pl. 5). In the mid-nineteenth century some 93 per cent of British exports were manufactured goods and about the same proportion of imports were unprocessed raw materials.[6]

The human relationship with nature forms an important thread in the book's narrative and the first three chapters begin with a brief overview of the ways in which people engaged with nature both physically and materially. Aspects of this relationship can be seen in the many garments in the Museum's collection whose materials, decoration or construction are inspired by nature. Although they were often collected to demonstrate the use of design sources and pattern-making, they also reflect the interest, delight and solace that we find in nature.

Research into a waistcoat embroidered with monkeys revealed several ways in which humans interacted with animals in the late eighteenth century (pl. 6). The embroidery design survives in the archives of the Musée des Tissus in Lyon,[7] and Paula Jenkins, Curator of Mammals at the Natural History Museum in London, identified the monkeys and their source. The monkey offering his companion a fruit is a crab-eating macaque (*Macaca fascicularis*); the other is a lion-tailed macaque (*Macaca silenus*). Both are derived from the multivolume *Histoire Naturelle, générale et particulière* (1749–88) written by Georges-Louis Leclerc (1707–1788), Comte de Buffon, and dedicated to Louis XV (1710–1774).[8] In 1766 the *Histoire Naturelle* was one of a number of imported books advertised for sale by the London booksellers T. Becket and P.A. Hondt, and by 1781 an eight-volume English translation (from the 4th French edition) with 300 copperplate illustrations was available. This was expanded to nine volumes in 1788.[9]

Because of their similarities to humans in their manual dexterity and sociable behaviour, monkeys were frequently depicted in allegories, fables and caricatures representing the more negative aspects of human nature. They were also fashionable pets and could be observed at

the Jardin du Roi (now the Jardin des Plantes) in Paris where Buffon was Director and at the Menagerie at the Tower of London. Choosing monkeys from Buffon's publication, which was translated into various languages, to create an embroidery pattern for a waistcoat reflected the fashionable success of Buffon's encyclopedic 'masterpiece' among Europe's educated, wealthy classes and the social kudos that the king's patronage brought Buffon and the study of natural history.[10] In turn, its wearer demonstrated his learning and awareness of the interest in natural history at the highest levels of society. Although the waistcoat's provenance suggests that the original owner was German, fashionable French waistcoats were popular among the British elite. Because of the high taxes on French silks they were sometimes the subject of smuggling.[11]

Since 1600 our knowledge of the world's geography, geology, flora and fauna has expanded significantly and the study of natural history has become professionalized. In the mid-nineteenth century the theories of evolution developed by Alfred Russel Wallace (1823–1913) and Charles Darwin (1809–1882) offered a new narrative of the history of the world. Darwin's seminal 1859 publication, *On the Origin of the Species by Natural Selection*, challenged traditional religious teaching and questioned the relationship of humans to other living creatures. Today technological advances are enabling us to explore the depths of the oceans and outer space as well as helping us to understand more about the astonishingly complex functions of 'everyday' nature, of the trees, plants and creatures among which we live. Yet although we know so much more about nature, and can see it in amazing detail on television and via the internet, we are probably less in touch with 'real' nature than ever before.

The authors of this book hope that it will inspire its readers to think more deeply about the relationship between fashion and nature and to examine the contents of their own wardrobe. If we know what our clothes are made from and how they were produced we can make better choices. Creating an environmentally friendly and socially aware fashion industry is a bold ambition that offers inestimable benefits for society, the health of the planet and those who inhabit it.

Chapter 1
1600 — 1800

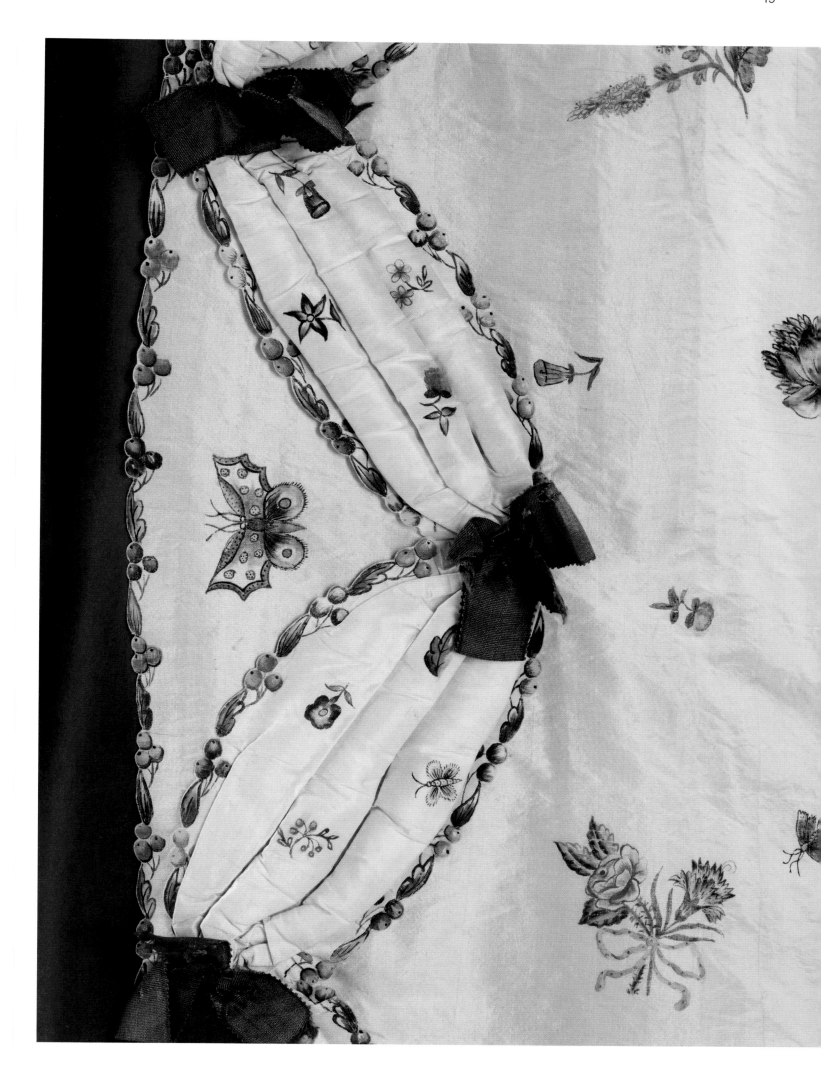

During the seventeenth and eighteenth centuries trade, exploration and wars, stimulated by competition between Europe's leading nations for commercial supremacy, opened up new sources of raw materials and enabled previously unrecorded territory, flora and fauna to be documented. This knowledge was visualized in maps (see pl. 7), which were published in sets and as individual sheets for framing, and in illustrated natural history books.[1] Newspapers, which proliferated

in the eighteenth century, provided factual information.[2]

BY

Edwina Ehrman

They published lists of imported materials and their countries of origin, articles about trade, overseas voyages and notices about travel books. It was also possible to purchase natural history specimens, as well as living plants and animals imported from overseas from dealers who advertised in newspapers.

Learning about the Natural World

The study of natural history was advanced in Britain by the Royal Society of London for Improving Natural Knowledge, which was founded by a group of natural philosophers and physicians in 1660. The Society and its publication *Philosophical Transactions* provided an opportunity for scholarly exchange and confirmed the study of botany and zoology as socially and intellectually respectable. A fascination with natural history was not limited to upper-class men. Regional and local societies, which were more focused on 'herborizing' (gathering specimens in the field), attracted men from many social and economic backgrounds. The botanist Sir James Edward Smith (1759–1828), who founded the Linnean Society in 1788, wrote of a group of artisans in his home town of Norwich who enjoyed herborizing in the countryside and identifying plants using plates in old herbals. They included tailors and weavers, who were known for breeding plants.[3]

Most women identified with the study of natural history came from the higher social classes, including the royal family. The interest of King George III's mother, Princess Augusta (1719–1772), in botany led to the foundation of the Royal Botanic Gardens at Kew. Margaret, Duchess of Portland (1715–1785), dedicated much of her fortune to the study of natural history, collecting specimens and creating a herbarium, aviary and menagerie at her estate at Bulstrode, in Buckinghamshire. Her passion led to her patronage of other collectors, plantsmen and artists, such as the flower painter Georg Dionysius Ehret (1708–1770) (pl. 8). The study of botany and flower painting were considered genteel accomplishments for upper-class women and lessons in painting on paper and fabric were available.[4] Women from this background set tastes in fashion.

A rare dress made from silk painted with butterflies, moths and flowers in the 1770s reflects this vogue. It was probably inspired by painted dress silks imported from China but the painting method is different. It might be an amateur work or from a professional workshop such as Mr Christian's British Painted Silk Manufactory, which traded in London in the 1760s.[5] Two hands, one less skilled, are evident and although some butterflies and moths can be identified as British, their delineation and colouring are fanciful (pl. 9). Entomology interested men and women. Two women, Mary Somerset (1630–1715), 1st Duchess of Beaufort, and the Hon. Mrs Walters, were known for successfully breeding insects. A quarter of the subscribers to Benjamin Wilkes's popular publication, *The English Moths and Butterflies* (1747–9), were women, and Moses Harris's proposal for *The Aurelian or, Natural History of English Insects; namely, Moths and Butterflies* (1766) recommended it as a source book for decorating 'ornamental furniture' and 'the Entertainment of those Curious & Ingenious Gentlemen & Ladies that Delight in the surprising Beauties of Nature'.[6]

Fashion: System and Practices

The production and consumption of fashion echoed the rhythms of nature and its yearly cycle through the seasons. It is self-evident that different temperatures and weather conditions require appropriate clothes and that the raw materials of fashion, whether they are of plant or animal origin, have their own cycles of growth and processing. However, fashion is time bound in other ways. Its dependence on innovation to remain current and appealing makes it particular to the present and subject to frequent change. In the early modern period lighter-weight fabrics of all kinds became fashionable. Being less durable and cheaper they prompted more frequent purchases and a greater attention among textile manufacturers to novelty, supporting and engendering a high turnover of patterns and colours. This production model was codified in the 1660s and 1670s when France rationalized the design of woven silks made at Lyon by instituting a system of annual change. The system enabled

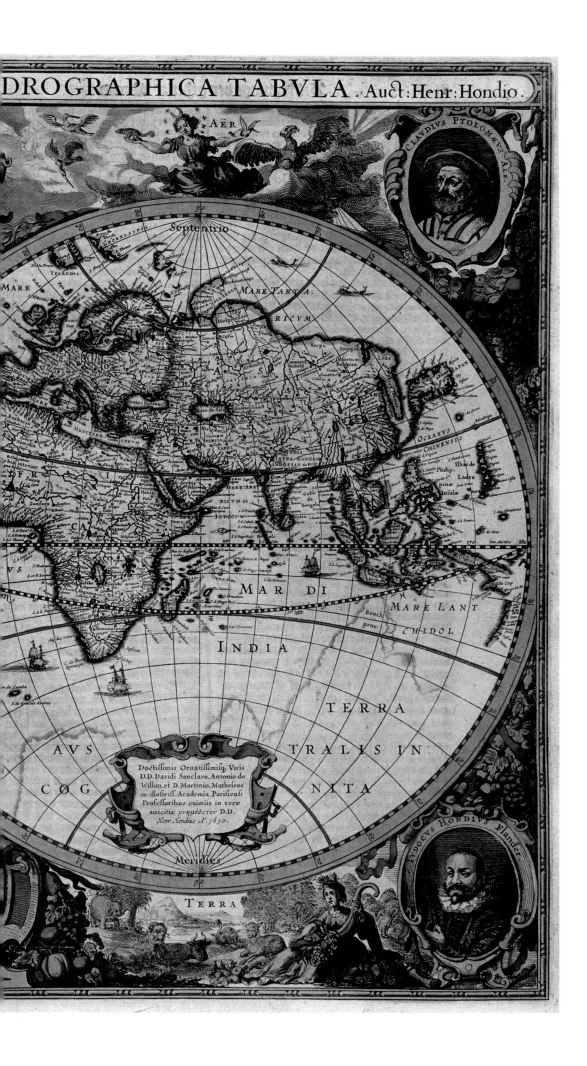

7 / LEFT Hendrik Hondius
(1597–1651), *Nova totius terrarum
orbis geographica ac hydrographica
tabula*. Hand-coloured engraving.
Amsterdam, 1630. Courtesy of the
University of Melbourne

8 / BELOW Georg Dionysius Ehret (1708–1770), Botanical study
of a Bull Bay (*Magnolia altissima,* now *grandiflora*). Watercolour
and gouache on vellum. London, 1743. V&A: D.583–1886

9 / RIGHT Gown. Painted silk. England, 1770s (silk), 1780–5
(garment construction). Replica petticoat and some bows.
Given by Mrs S. Clutterbuck, V&A: T.108–1954

MAGNOLIA *altissima Lauro-Cerassi folio flore ingenti candide*

The Lauret-leavec Tulip tree.

the design, marketing and manufacture of the complex, high-quality silks for which Lyon was renowned to be more logically planned and gave each year's designs invaluable kudos. At the same time Lyon's reputation for fashion leadership was bolstered by the reorganization of dress worn at the court of Louis XIV (1638–1715). Each year fresh silks were to be ordered for the royal wardrobe and the old discarded. Royal promotion of novelty thus provided the silk weavers with a steady stream of custom and a powerful advertisement for the latest patterns and colours. The shift to an annual cycle coincided with the launch of a new periodical, the *Mercure Galant* (1672–4; 1677–1714), which included regular fashion news and longer articles, usually published twice a year in spring and autumn. The periodical actively promoted the role of Paris and the French court in setting fashion and the organization of its content accustomed its readers to the new fashion cycle. The *Mercure Galant* set a precedent for disseminating and promoting fashion that would be realized in the late eighteenth century.[7] The French move to annualized production spread to other countries. In Britain it was adopted by manufacturers of patterned silks and of high-quality mixed fabrics woven with silk and wool. Yet as in France, most fashionable goods remained outside this system.[8]

In Britain men's and women's fashions were set at the highest level of society, by the court and nobility. The new trends then filtered down and across the social ranks in forms adapted to their taste and income. The influence of France was particularly pervasive after the Restoration of the monarchy in 1660 and the wealthiest and most fashion-conscious consumers, male as well as female, purchased textiles and dress in Paris as well as London. The latter was the centre of fashion manufacturing and retailing in Britain. Its population of 675,000 in 1750 encompassed the richest and poorest members of society, and its retail outlets and services were suited to every pocket. Regional centres such as York and Norwich served the fashion needs of the local gentry, merchants and wealthier tradesmen and their families. Nonetheless, some well-to-do people living in the provinces bought textiles and clothes in the capital in order to obtain the most fashionable styles. Those who could not visit in person sometimes sent an existing garment to a maker

to serve as a pattern, or commissioned a proxy to do business on their behalf.

As people acquired more disposable income, access to fashion grew, stimulating the growth of the industry. A rise in the population from the mid-century coincided with a better standard of living for most if not all social classes and trebled the number of potential consumers.[9] How far people followed fashion and how much they bought depended on variables including disposable income, social class, occupation, geographic location, moral outlook, sociability, gender and age. All clothes were hand-sewn and many items, particularly simply constructed garments like shirts, were home-made by family members, servants and hired seamstresses. The majority of towns had drapers, mercers and haberdashers who sold fabric, trimmings and accessories, tradespeople specializing in accessories (including ready-made items) and tailors and dressmakers ('mantua makers') who made to order. Peddlers served outlying areas. There was a growing trade in ready-made garments and a thriving second-hand sector particularly in urban areas and ports (pl. 10).[10]

At every level of society textiles and clothes had a monetary and moral value that went beyond the kudos and privilege fashion could express. Surviving garments reveal signs of reuse, documenting an economy of thrift that was promoted as domestic virtue well into the twentieth century. To be wasteful was against the laws of God and nature. Expensive silks were kept and reused long after their patterns went out of fashion: they were bequeathed in wills and donated to the Church to be made into vestments. Clothes were repaired, relined, retrimmed and altered to extend their use, cut down for children's garments, handed to relatives and dependants, and passed on as perks to servants to do with as they wished. Many of the latter were sold into the second-hand market, which at its highest level made good-quality clothes available to a wider range of people. The constituent parts of garments and textiles were recycled. Picking out or unravelling gold and silver threads from lace, silks and embroideries, in a practice known as drizzling, was a socially acceptable pastime among the elite of France and Britain. The gold threads were a valuable commodity purchased by goldsmiths to extract the metal content.[11]

10 / LEFT Marcellus Laroon (1653–1702), 'Old cloaks, suits and coats' (1688), from J.R. Green, *A Short History of the English People* (London 1874)

The Fabric of Fashion

From the early seventeenth century Britain began to play a much more prominent role in intercontinental trade with the Middle East, Asia and the Americas. Textiles were one among many commodities bought and sold, enabling new fashions to be introduced. In the Middle East the Levant Company (1592–1825) traded wool cloth and base metals from Britain, silver and cochineal from the Americas for dyes and valuable raw materials such as silk, cotton wool and yarn, cotton cloth and fine goatskin (*maroquain* or 'Morocco') for shoes and gloves. The English East India Company, founded in 1600, consolidated England's presence in Asia and by the 1700s trade with the region had become a key element in the economy and in Britain's identity as a trading nation. In 1672 the company won a valuable trading post in Taiwan and in 1699 it was granted a 'factory' (combined offices, warehouses and later, living quarters) in Canton on the Chinese mainland. In the eighteenth century, the company traded British woollens and Indian cottons for Chinese tea, porcelain, silk and fans (p. 42). Britain also acquired territory in the West Indies and colonies in North America, from Newfoundland to South Carolina, which gave it access to valuable furs, skins, dyes such as indigo and prized materials like turtle shell. This territorial expansion enabled London to become an entrepôt between Asia, North America and Europe.

The first stage in acquiring clothes was buying the material. The four principal fibres were the protein (animal) fibres silk and wool, and plant fibres cotton and flax, from which linen is made. Each fibre can produce textiles of varying qualities depending on the species, its cultivation and the way it is processed. They respond differently to dyes and some are more fitted to particular forms of decoration than others. Individually and as a group, they are very versatile, lending themselves to a variety of uses and incomes.[12] Examples of materials made from these fibres, annotated with their width, cost and the type of garment for which they were purchased, can be found among fabric samples dating from 1746 to 1823 preserved in an album by Barbara Johnson (1738–1825). Together they show how the fibres

contributed to the fashionable wardrobe. An unmarried daughter of a vicar, Johnson spent time with her family and a number of well-connected friends in the Midlands and London. Until late in life she lived on a 'slender income' of £60 a year and her notes on prices suggest careful budgeting (in 1760 a live-in maid could expect to earn about £5 a year). From 1764 to 1766 (pl. 11) she bought fabric for seven gowns at 2s. to 6s. 6d a yard. The widths of the fabric differ but even taking that into account the most expensive fabric was silk, and the cheapest wool. The three printed linens she chose were between 3s. and 4s. a yard. Although the wool purchased by Johnson in 1764 was modestly priced, the costliest fabric in her album was also wool: a broadcloth at 20s. a yard. This demonstrates the range of qualities that a fibre could encompass. The album contains 54 samples of silk and 37 of cotton. Most of the latter were printed and the quality of their colours and patterns and their prices, as well as cotton's practicality, explain its growing popularity in the fashionable wardrobe. Of the rest there are 11 examples of woollen fabrics, 7 linen and 13 silk mixes (mainly silk and wool). Mixing fibres combined the functional and aesthetic qualities of each component, creating materials of different weight, texture and appearance.[13]

Silk is a luxurious fibre: it is lustrous, strong, light, warm and gentle on the skin. It absorbs dye well and depending on the quality of thread and complexity of the weave can create fabrics of extraordinarily varied textures and visual effects. The cultivation of silk (sericulture), the fibre produced by the larva, or caterpillar, of the silk moth (*Bombyx mori*), began in China in the Neolithic period. Knowledge of sericulture reached the Middle East by the sixth century and Europe by the tenth century. The larvae feed on the leaves of the white mulberry (*Morus alba*), which is indigenous to northern China but can be naturalized in warm temperate climates. In sericulture the larvae grow in controlled conditions indoors. Once a larva is fully mature it extrudes fibres coated in gum (sericin) from two orifices on the side of its head, which it spins into a cocoon to protect itself as it metamorphoses into a pupa (pl. 12). Before the pupa can become a moth, it is killed by hot air or steam. The cocoons are then steeped in hot water to soften the

11 / LEFT Barbara Johnson (1738–1825),
page from an album of textile samples.
Britain, 1764–6. V&A: T.219–1973

12 / RIGHT A silkworm (*Bombyx mori*)
spinning its cocoon before pupating

sericin and enable the threads to be detached and processed. The silk threads from one cocoon are between 700 and 1,000 metres long. If the pupa is allowed to survive, or the insects are living in the wild, it makes a hole in the cocoon and emerges as a moth. This damages the silk resulting in much shorter lengths that have to be spun to produce a usable thread.

As Britain developed its silk weaving industry in Spitalfields, in East London, it had to compete for raw silk with other European silk-weaving nations. The British climate did not offer the conditions for successful large-scale sericulture. Raw silk was expensive and subject to fluctuations in supply because of diseases that affected the silkworm larvae. High-quality silk, required for the warp threads that are held in tension on the loom, was acquired from China and Italy, which also provided thrown silk prepared for the warp (organzine). Other silk was imported from Turkey and Spain.[14] Sir Thomas Lombe (1685–1739) built the first mill in Britain to throw and twist silk in preparation for dyeing and weaving. In use by 1719, the mill was powered by water and located on an island in the Derwent river in Derby.

The most technically accomplished silks, such as brocades, woven with metal threads and many colours, were very expensive. In January 1767 Lady Mary Coke (1727–1811), the widow of Viscount Coke, spent £70 on silk for a mantua (court dress) to wear with a new set of silver lace accessories for Queen Charlotte's (1744–1818) birthday celebration at court. The dress was evidently a success: Lady Powis (1735–1786) 'took my gown for imbroidery [sic], t'was indeed a beautiful silk. ... the King was particularly gracious & civil to me.'[15] Accounts of court dress in letters and diaries reveal competition between wearers and testify to silk's value as an indicator of wealth, taste and status. Men wore silk for court and formal dress, made into waistcoats, and informally at home as 'banyans' (a loose robe) (pl. 13). Both sexes wore knitted silk hosiery. Indeed, there were silks to suit almost every income, from ribbons and handkerchiefs to plain, checked and striped silk, silk blends, and simple and more complex brocades and velvets.

Wool was even more embedded in every wardrobe. At this period it was a European speciality. The fibre is valued for its insulating properties, absorbency, durability and elasticity. It is used for woven and knitted fabrics and the scales on its surface make it suitable for felting. Britain's woollen weavers drew almost entirely on home-grown wool. It had been a mainstay of the country's economy for centuries and some local sheep breeds were famous. The Ryeland, from Herefordshire, produced the finest wool but it could not quite match the greater softness and pliability of Spanish merino, which was imported to make the highest grade 'superfine' cloth. Lincoln and Leicester sheep were reared for their high-quality long wool. The wool industry was divided into two manufacturing branches: woollen and worsted. Woollens were, and are, wool cloths made from yarn of shorter-staple wool that has been 'carded' so that the fibres mingle and sit across each other. The resulting finish is fibrous and textured. Worsteds are wool cloths made from yarn of longer-staple wool that has been 'combed' so that the fibres sit in line with each other. The final appearance is smooth, lustrous and compact. Broadly speaking the woollen industry was located in the west of England, East Anglia, Yorkshire and Lancashire, and the worsted industry in Norfolk. However, during the eighteenth century Yorkshire and parts of Lancashire broadened their activities to encompass both types of cloth. The industry was based around the rivers Aire, Calder and Colne, which provided plentiful soft water for scouring, fulling and dyeing, and to power machinery.[16]

Wool's elasticity makes it particularly suitable for tailoring and it was an important staple of the male wardrobe. It was worn for informal wear, travelling, sport and, with suitable trimmings, for formal dress. As men's clothes became plainer towards the last quarter of the eighteenth century tailored coats, waistcoats and breeches made from very fine woollen cloth in single colours became fashionable (pl. 14). They were closely identified with British style and helped to establish Britain's reputation for men's tailoring and its wool cloth. Heavily fulled wool and tightly woven worsted cloths have rainproof qualities and were worn by both sexes for protection against the elements. Women's fashionable clothes were more suited to lighter fabrics and their use of wool declined in the later 1600s in favour of silk and the colourful, painted and

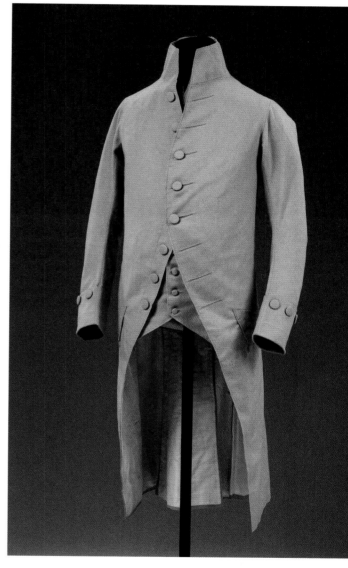

13 / LEFT Banyan. Silk damask. China (silk)
and Britain or the Netherlands (garment
construction), c.1720–50. V&A: T.31–2012

14 / RIGHT Coat and waistcoat. Wool. Britain,
1795–1805. Purchased with the assistance of
the Elspeth Evans Bequest, V&A: T.122–2015

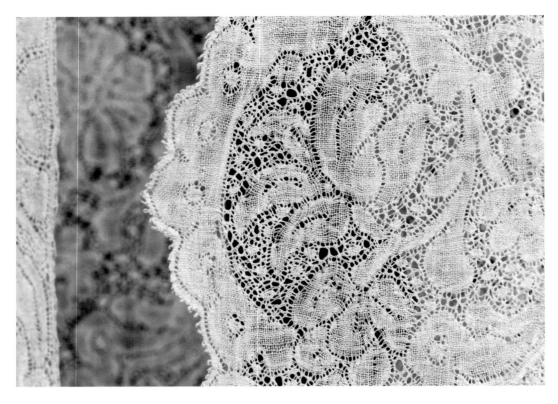

15 / LEFT Bobbin lace border
(detail). Linen. Valenciennes,
France, 1730s. Given from the
Everts-Comnene-Logan
Collection, V&A: T.64–2008

16 / BELOW Jacob van Ruisdael
(1628–1682), *View of Haarlem
with Bleaching Grounds*. Oil on
canvas, 1670–5. Mauritshuis

printed cotton 'chints' imported from India and their English imitations printed on cotton and linen.[17]

Linen, like wool, was a wardrobe staple. Archaeological evidence suggests that linen fibres have been made from flax (*Linum usitatissimum*) for about 34,000 years.[18] Flax benefits from rich soil, humidity, close planting to encourage height and timely harvesting before the seeds are fully ripe. It is composed of bundles of fibres, 1 to 2 metres long, that grow between a woody central core and an outer layer of tissue (epidermis). After harvesting, the dried stalks were retted in water to break down the woody parts. This was done using the morning dew supplemented by watering or plunging the stalks in pools or soft-water streams. Finally the dry stalks were beaten to remove the straw and combed to clean and align the fibres for spinning. The resulting fibres are strong, lustrous, absorb moisture and are good conductors of heat, but they lack elasticity. Dry spinning produced a stronger, firmer thread but wetting the fibres with saliva or water yielded the finest gauge.[19] Humidity is very important to the manufacture of linen to prevent it from becoming brittle. Once woven, linen can be washed at high temperatures making it a sensible choice for garments worn next to the skin.

At this date the highest-quality European flax came from Holland, Flanders (Belgium), France and Germany. Although flax was farmed in England, Scotland and Ireland, Britain relied heavily on imported European linen. Linen came in many qualities and prices. How the flax was grown and processed, the expertise of spinner and weaver, and how and where the cloth was bleached all affected its quality. The wealthy and fashionable put a premium on well-bleached linen woven with a fine even texture that retained its whiteness and body after laundering. The best bleaching grounds were located in the area around Haarlem in Holland. Jacob van Ruisdael's (1628–1682) *View of Haarlem with Bleaching Grounds* shows cloth laid out over the grassy dunes in the vicinity of Haarlem Lake (pl. 16). The complex bleaching process, which could take between six and eight months, drew on the local ecosystem. Buttermilk, from the dairy industry, combined with minerals present in the dunes, gave the cloth its superior whiteness.[20]

Linen was suitable for a wide range of garments: underwear such as shirts, shifts, breeches' liners, stays and underskirts; gowns and waistcoats; and accessories such as aprons, handkerchiefs, caps, cravats and lace. Lace was the essential finishing touch for those who aspired to a fashionable appearance and could afford it. The finest linen thread for lacemaking came from Flanders and by the late seventeenth century different styles of Flemish bobbin lace were associated with particular places, such as Brussels and Mechlin (Mechelen). In France the area around Valenciennes, which was formerly part of Flanders, made lace in the Flemish tradition with exceptionally delicate thread. Because of the quality of the thread, its detailed patterns and creation in a single strip, rather than in sections by multiple hands, Valenciennes lace was very slow to produce. A lace edging worked in this region, now in the V&A's collection, epitomizes the density of pattern that could be achieved when using such fine threads (pl. 15). Unusually, it has not been cut and measures more than 5 metres in length.

Cotton was employed alongside linen in Britain, initially mainly for household uses and furnishings, from the 1500s.[21] Like silk, it was the object of global trade, with most cottons originating in India. It is soft, comfortable and lightweight. It can absorb a high proportion of water before becoming damp and it has low thermal conductivity making it cool in hot weather and warm in cold temperatures. It is easy to wash, dries relatively quickly and can be ironed at high temperatures. The cotton plant belongs to the genus *Gossypium*. It is planted in the spring and harvested six to seven months later. It flowers eight to ten weeks after planting and seed pods (bolls) develop from the fertilized flowers. When the bolls are ripe they burst open to reveal the fine downy cotton (lint) that covers the seeds. Before mechanization the technology used to remove the fibre from the seeds, prepare, spin and weave it varied by place and according to the cloth to be produced.[22]

Britain imported raw cotton, yarn and cotton cloth. Today, in a world of vividly coloured, digitally printed fabrics, it is hard to imagine the excitement generated by the painted and printed calicoes (cottons) imported from India in the seventeenth century. In 1696 the author

of *The Merchant's Ware-house Laid Open* praised their patterns and dyes, 'Painted with very fine Colours all of Indian figures, either of Birds, Beasts or Imagery, which if washed never so often, still retain their colours till they are worn to pieces'.[23] Their exotic patterns, albeit modified to suit British taste, created a new design vocabulary (pl. 17). The East India Company imported a great assortment of cotton fabrics from India, varying in weight, texture, colour, pattern, purpose and price, enabling them to meet the needs, desires and pockets of the middling and lower classes as well as the upper ranks of society.[24]

The immense popularity of the painted and printed Indian fabrics provoked the silk and wool industries to lobby for government protection and in 1700 an Act of Parliament banned all Asian textiles apart from unfinished and plain cottons. The domestic textile printing industry, located along tributaries of the river Thames in London, was an immediate beneficiary. Adopting improved dyeing techniques learned from India, the printers used the traditional European method of block printing to transfer pattern to cloth. One estimate suggests that their success resulted in a four-fold growth in imports of white cotton goods to over 2 million pieces by 1719 and an intensified campaign against their products by the silk and wool industries.[25] Further legislation in 1721 prohibited the import, sale, use and wear of all printed cotton in Britain. However, textile printing was permitted on linen and fustian, a fabric with a linen warp and cotton weft. Although it took time for printers to become proficient in dyeing and printing, their goods had a similar appeal for the consumer to the Indian fabrics on which they were modelled. They were practical, produced in a variety of colours and patterns, and above all affordable.[26]

Cotton manufacturing was based in Lancashire. A wide range of mixed fabrics was produced from cotton and linen and, imitating another Indian fabric, cherryderry, which was woven with a silk warp and cotton weft. Cherryderry was used for women's dresses and handkerchiefs. Pure cotton fabrics included 'Manchester velvet', which was popular for breeches and waistcoats. A waistcoat with front panels of silk velvet and back panels of cut cotton velvet (pl. 18) shows how the fabric could be employed as a luxurious alternative to the

usual plain linen and fustian back panels that, being hidden from view by the wearer's coat, were made of cheaper fabric. After 1774 all cotton goods could again be printed for domestic consumption.

Pure cotton goods were made with cotton warp threads imported from India as the hand-spinning techniques employed in Britain were unequal to the task of creating the consistency and strength required for the warp. The invention of a series of increasingly efficient spinning machines from James Hargreaves's spinning jenny (1765, patented 1770) and Richard Arkwright's water frame (1767, patented 1769) to Samuel Crompton's spinning mule (1779) resolved this. When Edmund Cartwright patented his steam-driven power loom in 1785 it heralded the mass production of pure cotton goods realized in the nineteenth century. In areas with fast-flowing rivers water power offered a cheaper alternative to steam. In 1771 Arkwright built the first water-powered spinning mill at Cromford in Derbyshire's scenic Derwent Valley. A second mill, Masson, followed in 1783. Steam power, whose cost depended on local coal prices, was used from the late 1790s, but it remained expensive in comparison with water.

Alongside the four principal fibres many other materials contributed to the fashionable wardrobe. Whalebone was used to stiffen and shape women's stays (the antecedent of the corset) (pls 19 and 20) and the hooped petticoats that supported the exaggerated width of women's skirts from the late seventeenth century to about 1795. Whalebone is a colloquial name for baleen, the keratinous plates found in the upper jaw of baleen whales. The plates, which can be up to 3.5 metres long, encase bristles that act like a sieve, sifting seawater from the whale's food of plankton and krill. Baleen is strong, durable and lightweight. Once the plates had been divided, the bristles removed and the baleen cleaned, it was soaked in hot water to make it soft enough to cut and manipulate.

Riding whips, stretchers for umbrellas and the arched supports of a hood-shaped bonnet called a calash were made from baleen too. The price of baleen depended on the supply of whales. In 1736 a newspaper reported, 'The Number of Whales taken by the Dutch this Year on the Greenland Coast, not being above half

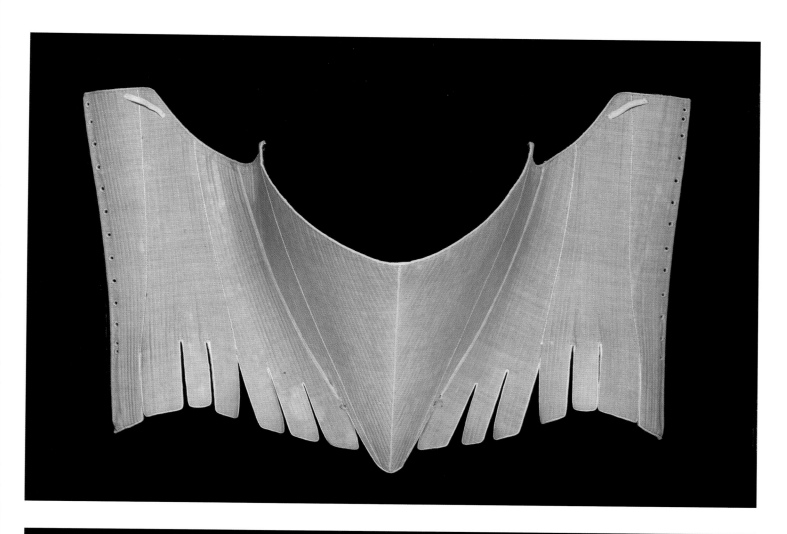

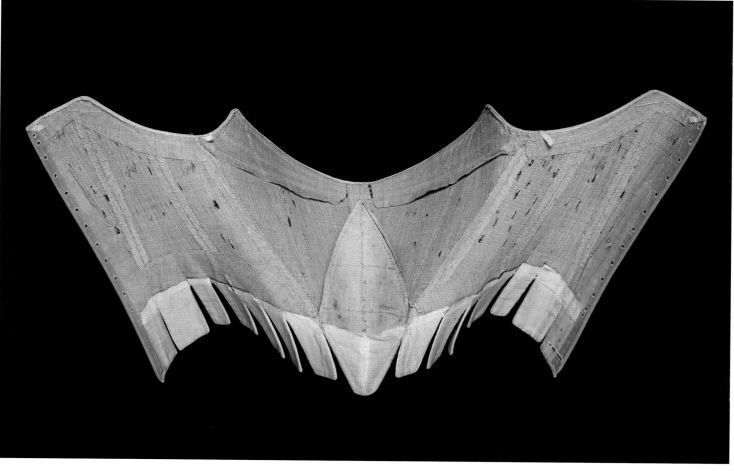

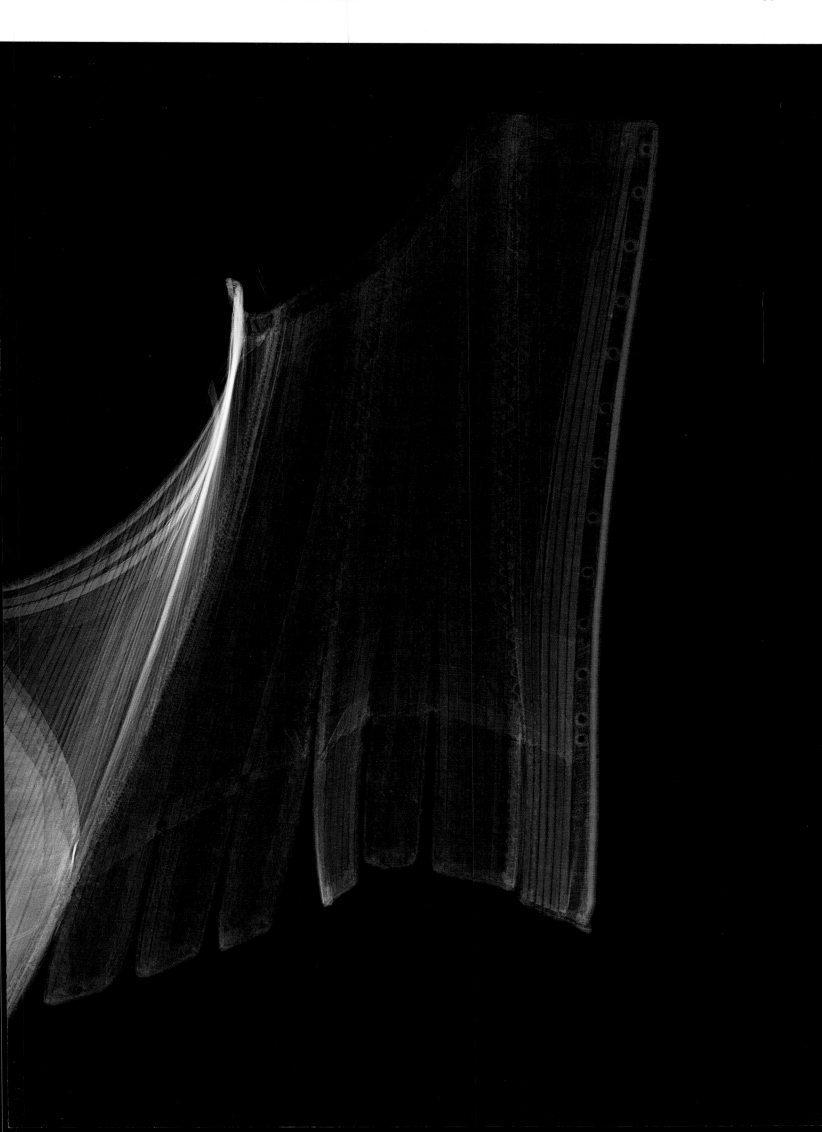

what they took last year, Whalebone has risen Thirty Per Cent here within a short time; but the Ladies wearing Cane Hoops so much, will occasion less Demand for that Commodity'.[27] Many whalebone merchants sold cane (rattan, imported from the East Indies) because it was interchangeable with baleen for hoops.[28] Whales were also hunted for their valuable oil and blubber, which were used for lighting, making soap, lubricating machinery and preparing leather and cloth. The bristles were utilized for upholstery stuffing. Walking sticks could be fashioned from the jaw bones of sperm whales.

Other creatures provided their skins for fashion, both sexes wearing fur-lined garments, fur muffs and felted hats. Trimmings and tippets, which sometimes incorporated the animal's head, paws and tail, were popular for women. Using the whole pelt revealed the species, and its value, while varying the fur's form, texture and weight, and reducing waste. Fur had a sensual, erotic appeal driven in part by its association with wild untamed nature. Wenceslaus Hollar's (1607–1677) extraordinarily realistic etchings of fur convey its materiality: the contrasting textures of stiff glossy guard hairs and soft underfur, the depth of colour and its limp animal bulk (pl. 23). Furs were valued for their warmth, luxurious appearance and, in the case of the most costly such as sable and ermine, their exclusivity.

Britain had few fur-bearing animals in the quantities required by the trade apart from rabbits, which were bred in warrens in Lincolnshire, so much fur was imported from Russia, Scandinavia and the Baltic. The falling numbers of European beaver (Castor fiber), which was used principally for felt hats, led the British and French to compete to secure new supplies in the north of North America. Both countries set up trading companies to buy pelts from the Native Americans who understood the local ecology, were skilled trappers and could survive the harsh winters. By the 1680s Britain's Hudson's Bay Company was shipping home enough pelts to supply the domestic hatting market and develop a significant export trade, which thrived until the mid-eighteenth century.

Beaver was prized for hat-making, with men and women at the highest levels of society wearing such hats for riding and walking. Samuel Pepys (1633–1703), whose diary shows

the importance of a fashionable appearance to his sense of identity and professional ambitions, noted the purchase of several beaver hats and the acquisition of a second-hand one in 1662: 'an old one but a very good one, of Sir William Batten; for which I must give him something, but I am well pleased with it'.[29]

The beaver's woolly underfur is ideal for felting (pl. 21). After the guard hairs had been removed the underfur was cut or pulled from the pelt. The felting process began with the hairs being agitated to make the scaly keratinous fibres mat evenly together. Moisture, heat and pressure were applied to shrink, consolidate and shape the felt, before dyeing and finishing. Beaver felt can support wide brims and high crowns (pl. 22) and will retain its shape even when exposed to wet weather and long wear.

Accessories provided the important finishing touches to a fashionable appearance and many were made in luxurious imported materials. These included ivory, 'tortoiseshell' and mother-of-pearl. Ivory comes mainly from the teeth or tusks of the African and Asiatic elephant. It is a dense material and can be sawn and shaped, turned, drilled, pierced, carved and engraved to create fine details. A very thin cross section will not fracture easily and can be permanently curved by being exposed to steam. Britain imported ivory from Asia and, like France, from West Africa via the Caribbean on slave ships.[30] In France, Dieppe excelled at ivory carving. Chinese craftsmen used ivory from Africa, India and South-East Asia. From the early 1600s Portuguese, Dutch and British traders brought ivory to Canton, which became China's most important centre for ivory working for the home and export markets. Canton workshops also produced and decorated objects with mother-of-pearl, a soft, layered substance secreted inside the shells of certain molluscs. Pinctada margaritifera, found in waters including the South China Sea, the Indian Ocean and the Persian Gulf, was the usual source. It was valued for its iridescence and range of colours. Following the removal of the hard outer shell, the material can be carved and polished. Mother-of-pearl for working in Britain was shipped by the East India Company.

'Tortoiseshell', more correctly known as turtle shell, is obtained from the enlarged plates that form the protective outer shell of certain

21 / ABOVE LEFT Wild beavers

22 / ABOVE RIGHT Man's or woman's hat. Beaver felt. Britain, 1590–1670. Given by Lady Spickernell, V&A: T.22–1938

23 / RIGHT Wenceslaus Hollar (1607–1677), Group of muffs and articles of dress. Antwerp, 1647. V&A: E.7095–1908

Wfollar fecit Aqua forti. 1647.   Antuerpiæ,

24 / RIGHT Fan depicting Belshazzar's Feast.
Watercolour on vellum, carved ivory (probably
Loxodonta sp.) sticks and guards. Flanders or
Italy (leaf), China (sticks and guards), 1700–25.
Given by Admiral Sir Robert and Lady
Prendergast, V&A: T.22–1957

25 / NEXT PAGE Joachim Wichmann
(fl.1670–1680s), *The Whale Fishery*.
Engraving, *c*.1683. Peabody Essex Museum

species of tropical and subtropical marine
turtles. The plates on the turtle's back (carapace)
are coloured in shades of dark brown, amber
and red while those on its underside (plastron)
are usually clear and yellow ('blonde'). Three
species were used to create decorative art
objects: the Hawksbill (*Eretmochelys imbrica-
ta*), which has the finest scales, the Loggerhead
(*Caretta caretta*) and the Green turtle (*Chelonia
mydas*). The shell is valued for its colours,
translucency and the sheen it acquires when
it is polished. Like baleen, it is a keratinous
material, which is easily sawn, and it has ther-
moplastic properties. When heat is applied to
the plates they become soft and can be shaped
and fused together; once cooled they retain
their new form. Britain imported turtle shell
from the Caribbean.

All these materials were used to make and
decorate fashion accessories, including fans,
snuff boxes and walking sticks, elevating these
objects from practical to luxury items for
display. The importance of walking sticks to
the fashionable appearance sometimes led to
multiple purchases. Voltaire (1694–1778), the
French philosopher and writer, is said to have
owned 80.[31] The shaft and rondel (knob/handle)
were commonly assembled from different
materials. Cane (rattan), hardwoods, ivory and
horn were employed for the shaft. For the
rondel, ivory and turtle shell, often inlaid with
silver or mother-of-pearl, were common. Fans
also had several components, which were
usually crafted from a variety of materials. The
sticks and guards of the most decorative and
costly fans are frequently made of ivory, turtle
shell and mother-of-pearl or combinations of
these materials. Some are additionally embellished with carving, gilding, paint, foil and
jewels. Brisé fans comprising only of sticks and
guards were very popular in the eighteenth

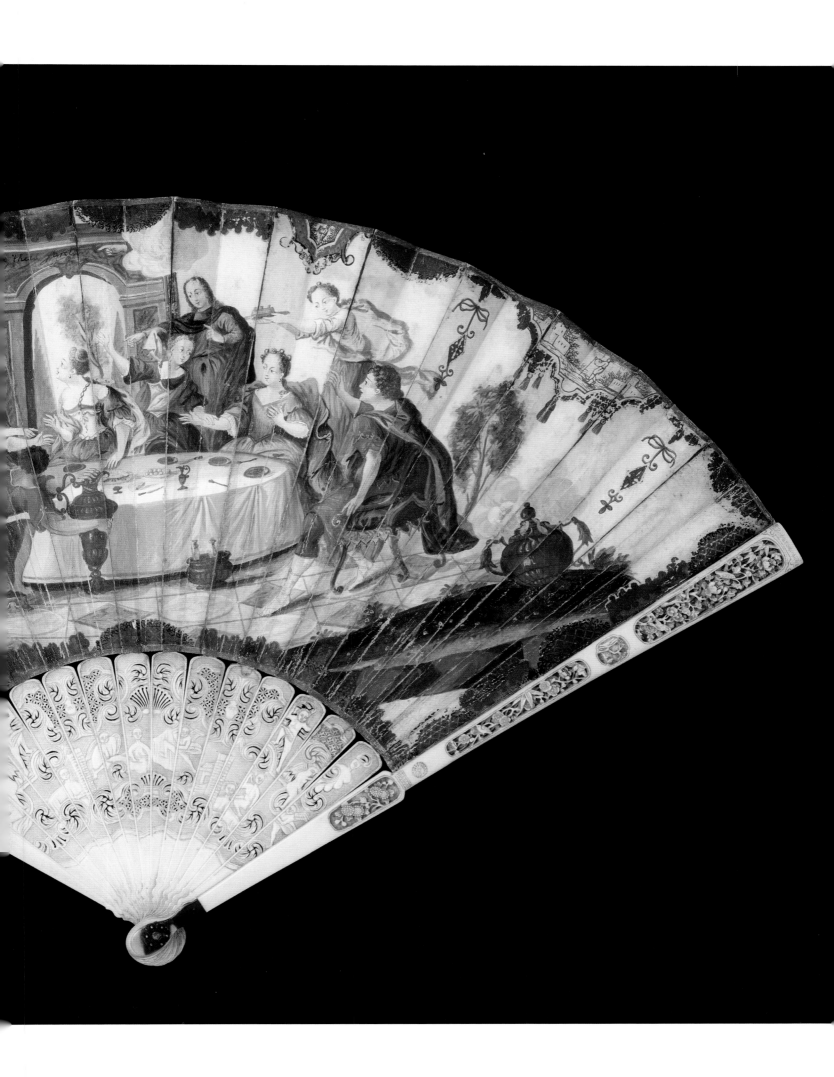

century. In the folding fan, the leaf, or mount, which is attached to the sticks, has to be of a material that can be pleated, such as vellum (calf skin), paper or fabric. Generally painted, it may also be decorated with slivers of mother-of-pearl, straw and metal spangles (sequins), whose shiny surfaces catch the light. Many fans, and sets of sticks and guards, were produced in China for the European market. They were elaborately carved to reflect western taste and notions of the East (pl. 24).

The Impact of Fashion on the Natural World

By 1800 the processes that supported the fashion industry and its rising demands for raw materials were beginning to have an impact on the environment and some animal populations. Evidence of public disquiet about pollution from the textile industry can be found in newspapers. There were also social and aesthetic concerns about the spread of industrialization, particularly in areas of natural beauty, but for most people these were outweighed by its economic benefits.[32] Attitudes to animals were complex but in the second half of the eighteenth century religious, moral and political questions were raised about the relationship between humans and animals. Non-conformists, particularly Methodists, condemned cruelty to animals and argued that domestic and wild animals alike should be treated humanely. The radical philosopher Jeremy Bentham (1748–1832) went further, proposing that animals should be protected from cruelty by legislation.[33] Although their views were influential, for merchants and manufacturers the economic value of animals was paramount. Images of whale fishing often include a whale's bloodied corpse but their perspective is anthropocentric. They celebrate the courage of the men who risked and lost their lives braving dangerous seas and cruelly bitter weather to bring home products that benefited industry and contributed to the nation's wealth (pl. 25).

The effects of overhunting species were already apparent. As early as the 1600s the demand for beaver could no longer be met by the European beaver whose numbers had diminished drastically because of it. Similarly,

as the demand for whale products grew, whales swimming close to the shore in the seas around Greenland and Spitzbergen became fewer. This pattern was repeated as whaling vessels went further afield: from the waters of the Arctic into the North Atlantic and eventually as far north as the treacherous pack ice of Baffin Bay. Whales were subjected to a cruel and protracted death. The first contact was made with barbed iron harpoons fixed to lengthy ropes that were hurled from fast rowing boats. The harpoons caught in the whale's flesh, tethering the boats to it. As the whale tried to escape by diving, the boats remained attached to it at a distance, closing in to kill it with lances when it tired. Elephants also suffered from the demand for ivory. Until the introduction of large-calibre elephant guns in the later 1800s many rounds of shot were needed to kill an elephant. Experienced hunters aimed for the animal's lungs.[34]

At home, the textile industry's dependence on water impacted on the environment: several of the processes involved in preparing and finishing textiles caused water pollution. Retting flax stalks to break down the woody parts in pools or streams caused the fibre to putrefy producing a pungent smell. As the bundles of stalks rotted they affected the flow and quality of the water. Dyeing caused the most damage because of the chemicals involved, for instance in Yorkshire, in Leeds and the neighbouring villages along the river Aire and its tributaries, where coloured wool cloth was produced. In 1783 the *Leeds Intelligencer* published a letter purportedly from an anonymous correspondent concerned about the risk to public health from water tainted by dyeing. It urged the town's magistrates and principal inhabitants to address the water supply, which was 'polluted by the many Dye-Houses with their noxious contents, such as Aqua-Fortis, Spirits of Vitriol, Verdigrease [*sic*], Copperas, and many other thing of a poisonous or pernicious quality', including human waste.[35] Fouling the water in this way affected human communities and the rivers' ecosystems.

From Cocoon to Court:
An Eighteenth-Century Mantua

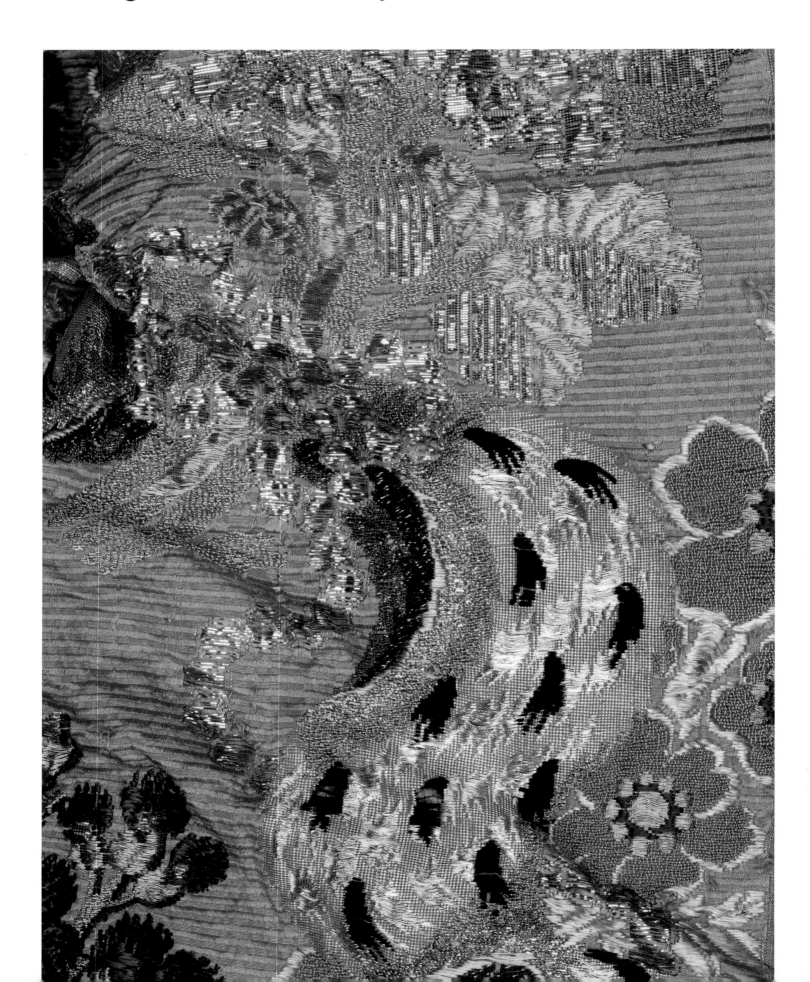

BY
Lesley Ellis Miller

This splendid court mantua is a truly global ensemble (pl. 31): its raw materials originated in the Americas, Eurasia and the Middle East; its fabric and trimmings were probably made in France and Britain; and its construction into apparel was almost certainly undertaken in London. The substantial textured silk remains buoyant despite spending the best part of 250 years in storage. Many of its silver and silver-gilt threads still sparkle, and dark fur tails peek perkily from the slightly tarnished silver lace trimmings. The original cut and construction conformed to the fossilized dress requirements for attendance at court in eighteenth-century London.[1] Later alterations, probably for nineteenth-century fancy dress, adapted its cut to a new wearer and purpose.

It was most likely first created for a member of the British social or political elite who attended 'drawing rooms' at St James's Palace, among other royal occasions (pl. 27).[2] Fashionable silks and trimmings were often used for the antiquated style of such attire, the future wearer choosing them from a silk mercer's stock or ordering them from a range of samples. The material would then be taken to a mantua maker to be made up into a perfectly fitting garment. The fabric was so expensive that the dressmaker did not cut into it unless absolutely necessary, but rather pleated it into shape, attaching widths of fabric to each other using running stitches that could be taken apart easily at a later date when the fabric was recycled.

Silk designs changed seasonally during this period, so the fabric – especially one as distinctive as this – would immediately tell the fashion cognoscenti whether or not a lady was wearing a new mantua. The first possible airing of this item was about 1760–5, when a variety of motifs comprising curvaceous scrolls interspersed with bouquets of flowers ornamented many European silks.[3] This particular silk was probably woven in Lyon – the major French silk manufacturing centre renowned for silks with gold and silver threads and novel designs[4] – even though at this date Queen Charlotte was encouraging her ladies to 'buy British' in order to support the Spitalfields weavers in London who thought their livelihood threatened by French silk imports.[5]

Such textiles were suitable only for court dress or ecclesiastical vestments and do not survive in great quantities as they were often recycled to regain the metal that was essentially hard cash.[6] They were extravagant even in court circles, as Elizabeth Montagu's (1718–1800) description of her own relatively plain dress of 1769 suggests: 'A corded blue tabby [plain blue silk] trimmed with Ermine, which with fine lace and jewels, makes a respectable figure and as I had the Ermine cost me little'.[7] At this level of society, ermine edged dresses (pl. 28) and fashionable capes, but it lined only exceptional garments, such as royal coronation mantles.[8] Imported to Western Europe from North America or Russia,[9] ermine, the stoat in its winter coat, was distinguished by its black tail protruding from the white pelt.

In this mantua, only black tails were used, set into a silver lace trimming round the neck and down the front. This design conceit harmonized perfectly with the silk's brocaded pattern, which represents ermine in a similar way: black tails in an undulating textured silver band (pl. 26). The precious metal had travelled from more southern climes than the ermine, probably from the famed Potosí mines (in present-day Bolivia), exploited by the Spanish since their colonization of Peru in the sixteenth century.[10] It is employed generously in four different metal threads, thus locating the silk in the second most expensive category woven in Europe at the time.[11] In Britain, a similar English-woven dress length might have cost as much as a skilled artisan earned annually, while a French-woven legal import might have been double that amount.[12]

Metal content apart, the fabric was expensive because raw silk was imported and was then transformed into fabric via a number of time-consuming and skilled processes. Sericulture – the cultivation of the silkworms that provided the silk filament – was never successful enough in France to serve the needs of its domestic weaving industry (pl. 29). By the middle of the century, according to Denis Diderot's *Encyclopédie*, 6,000 bales of silk entered Lyon each year: 1,600 from Sicily, 1,500 from Italy, 1,400 from the Levant (Middle East), 300 from Spain and the remaining 1,200 from the south of France.[13] Having been transported by sea and land in sailing ships, horse-drawn barges and coaches, once the silk arrived,

26 / LEFT Court mantua (detail).
Silk, silver and silver-gilt threads.
France, 1760s. V&A T.252-1959

27 / ABOVE George Noble (fl.1795–1806),
View of the Court of St. James's with the
Ceremony of Introducing a Lady to her
Majesty. Britain, late 1770s to early 1780s.
Royal Collection: RCIN 750504

28 / RIGHT Allan Ramsay (1713–1784),
Mrs Everard. Oil on canvas, c.1768–9.
Given by William Freeman, V&A: 1147–1864

it was thrown and twisted into threads; hanks of thread were dyed for warp and weft; and the drawloom was threaded up to execute the design. The weaver and his assistant (the drawgirl) then proceeded to weave up the fabric at the rate of only a few centimetres per day. As a result, a dress length of this pattern probably took up to a month and a half to weave.[14] Compare this timescale with the speed at which the dressmaker and her assistant(s) turned the fabric into a garment: just three days.[15]

The process most detrimental to the environment was probably dyeing, which required the submersion of silk in a sequence of degumming and dyeing vats (pl. 30). The dyestuffs all came from plants and insects; some were native to Europe and others were imported from the Middle East and South America.[16] They were fixed on the silk by the use of mordants or fixing agents, also from natural sources. The French silk dyers emphasized that the lustre of silk was of primary importance in creating a good colour and that thorough degumming of the silk prior to dyeing was essential. This involved 'cooking' the silk in boiling water with white soap for at least three and a half hours, emptying the contents into the river, and washing and beating the soap out of the silk before putting it into a solution of cold water and alum. Dyeing a good black took more than four days.[17]

The colours in this mantua conform to those recorded in the *Encyclopédie*: the dusky pink ground comes from a redwood, probably brazilwood; the brownish-black from a combination of redwood and young fustic, and there are some traces of iron that might have been employed to fix the colour; other dyestuffs include indigo or woad, and lichen.[18] The Lyonnais were proud of the quality of their colours, vaunting the optimal conditions provided by the city's two rivers and petitioning the authorities to ban the export of their dyed silk hanks for use by competitors.[19]

This dress embodies some of the characteristics of fashion production that cause concern today: the exploitation of non-renewable global resources, the promotion of built-in obsolescence and the release of pollutants into air and water supplies.[20] At the time, however, their impact on the environment was probably minimal as rapidly changing fashion was still the preserve of a small elite and transportation made no use of fossil fuels.

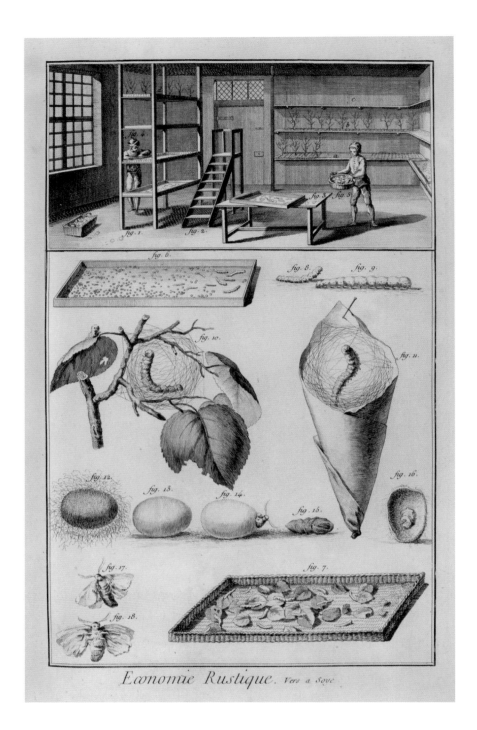

Eœnomie Rustique. Vers a Soye

29 / ABOVE *Vers a Soye*, Sericulture. Denis Diderot and Jean Le Rond d'Alembert (eds), *Recueil de Planches sur les Sciences, les arts libéraux et les arts méchaniques avec leur explication* (plates to the *Encyclopédie*), vol. 1, Briasson (France, Paris 1762–72). V&A: National Art Library

30 / BELOW *Teinturier de Riviere, Attelier et différentes Opérations pour la Teinture des Soies*, Dyeing. Denis Diderot and Jean Le Rond d'Alembert (eds), *Encyclopédie Recueil de planches, sur les sciences, les arts libéraux et les arts méchaniques, avec leur explication*, vol. 10, Briasson (France, Paris 1762–72). V&A: National Art Library

Teinturier de Riviere, Attelier et différentes Opérations pour la Teinture des Soies.

31 / LEFT Court mantua and petticoat.
Silk, silver and silver-gilt threads and
ermine fur. France (silk) and Britain
(garment construction), 1760s, altered
1870–1910. V&A: T.252 to C–1959

Drawn from Nature: 1600–1800

BY

Clare Browne

For almost as long as patterned textiles have been produced, the natural world has provided inspiration for their designs.[1] In medieval and Renaissance Europe, the scientific study of nature had been advanced by the development of book printing, allowing for the circulation of illustrated works that widened enormously the pool of animals, plants and other types of creature whose images could be copied as decoration. Conrad Gesner's (1516–1565) *Historia Animalium* (1551–8), the most important zoological work of the Renaissance, had far-reaching influence; Mary Queen of Scots (1542–1587) chose from among its extensive illustrations for motifs to embroider during her years of captivity in the later sixteenth century.[2] But although Gesner presented his work as the state of current knowledge, he was typical of his time in drawing extensively on the writings of classical and medieval authors (he offered, for example, proof that unicorns had existed). John Gerard (*c*.1545–1612), in his *Herball*, or the *Generall Historie of Plants* (1597), included some 1,800 illustrations, making a pleasing connection between flowers and their depiction in fashion in his description of 'the earth apparelled with plants, as with a robe of embroidered worke'. The *Herball*'s plates could be adapted to provide stylized motifs for textile patterns, but only a tiny number had been newly drawn from living plants; the rest were copied at second or third hand from older woodcuts.[3]

In the later sixteenth and early seventeenth centuries new types of work describing the natural world began to appear, moving away from copies of earlier models towards observational accounts of plants, animals and other types of creature. This was part of a collecting and cataloguing impulse that underlay so many scientific developments in the seventeenth century. Flower books, known as florilegia, illustrated plants that were increasingly grown purely for their decorative qualities, rather than practical use. There was a direct connection between florilegia and pattern books. Pierre Vallet (1575–1650), the first botanical painter appointed to the seventeenth-century French court, also served as royal embroiderer; his work, *Le Jardin du Roy Très Chrestien Henri IV* (1608), based largely on plants in the gardens of the Louvre Palace, was specifically intended to be a pattern book for painters, embroiderers

and tapestry weavers.[4] Other works of natural history could provide sources for textile designers in a more incidental but equally fruitful way. The pattern drawer of the embroidered decoration on the sleeve in plate 34 included a realistic and diverse range of insects in the design. These are likely to have been copied from or inspired by a work like Thomas Moffet's (1553–1604) *Theatrum Insectorum* (published posthumously in 1634) (pl. 33), which gave prominence to 'lesser living creatures' recorded with new methods of classification.

The climate of interest and enthusiasm for the study of natural history continued to grow in the eighteenth century. Colonial expansion and exploratory travel supplied evermore new material, including both the specimens – plants, animals, birds and insects – themselves, and images of them recorded by artists sent on expeditions. Advances in their study increasingly widened the range of published works, so that by 1746 the plant collector Peter Collinson (1694–1768) could report to the Swedish naturalist Carl Linnaeus (1707–1778) that books on the subject of natural history sold the best of any in England.[5] Collinson was a wealthy textile merchant, and his connections both with distinguished naturalists of his day, like Linnaeus and Sir Hans Sloane (1660–1753), and several leading designers for London's silk industry provide evidence of a network disposed to share its knowledge and enthusiasm.

The master weaver and silk designer James Leman (*c*.1688–1747) and the silk designer Joseph Dandridge (1668–1746), both key figures in the production of highly fashionable English dress fabrics, were fellow members with Collinson of the Aurelian Society, the earliest specialist entomological society in Britain. Dandridge was also a noted botanist, ornithologist and entomologist in his own right. Anna Maria Garthwaite (1689–1763), designer of some of the most exquisite floral-patterned silks ever produced in England, also had direct contact with this community of naturalists through her brother-in-law, Vincent Bacon (d.1739), an apothecary and member of the Royal Society. From her earliest work, Garthwaite in particular among the designers displayed a perceptiveness of botanical form that came to be seen as characteristic of English silks, compared with their European counterparts, in the first half of the eighteenth century.

32 / LEFT Bodice. Linen embroidered in silk and silver-gilt thread. England, 1600–25. V&A: 1359–1900

INSECTORVM
SIVE
Minimorum Animalium
THEATRVM:
Olim ab

EDOARDO WOTTONO.
CONRADO GESNERO.
THOMAQVE PENNIO
inchoatum :

Tandem
THO. MOVFETI Londinâtis operâ fumptibufq; maximis concinnatum, auctum, perfectum :
Et ad vivum expreffis Iconibus suprà quingentis illuftratum.

Londini ex Officinâ typographicâ *Thom.Cotes.* 1 6 3 4.

7

33 / LEFT Thomas Moffet (1553–1604), *Insectorum sive Minimorum Animalium Theatrum* (London 1634)

34 / RIGHT Sleeve panel (detail). Linen embroidered in silk. England, 1610–20. V&A: T.11–1950

35 / RIGHT Anna Maria Garthwaite (1689–1763),
design for woven silk. Watercolour on paper.
England, 1727. V&A: 5970:46

36 / OPPOSITE Pierre Pomet (1658–1699),
A Compleat History of Druggs
(London 1712), plate 33

Her natural history knowledge is likely to have
been gained both from personal observation,
and from botanical or scientific works showing
rarer and non-native plants. A silk design of
hers from 1727 (pl. 35) incorporates a harmo-
nious scattering of wild flora that might well
have been inspired by the plates in a work like
Pierre Pomet's (1658–1699) *A Compleat History
of Druggs* (1712) (pl. 36).[6]

Later in the century, technical advances in
the field of textile printing allowed for greater
intricacy in the depiction of fine details, which
the calico printer William Kilburn (1745–1818)
superbly realized in his inclusion of the feathery
strands of seaweed and ferns in his designs (pls
37 and 38).[7] Kilburn's skill as a botanical artist
led to a commission to provide many of the
illustrations for William Curtis' (1746–1799)
Flora Londinensis, a record of plants growing
within 10 miles of London, published between
1777 and 1798. His work exemplifies the advice
in a mid-eighteenth-century manual for
'designing and drawing of ornaments, models
and patterns, with foliages, flowers, etc. for the
use of the flowered-silk manufactory, embroidery and printing'. It goes on to state:

But why should we plague and torture our
brains, for whims of our own, when nature
so bountifully has furnished us with
endless varieties of subjects, which only
want to be well composed, by a bright
imagination and an artful hand. Each
season of the year produces vegetative
plants, flowers, and shrubs, as afford far
greater varieties than we are able to
imitate, though we lived to the years of
Methusalem. The Spring opens her boun-
tiful treasure every year, and clothes and
enamels the earth with endless charms of
beauty; she invites us to imitate her as
near as possible in all her splendour.[8]

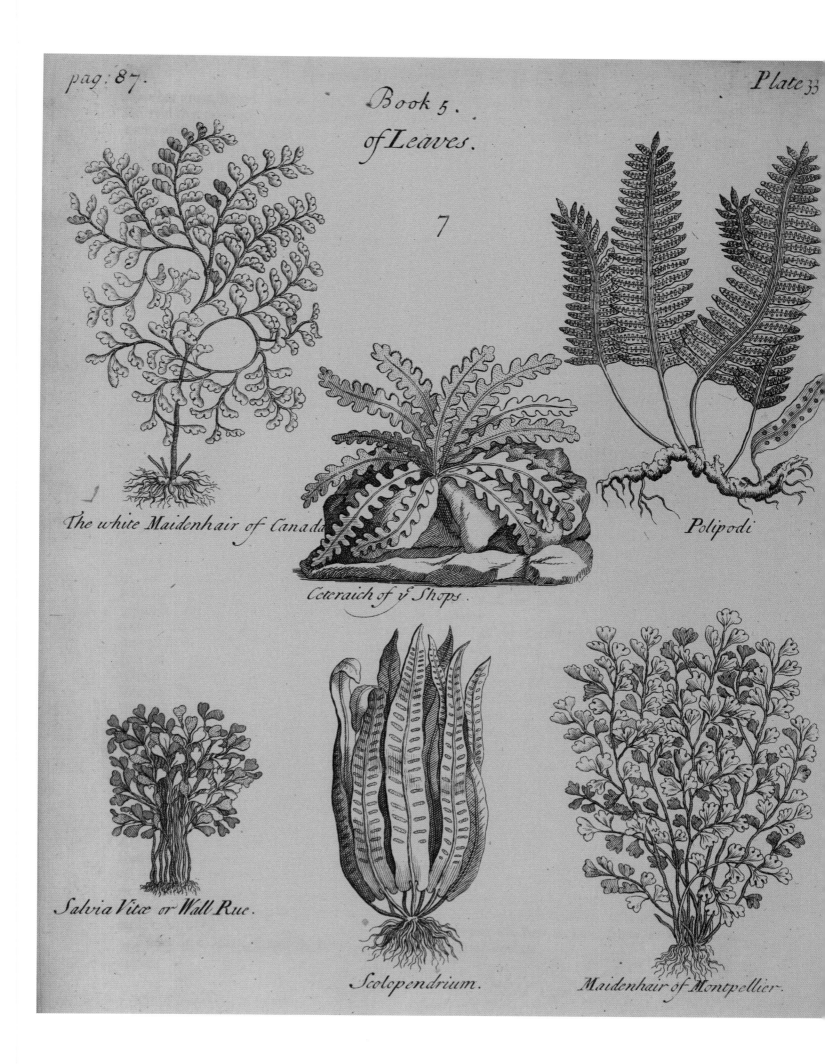

pag: 87.

Book 5.
of Leaves.

7

Plate 33.

The white Maidenhair of Canada

Ceteraich of ẙ Shops.

Polipodi

Salvia Vitæ or Wall Rue.

Scolopendrium.

Maidenhair of Montpellier.

37 / BELOW Gown (detail). Block-printed cotton to a
design by William Kilburn (1745–1818). England,
*c.*1790. V&A: T.84–1991

38 / RIGHT William Kilburn (1745–1818), design for
printed cotton. Watercolour on paper. Britain,
*c.*1788–92. Purchased from the funds of the
H.B. Murray Bequest, V&A: E.894:49/1–1978

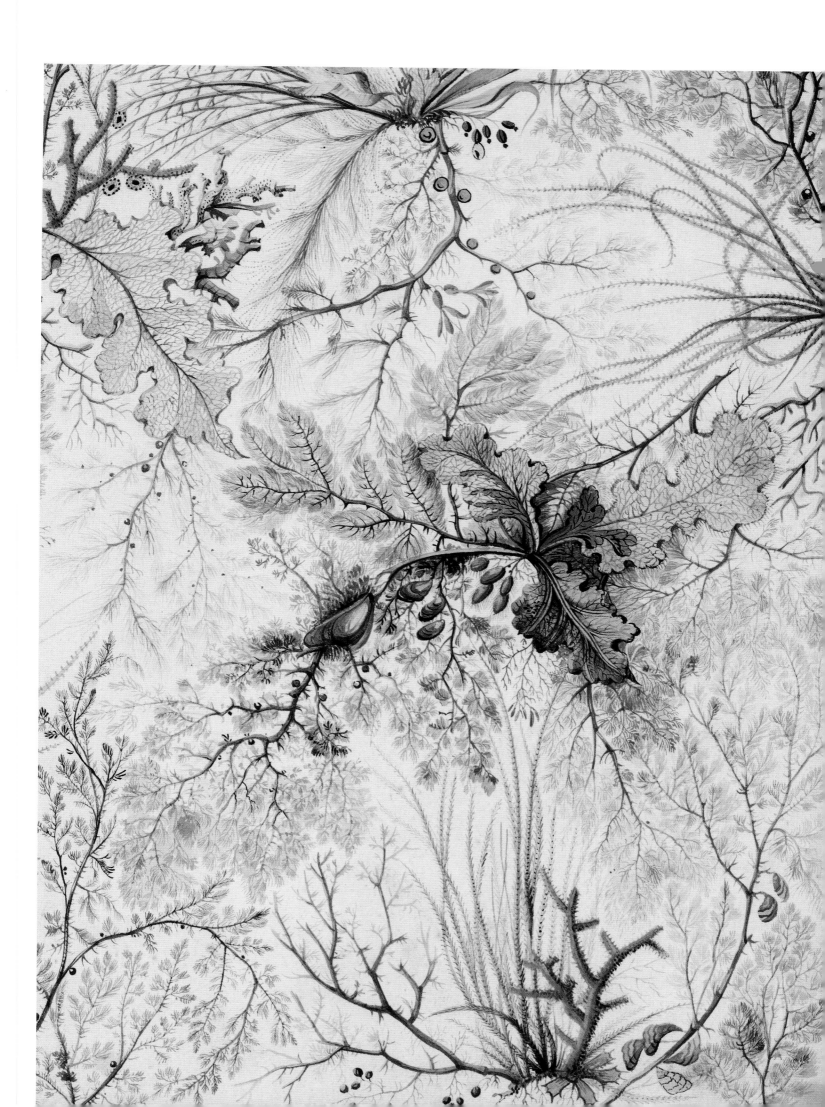

Chapter 2
1800 — 1900

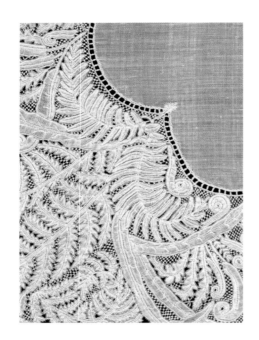

In the nineteenth century new methods of transport, cheaper books and periodicals and the establishment of museums with natural history collections created greater opportunities for middle- and working-class people to learn about natural history and enjoy the countryside and its flora and fauna. The railway network, which expanded rapidly in the 1840s, took travellers to the seaside and areas of natural beauty and scientific interest.[1] From the late nineteenth century safety bicycles, whose price made them affordable to the working classes by the mid-1890s, offered an alternative to rambling on foot.

BY

Edwina Ehrman

Searching woods, hedgerows and rock pools, collecting shells, fossils, seaweed, wild flowers and ferns, identifying and preserving them, became popular hobbies for which women's fashions were lamentably ill-suited. Margaret Gatty, author of *British Sea-weeds* (vol. II, 1872), offered stern advice:

> Let woollen be in the ascendant as much as possible; and let petticoats never come below the ankle. ... Cloaks and shawls, which necessarily hamper the arms ... cannot fail to get soaked and should be avoided as much as possible; ... a hat is preferable to a bonnet, merino stockings to cotton ones, and a strong pair of gloves is indispensible. All millinery work – silks, satins, lace, bracelets, and other jewellery, &c. must and will, be laid aside by every rational being who attempts to shore hunt.[2]

The railways also enabled excursions to London to visit events like the international exhibitions of 1851 and 1862, which showcased raw materials as well as the latest manufactured goods, and to browse in the capital's shops. The Zoological Society's Gardens in Regents Park, which opened to the public in 1828, were popular with tourists and London families.[3] The zoo, with its architect-designed animal houses, combined education with more anthropocentric activities like feeding cake and buns to the zoo's 'pets': an Indian elephant called Jack and Toby the Russian bear. The Natural History Museum in Exhibition Road (1881) offered other ways of encountering animals, principally through taxidermy. The collection, owned by the British Museum, was formerly kept at Montagu House, where three stuffed giraffes and a rhinoceros stood on a landing above the entrance hall.[4]

Exploration within and outside the British Empire and Britain's commercial and cultural links overseas led to a boom in collecting natural history specimens, especially plants. This coincided with affordably priced publications that benefited from tax reductions on printed paper and the lower costs made possible by steam-powered presses. Many titles were dedicated to natural history and gardening, which found an eager audience among middle-class families living in the leafy suburbs expanding around major cities. Sir Joseph Paxton (1803–1865), Head Gardener at Chatsworth House, architect of the Crystal Palace and from 1854 Member of Parliament for Coventry, developed a substantial publishing portfolio including *Paxton's Magazine of Botany and Register of Flowering Plants* (1834–49). A figured silk waistcoat from the 1840s, its pattern probably drawn from a Paxton plate illustrating *Rhodochiton volubile* (now *atrosanguineus*), shows that textile designers continued to use botanical illustrations. Unfortunately, the tailor's knowledge did not match the designer's and he placed the silk so that the flowers of the Mexican climber look up rather than hang down (pls 39 and 40).

Fashion: System and Practices

In the nineteenth century British fashion continued to be led by the tastes of the royal family, nobility, aristocracy and those eligible to attend court, who were collectively described as 'society'. Concerns about threats to the exclusivity and privilege of the upper ranks from newly wealthy families whose money had been acquired through commerce and industry prompted a greater emphasis among the established upper class on privacy and control. This powerful elite was not static or impermeable but admission was carefully controlled and those with the means and aspiration to join had to be approved and invited.[5] The group's adherence to a ritualistic cycle of social events, from court functions to taking part in the morning ride in Hyde Park's Rotten Row, yachting at Cowes in early August and shooting game in Scotland, ensured its social visibility. Each gathering had its own etiquette of dress for which participants needed an extensive occasion-specific wardrobe. As these members of high society travelled around the country or went abroad, to Paris, Baden-Baden and Biarritz, their journeys were documented by *The Times* and society magazine *The Queen*. The latter devoted many columns to the details of their dress for the benefit of subscribers who did not belong to this tight-knit circle.

Within this elite group Princess Alexandra (1844–1925), wife of future King Edward VII,

39 / LEFT Waistcoat. Silk. Britain, 1840–60.
Given by Mrs P.M. Rumbold, V&A: T.19–1984

40 / RIGHT Frederick William Smith
(1797–1835), 'Rhodochiton volubile', *Paxton's
Magazine of Botany and Register of Flowering
Plants* (London 1836), vol. 2, p. 27

was widely admired for her beauty and style. At the end of the nineteenth century celebrities from other spheres, particularly actresses starring in lightweight plays and musical comedies with contemporary plots, exerted an influence on fashion. Several worked with dressmakers, including French fashion houses such as Worth and Doueillet, to create their on-stage wardrobes. Photographs and detailed descriptions of their outfits were published in the media offering both actress and fashion house widespread publicity.[6]

The annual fashion system, whose first manifestation was described in Chapter One (p. 27), was now embedded in the promotion of women's fashion. The fashion media continued to reinforce the leadership of Paris while acknowledging London's role as the centre of British fashion. Magazines included lengthy descriptions of French styles illustrated with fashion plates originally prepared for a French audience, and there were English-language versions of French magazines like *Le Follet* (1829–92), which were read by milliners and dressmakers, whose clients expected them to be well-informed, and fashionable consumers.[7] Regional newspapers across the country reprinted extracts about the latest styles from the periodicals, potentially reaching readers who could not afford or did not wish to subscribe to the original source. The fashion trade itself was becoming increasingly sophisticated, driving sales through advertising and editorials in the media and adopting new methods of selling, particularly via the department store, which offered a wide range of goods and services under one roof and encouraged customers to browse (p. 95).

The methods of making and buying clothes were similar to those of the previous century. Dressmakers and tailors, catering for a range of needs and income levels, continued to make garments to order. There was a thriving ready-made industry and a well-organized trade in second-hand clothes. Many clothes were home-made. What was different by the late nineteenth century was the scale, organization and marketing of ready-made menswear and a new concept of the role of the dressmaker, which was introduced at the highest level of the fashion system.

When Englishman Charles Frederick Worth (1825–1895) opened Worth et Bobergh in Paris

in 1858, he offered his clients original designs from which they could order a custom-made copy. These garments were constructed from fabrics and trimmings that Worth selected and often commissioned from French textile companies, and were made in his ateliers. This complemented the most common practice at the time, which was for the client to buy her own choice of fabric and take it to a dressmaker, who worked according to the client's directions and requirements. Worth's business provided all the many garments and accessories that contributed to the fashionable wardrobe, including ready-made items such as cloaks. He also introduced the practice of showing his collections in advance of the season for which they were designed, launching his Spring/Summer collection in January to enable time for the pieces to be made up for individual clients. The organization of his house laid the foundations of the Paris haute couture. His characterization of his role as an originator of fashion was novel and his success brought him authority, influence and celebrity status.[8]

In Britain 'court dressmakers' catered for women in high society. They understood the regulations governing court dress and had staff with the expertise to create the etiquette-correct, occasion- and season-specific garments that their clients required. They held stocks of fabric but advised and collaborated with their clients rather than dictating to them. Men with a similar background and lifestyle patronized the bespoke tailors in and around Savile Row in London's West End.

The concept of a wardrobe of seasonal clothes appropriate for a wide range of formal and informal activities was adopted by the cost-conscious ready-made tailoring trade, which developed rapidly, particularly for men's and boy's clothing, in south-east England from the 1830s. The growth in ready-made clothing was facilitated by the falling cost of textiles as the industry mechanized. Improved methods of pattern cutting, the adoption of new technologies such as the sewing machine (commercially produced from the 1850s) and band knife (1860), and subcontracted, subdivided, cheap 'sweated' labour all contributed. The business strategy of this growing sector focused on fixed prices, cash sales and a fast turnover supported by low costs and margins, eye-catching advertising and well-appointed

41 / NEXT PAGE Fashion plate showing ready-made tailored clothing. Lithograph, coloured by hand. England (probably), c.1845. V&A: E.1501–1954

retail outlets on busy shopping streets. The largest companies, like Hyam & Company and Elias Moses & Son, had shops in the City and West End of London, in regional centres such as Manchester, and in Australia, from where Moses imported wool and hides. The scale of their operations was ambitious, integrating manufacturing, retail, tailoring and outfitting, and the sale of bespoke as well as ready-made garments. Importantly, they had the financial backing to take advantage of fluctuations in the market and to buy in bulk when prices were favourable, enabling them to pass on savings to the consumer.[9]

The ready-made trade benefited from Britain's rising population. In England it grew from 8.3 million in 1801 to 30.5 million a century later. Scotland and Wales saw similar expansion with 2 million people living in Wales and 4.5 million in Scotland in 1901.[10] Of these, the 'massed ranks of the moderately wealthy', whose varying incomes enabled them to follow fashion to a greater or lesser degree, grew more rapidly than any other group.[11]

The stock sold by manufacturers like Hyam, Moses and H.J. & D. Nicoll included imaginatively named standardized clothing and more fashionable garments. Their advertising played heavily on the appeal of novelty. Seasonal advertisements encouraged the purchase of leisure wear, for an excursion to the seaside or a day at the races, and of sportswear, for walking and the traditional country sports of hunting, shooting and fishing (pl. 41). The leading firms also promoted garments whose design they had registered under the 1839 Design Copyright Act, drawing attention to the originality of their stock and enhancing the public perception of their 'brand'.[12] Very few clothes made by these companies have survived, possibly because of their built-in obsolescence, cheaper and less durable fabrics or because their affordability diminished their status as items to cherish.

Moses and Hyam sold women's riding habits, traditionally made by tailors, and by 1851 Moses was offering furs, shawls, hosiery, footwear and parasols. A decade later Thomas Ford of Oxford Street was selling more fitted, ready-made womenswear. As the fashion industry escalated in scale to meet the physical, social and cultural needs and ambitions of the growing population, its demand for raw materials grew.

42 / ABOVE Bodices. Cotton. Britain, 1860s.
Given by Miss Juliet and Messrs G.F. and
A.L. Rickitt, V&A: T.132 and 134–1923

43 / RIGHT Cotton picking in Savannah,
Georgia, USA, c.1890

The Fabric of Fashion

In the nineteenth century cotton was worn by every social class, taking the place of linen for many garments and accessories. Among the working classes it also substituted for wool. Silk and wool, however, retained their importance in the fashionable wardrobe. Silk was the focus of a search for alternative fibres because of shortages caused by silkworm diseases such as pébrine, while wool's significance here rests on the effect of its processing on the environment. Rubber and chemically created aniline dyes reflect the economic importance of new technologies and scientific discoveries to the fashion industry. Some forms of colour were difficult to create. Iridescence, found in certain birds, beetles and shells, was highly prized. By the close of the century the vogue for feathers of all kinds, and fur, was so widespread that some species and the ecosystems that they supported were endangered.

Cotton became Britain's most important textile industry in the nineteenth century. The mechanization of spinning and transition from hand to power looms, which accelerated in the 1830s–40s, gave Britain a huge competitive advantage, enabling the fast production of much greater quantities of cloth to a higher standard. Between 1816 and 1850 cotton products contributed nearly 50 per cent of the value of all British exports.[13] They were sold throughout the world and effectively destroyed India's centuries-old industry.

Imports of raw cotton to feed the mills of the north of England, and Glasgow and Paisley in Scotland, rose from 11 million pounds in weight in 1785 to 588 million in 1850.[14] From the early 1800s the USA was the main source of the raw material, where various Old and New World species had been grown from the sixteenth century. Its stocks of upland cotton cultivated in the western states away from the Atlantic coast, were, however, significantly improved by successive introductions of Mexican cotton varieties in the 1800s.[15] Eli Whitney's (1765–1825) invention of the cotton gin (1793), which separated seeds from lint, mechanized one of the most time-consuming processes in the production of cotton. The continual weeding of the cotton fields still had to be done by hand. Before the Civil War the plantation owners relied on the back-breaking physical labour of slaves who endured brutal treatment, and afterwards they exploited disadvantaged sharecroppers (pl. 43).

Refinements to the chemical bleaching of cotton, which reduced the time taken to bleach cloth from months to hours and brought the process indoors, contributed to the faster production of cotton textiles. In 1799 Charles Tennant (1768–1838), in partnership with the chemist Charles Macintosh (1766–1843) (p. 75), patented a method for making dry bleaching powder by reacting chlorine with dry slaked lime. In 1800 he founded a chemical plant at St Rollox near Glasgow to manufacture bleaching powder, soda ash and other alkali substances. Soda ash was used in the production of soap, which was widely employed in the textile industry for scouring (aqueous cleaning). Hydrogen chloride fumes emitted while making these substances were converted in the atmosphere to hydrochloric acid, which caused atmospheric and environmental pollution. The Alkali Act (1863), which was designed to combat air pollution from alkali manufacturing, diminished this problem.[16]

Cotton of all kinds and qualities was produced to meet the requirements of the burgeoning ready-made industry and higher levels of the clothing trades. Cotton and muslin, whether plain, figured, printed or embroidered, were rarely out of fashion for women (pl. 42). Men too wore muslin in the form of cravats, shirt ruffles and exquisite hand-embroidered shirt fronts, and shirts themselves were increasingly made from cotton rather than linen. Newly introduced machine-made cotton net, lace and embroidery consumed even more of the fibre, serving the demand for affordable fashion.

During the Crimean War (1853–6), when Britain was cut off from Russian supplies of flax and hemp, there was a burst of interest in lesser-known plant fibres and their suitability for growing and processing in India and manufacture in Britain. Those under consideration included pineapple fibre. Pineapple leaves contain coarse fibres, used to make twine, and fine white fibres, which can be woven on their own or mixed with another fibre to make pineapple cloth. The use of pineapple fibres for cloth in South America and the Caribbean predates the Spanish conquest. In nineteenth-century Europe, where it is often given its French name of *batiste d'ananas*, it was associated with Asia, particularly the Philippines where it is called *piña*. Fashionable in France in the early 1840s, particularly woven into handkerchiefs, it was described by the writer Delphine de Girardin (1804–1855) as 'white, smooth and shiny, with the freshness, transparency and brightness of the purest wave of water'.[17]

Pineapple cloth and thread from Java, the Celebes (present-day Sulawesi, Indonesia), Singapore, Madras and other parts of India, and embroidered handkerchiefs from the Philippines and China, were exhibited at the Great Exhibition in London in 1851. The cloth's potential use to Britain as a fashion fabric was flagged by *The Illustrated London News*, which described it as 'pretty' and apparently 'capable of being worked into useful fabrics and [meriting] attention, especially as they can be produced at a low rate'.[18] Small quantities of pineapple fibre were imported into London and Liverpool in the 1850s but how they were employed is unknown.[19] Ships crossing the Atlantic docked at Liverpool, which suggests that some fibre may have been sourced in South America or the West Indies.

In 1828 Isabella Davison (1809–1883) wore a dress of conventionally fashionable cut, made of silk woven with pineapple fibre, when she married Thomas Forster (1797–1878) of Burradon Hall, Northumberland (pl. 44). The unusual fabric is figured with trails of flowers and voided, semi-transparent leaf shapes of pure *piña*. Nothing is known about the fabric's source so we can only speculate that it came from Asia. The infrequent references to pineapple fibre in newspapers of the time suggest that its role in European fashion was slight but further research may uncover more evidence of its use as an exotic fabric.

Fluctuations in the supply and price of raw silk led to experiments with spun glass. Silica, found in quartz and some sands, is the main constituent of glass. Spinning glass creates a soft, fine flexible thread that breaks only when pressure is placed on it (pl. 46). Glass had many advantages: it cost less than silk; its colours did not fade or tarnish; it was not susceptible to moth, rust or mould; and it was water- and fire-proof. Patents for fabrics woven with spun glass were registered in France and

Britain in the 1830s. The principle challenge for the manufacturer was to form a very fine, strong, elastic thread. Louis Schwabe (1798–1845), a weaver and inventor in Manchester, manufactured glass tissue for Williams & Sowerby, which retailed the fabric in its store in Oxford Street in London. Schwabe's innovative research into spinning glass anticipated the technology used to produce man-made fibres. Spun glass was traditionally made by heating a glass rod, drawing a thread and attaching it to an iron drum that revolved at high speed, pulling out and reeling the glass fibre, which cooled and solidified in contact with the air. Schwabe invented a spinning machine that forced the molten glass through fine holes, 'separat[ing] the fibres whilst spinning ... the weft, requiring, as it does, one hundred of these fibres to form one pick or shoot'.[20] Other travelling flame-workers and manufacturers besides Schwabe succeeded in producing longer, more flexible and stronger threads.

The royal family and the Duke of Wellington (1769–1852) were quick to endorse glass tissue, made with a silk warp and glass wefts, purchasing hangings from Williams & Sowerby in 1840.[21] Although the fabric was principally marketed for furnishing, the Duke's daughter-in-law, the Marchioness of Douro (1820–1904), appeared at court in 1840 in a blaze of diamonds wearing a pale green watered silk dress trimmed with gold lace with a train of 'magnificent gold and white glass tissue'. The train was embellished with more gold lace and diamonds, and bouquets of myrtle and pale pink roses.[22]

Glass cloth was sufficiently successful for its manufacture to continue and the London silk mercers and drapers Grant and Gask exhibited a glass furnishing fabric called 'Royal Tissue de Verre' at the 1862 International Exhibition. In the 1890s the Libbey Glass Company of Toledo, Ohio, manufactured glass cloth suitable for dressmaking (pl. 45), patented by Hermann Hammesfahr (1845–1914) in 1880, although this was undoubtedly a novelty.[23] Glass fibre was also crafted into 'feathers' and millinery trimmings from the 1820s to the early 1900s. In 1898 they were recommended as an ethical alternative to real feathers.[24] Further interest in spun glass as a fibre for textiles was probably limited due to

44 / RIGHT Wedding dress, worn by Isabella Davison when marrying Thomas Forster at Morpeth, Northumberland. Pineapple fibre and silk. India (fabric, possibly) and Britain (garment construction), 1828. Bowes Museum: 2003.2332.1

45 / LEFT A 'cabinet card' from the World's
Columbian Exposition, Chicago, depicting
Princess Eulalia of Spain (1864–1958) wearing
a dress of glass fibre made by the Libbey Glass
Company, 1893. Ink on paper. Corning
Museum of Glass: 134150

46 / BELOW Skein of spun glass. Britain, c.1847.
Given by Captain T.T. Barnard, V&A: T.11–1951

the production of artificial silk from chemically modified cellulose in the last two decades of the century. Count Louis de Chardonnet (1839–1924) produced the first multi-filament man-made fibres in 1884. Although initially successful, 'Chardonnet silk' was highly flammable. It was followed by the invention of viscose rayon, which was patented in 1892 and manufactured commercially from 1905 (p. 128).

Chemistry was also important in the commercial development of rubber. Rubber is derived from the milky sap (latex) found in several varieties of plants. Its principal source is the Para rubber tree (Hevea brasiliensis), which is native to the rainforests in the Amazon regions of South America. It is extracted by making an incision in the bark that cuts through the latex vessels. In the nineteenth century the latex was coagulated by exposure to heat and smoke and then formed into a ball or 'biscuit', which might eventually weigh 50 pounds. Native peoples in Central and South America knew of rubber's elasticity, resilience and waterproofing qualities and used it to make balls as well as for more practical purposes. It was first employed in Britain in the 1770s as an eraser, or 'rubber', to rub out pencil marks on paper.

In 1823 Charles Macintosh (p. 71) patented a method of dissolving solid rubber in naptha, a byproduct of coal gas. By spreading the solution between two layers of cloth he made the first truly waterproof fabric, which acquired his name, although in the modified form of 'mackintosh'. (The Oxford English Dictionary's first example of the use of the word as a noun dates to 1835.) The process of vulcanization was discovered by Charles Goodyear (1800–1860) in the USA, although Thomas Hancock (1786–1865) in Britain was the first to secure a patent for the method in 1843.[25] It improved the properties of rubber, making it more stable and less susceptible to temperature change. Rubber's disadvantages – its strong smell, sweat-inducing warmth and impermeability – were mitigated in fashionable clothing by the looser styles of the 1850s and '60s and the introduction of eyelets to enable air circulation.

Vulcanization also improved the quality of the elastic threads knitted into hosiery, haberdashery elastic and webbing. The very first registered design to include elastic was an ankle boot by Joseph Sparkes Hall (1811–1891) in 1840, which had side gores made from elastic web. Sparkes Hall numbered the young Queen Victoria (1819–1901) among his clients and had a shop in Regent Street, London's premier shopping destination.[26] Elastic-sided boots for men and women survive in many museum collections (pl. 47). The elastic is often degraded and unattractively loose and puckered. Another London shoemaker, Jean Georges Atloff (c.1809–1876), claimed to have overcome the 'gouty appearance' developed by side gores during wear by placing the web on the boot's throat 'to allow the free rising of the instep, and produce that … *cambré* (arched) shape which is always so greatly admired'.[27]

Rubber was utilized to make a variety of waterproof protective clothing (pl. 48). In 1857 Barbara Leigh Smith Bodichon (1827–1891) declared that 'No woman ought to be without a waterproof coat with a hood. The best can be procured for £2, common ones for £1.' As a feminist campaigning for women's rights to education, legal independence, access to the professions and waged work for all social classes, Bodichon took a dim view of the conventional fashions of her period. Women needed waterproofs to protect them from colds just as they needed work for the health of their minds and bodies.[28]

The increasing demand for rubber for industrial purposes led to government-backed attempts to establish a stock of *Hevea brasiliensis* in order to introduce its cultivation into the Empire. In 1876 botanists at Kew succeeded in germinating enough seeds to send seedlings, packed in Wardian cases (p. 101), to the botanic gardens in Ceylon (Sri Lanka) and Singapore. The first Asian rubber plantation was established in Malaya (now part of Malaysia) in 1896.

Another byproduct of the gas industry, coal tar, was integral to the manufacture of man-made aniline dyes, which transformed the colour palette of textiles. Aniline dyes are cheaper and easier to apply to fabric than traditional dyes derived from plants, insects and shellfish and in the twentieth century they became the mainstay of commercial dyeing. William Henry Perkin's (1838–1907) serendipitous discovery of synthetic mauve (mauveine) in 1856 focused attention on the potential of aniline dyes and drove the development of new

47 / BELOW Boot. Wool, canvas and rubber elastic. Britain, 1845–65. Given by Mr A.L.B. Ashton, V&A: T.24–1936

48 / RIGHT Advertisement for J.C. Cording, 'Manufacturer of Waterproof Goods, Warranted to Resist the Effects of any Climate', from *Prospectuses of Exhibitors at the Great Exhibition* (Britain 1851), vol. 16. V&A: National Art Library

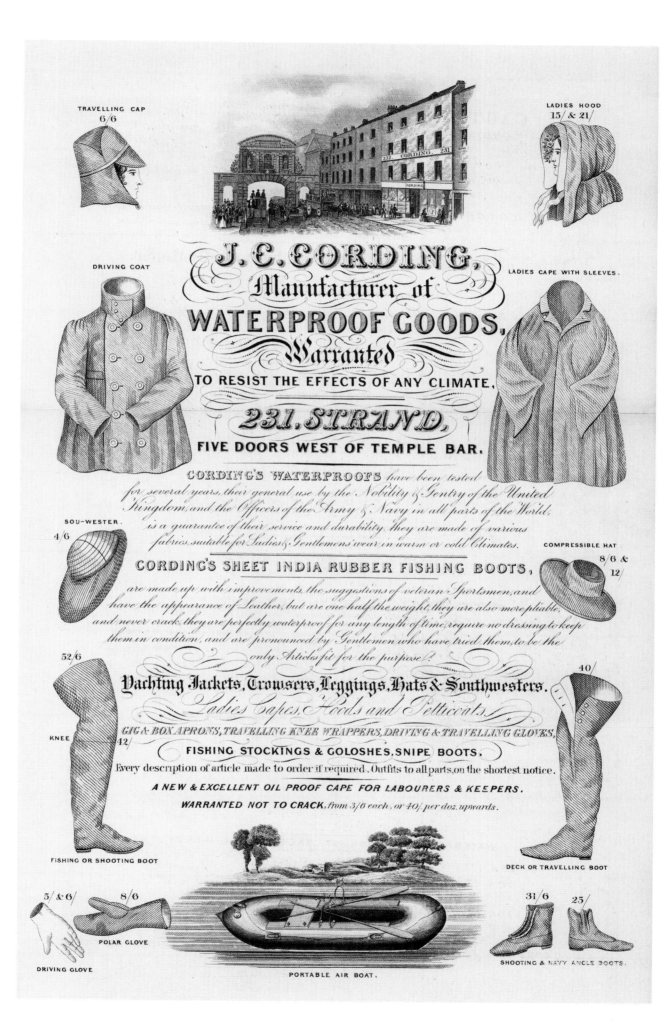

TRAVELLING CAP
6/6

LADIES HOOD
15/ & 21/

DRIVING COAT

LADIES CAPE WITH SLEEVES.

J.C. CORDING,
Manufacturer of
WATERPROOF GOODS,
Warranted
TO RESIST THE EFFECTS OF ANY CLIMATE,
231. STRAND,
FIVE DOORS WEST OF TEMPLE BAR.

CORDING'S WATERPROOFS have been tested for several years, their general use by the Nobility & Gentry of the United Kingdom, and the Officers of the Army & Navy in all parts of the World, is a guarantee of their service and durability, they are made of various fabrics, suitable for Ladies & Gentlemens wear in warm or cold Climates.

SOU-WESTER.
4/6

COMPRESSIBLE HAT
8/6 & 12/

CORDING'S SHEET INDIA RUBBER FISHING BOOTS,
are made up with improvements, the suggestions of veteran Sportsmen, and have the appearance of Leather, but are one half the weight, they are also more pliable, and never crack, they are perfectly waterproof for any length of time, require no dressing to keep them in condition, and are pronounced by Gentlemen who have tried them, to be the only Articles fit for the purpose.

52/6

40/

Yachting Jackets, Trowsers, Leggings, Hats & Southwesters.
Ladies Capes, Hoods and Petticoats.
GIG & BOX APRONS, TRAVELLING KNEE WRAPPERS, DRIVING & TRAVELLING GLOVES,

KNEE
42/

FISHING STOCKINGS & GOLOSHES, SNIPE BOOTS.
Every description of article made to order if required. Outfits to all parts, on the shortest notice.

A NEW & EXCELLENT OIL PROOF CAPE FOR LABOURERS & KEEPERS.
WARRANTED NOT TO CRACK, from 3/6 each, or 40/ per doz. upwards.

FISHING OR SHOOTING BOOT

DECK OR TRAVELLING BOOT

5/ & 6/

8/6

31/6

25/

DRIVING GLOVE

POLAR GLOVE

PORTABLE AIR BOAT.

SHOOTING & NAVY ANCLE BOOTS.

49 / ABOVE Day dress. Silk dyed with methyl
violet (synthetic dye). Britain, c.1873. Given by
the Marchioness of Bristol, V&A: T.51&A–1922

50 / RIGHT Nursing dress. Block- and
roller-printed cotton dyed by the Turkey red
process. Britain, 1825–30. Given by Miss
D.A. Frearson, V&A: T.74–1988

colours particularly in Germany and Switzerland. Formulating dyes that were suitable for silk, wool, and especially cotton, which was of far greater commercial importance, was an important part of this research.

In 1868 two German chemists analysing the chemical structure of alizarin showed that it is derived from the coal tar hydrocarbon anthracene. Alizarin is present in the root of the madder plant, which was widely used for calico printing and Turkey red dyeing on cotton (pl. 50). This discovery enabled the synthesis of alizarin and after further experimentation by Perkin in Britain and the Hoechst dyeworks and Heinrich Caro (1834–1910) at BASF in Germany an economical way of producing it was found.[29] Dyes based on alizarin, whether derived from madder or man-made, are fast.

The advent of the first brilliantly coloured synthetic dyes coincided with the vogue for voluminous skirts supported by crinoline frames. The fashion was the perfect advertisement for the exciting new colours so miraculously derived from coal tar. Together they were an assertion and embodiment of modernity. Yet many aniline dyes, although originally touted as fast, including mauveine, magenta, malachite green and methyl violet (pl. 49), proved disappointingly fugitive. Some became unstable when exposed to sweat and body heat, causing swelling, sickness and rashes. Aniline poisoning became an occupational hazard for dyers.[30] In 1890 Professor John James Hummel (1850–1902), first Professor of Dyeing at the Yorkshire College of Science and an expert on fast and fugitive dyes, was driven to defend coal-tar dyes. Of approximately 30 natural dyes, 10 gave fast colours; of the 300 coal-tar dyes in use in 1890, about 30 had proved extremely fast and an equal number moderately fast giving the dyer far more choice.[31] Natural dyes continued to be used independently of and combined with synthetic dyes into the early 1900s (p. 98), but the latter delivered a consistent strength and were cheaper.

The ability to draw on innumerable colours is one of fashion's most useful tools for introducing novelty and the appearance of change. Given the susceptibility of dyes to fading, it is no surprise that raw materials with naturally beautiful, longer lasting colouring were prized for clothing and accessories. Iridescence was

51 / LEFT Day dress. Moiré silk.
Britain, c.1858. Given by Miss
Janet Manley, V&A: T.90&A–1964

52 / ABOVE Pair of earrings. Gilt metal,
glass and the heads of red-legged
honeycreepers (*Cyanerpes cyaneus*).
Britain, c.1875. V&A: AP.258–1875

particularly admired. It is difficult to simulate in textiles although both shot silk, woven with warp and weft threads of contrasting colours, and moiré silk (pl. 51) create similar optical effects. Iridescence results from colour that is produced by minute structured surfaces that are fine enough to interfere with visible light. It changes with the angle of light falling on the surface and the angle from which it is viewed.[32] Mother-of-pearl (pl. 55), the feathers of certain birds (pl. 52) and the vivid, metallic wing cases of jewel beetles (*Buprestidae*) owe their shimmering colours to this interaction (pl. 53).

Buprestidae are wood-boring insects that are found in many parts of the world, including Europe. The beetles have been utilized in many cultures to embellish clothing and indicate high rank, and their vivid effects led to their use in fashion. Both the hard forewings that protect the flying wings when the beetle is at rest and whole beetles are found decorating garments and dress accessories such as stoles, fans and purses. In 1828 the Hon. Mrs Edward Cust (1800–1882) ordered a pink silk court dress, 'embroidered with gold and beetle's wings, [with] tassels of green and gold', and a green silk train to honour the king's birthday. Her choice of pearl and emerald jewellery and the materials of her costume reflected her family's wealth and colonial ties.[33] Mrs Cust's father, Lewis William Boode (d.c.1800), belonged to a leading family of slave and plantation owners in British Guiana in South America. India developed an export trade in muslin stoles, dress panels and flounces embroidered with wing cases and silver-gilt metal thread and its success inspired British dressmakers to copy the embroidery (pl. 54) with imported wing cases. In 1867 a single shipment numbered 25,000 wings.[34]

Fashion's constant quest for novelty also led to living insects being worn. The brief American fad in the late 1880s for wearing makech beetles (*Zopherus chilensis*), ornamented with jewels and attached by a chain to a lapel or corsage, was met with disbelief: 'the poor little wretches are treated … as if they were lumps of gold, not living creatures'.[35] There are also accounts of evening dress adorned with fireflies creating a mesmerizing natural light show that quite literally put their wearer in the spotlight.[36] Both customs were appropriated from traditional practice in Central and South America.

Of the multitude of birds imported to ornament dress, those with iridescent feathers were among the most desirable. Although pigment colours fade, the iridescence is retained because of the feathers' structure. Peacocks, hummingbirds from South America and Impeyan pheasants from the Himalayas were prized for their feathers' vibrant, shimmering colours. Possibly the most artful use of hummingbirds was their incorporation into fans (pl. 56). Manipulated with a deft hand the stuffed and lifeless bird might almost seem to hover again in flight. Some fans feature beetles and beetle wing cases whose prismatic colours echo the hummingbird's sheen.

From the 1770s to 1914 birds, bird parts and feathers were employed in astonishing quantities to dress hair, ornament bonnets, hats and ballgowns, and create delicate accessories such as boas, muffs and fans. Two trends stand out: the fashion for using whole birds and the impulse to improve on nature. An early instance of the former occurred in 1829–30 when millinery decorated with pairs of birds of paradise was heralded as the latest novelty. No doubt their cost as well as their appearance distinguished them from mainstream styles that merely incorporated the birds' plumes.[37] The vogue was reignited in 1859 when the style-setting Empress Eugénie (1826–1920), wife of Napoleon III of France, wore a bonnet decorated with a hummingbird perched on a spray of lilac.[38] The bird was probably a stuffed specimen of the violet-throated Empress Brilliant (*Heliodoxa imperatrix*), which the ornithologist, taxidermist and publisher John Gould (1804–1881) dedicated to the Empress in 1856. This widely reported 'fashion moment' seems to have launched a fad for utilizing small birds like hummingbirds, tanagers, swallows and robins to decorate dress and millinery that led to the death of millions of birds.

The starling-trimmed hat described by Veronica Isaac (p. 98) is a good example of the desire to improve on nature. Dyed and painted feathers from another bird supplement the starling's recoloured feathers in a form of sartorial crossbreeding, creating a new 'fancy' species. The instinct to impose a human aesthetic of beauty on nature through artifice and intervention goes to the heart of our

53 / ABOVE Jewel beetle in the Sanjay
Gandhi National Park, Mumbai, India

54 / RIGHT Bodice and skirt. Cotton
muslin decorated with jewel beetle
wing cases (*Sternocera aequisignata*).
Britain (probably), 1868–9. Given by
Kathy Brown, V&A: T.1698:1 to 5–2017

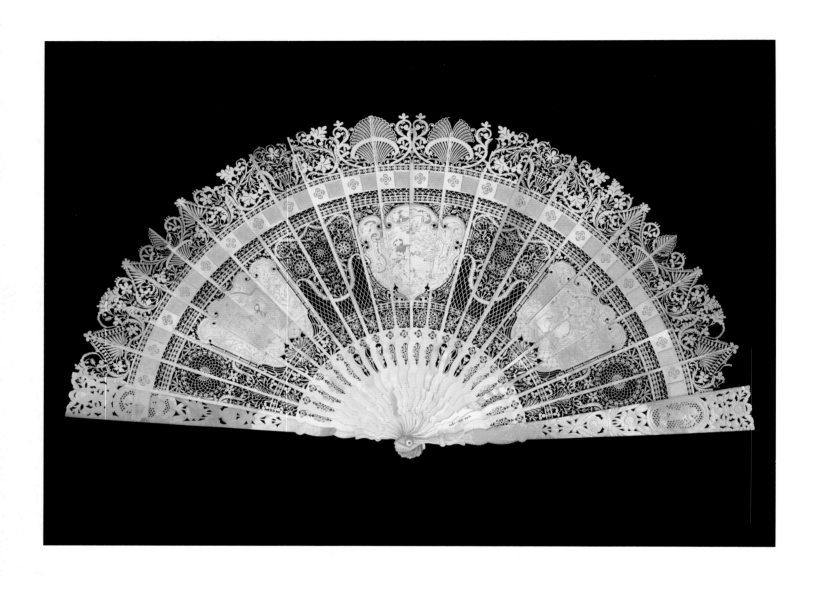

55 / ABOVE Fan. Pierced and carved
mother-of-pearl. France, 1800–50.
Given by HM Queen Mary,
V&A: CIRC.248–1953

56 / RIGHT Mesdesmoiselles M. & E.
Natté, feather fan decorated with a
stuffed hummingbird and jewel beetles.
Brazil, 1880s. Given by Margaret S.
Perkin, V&A: T.15–1950

relationship with nature. The hat demonstrates the impulse to control and manipulate nature to make it more 'useful', 'beautiful' or 'rare'.[39]

In the nineteenth century new ways of processing fur, which made it more supple, led to the development of fur coats. Fur had previously been used only to line and trim garments. Sealskin, from the northern fur seal (*Callorhinus ursinus*), which lives in cold northern waters, was among the first furs to be tailored into outerwear. When employed for clothing the dark, coarse outer guard hairs are removed to reveal the soft, silky underfur, which is a rich chestnut brown. Sealskin jackets and accessories were enormously popular from the middle of the century and there are records of proud owners in fact and fiction.[40] The best-quality coats were luxurious. They were often dyed to enrich their colour, were soft, warm and, in the hands of a skilled furrier, well-fitting and stylish. A fine example in the V&A's collection, made in about 1905 by the Parisian firm of Pfeiffer-Brunel and worn by Elizabeth Lindsay de Marees Van Swinderen (1878–1950), incorporates skins with and without the guard hairs (pl. 58). The former are used for the collar, cuffs and matching muff, creating a visual and textural contrast with the short velvety fur of the jacket's body.

Fur garments and accessories, like stoles and muffs, trimmed with tails, paws and heads, were a feature of late Victorian and Edwardian fashion. Ermine, of which the best though most expensive quality was sourced in Russia, Norway and Sweden, foxes, mink and martens (pl. 59) imported from Canada and raccoons from North America were common subjects for this treatment. Stuffed animals, such as fur seals, ermine (stoat) and bears, featured as decorations in fur showrooms (pl. 57). When so many furs of lesser value were used as alternatives to more costly and exclusive pelts, such as pine marten for sable and, at the lowest level, 'seal coney' (made from rabbit fur) for sealskin, the presence of a real, if stuffed, animal may have been designed to reassure customers of the quality and authenticity of a retailer's stock. The fashions themselves were ostentatious, and were offensive and unethical to those who condemned cruelty to animals and blood sports.

57 / ABOVE Harrods, *London's Centre for Fashionable Peltry*. Advertisement. London, 1901–14. V&A: Textiles and Fashion archive

58 / BELOW Pfeiffer-Brunel, jacket with muff. Sealskin. Paris, c.1905. Given by Lady Hoyer Millar, V&A: T.49 and 50–1961

The Impact of Fashion on the Natural World

The formation of societies such as the Society for the Prevention of Cruelty to Animals (SPCA, 1824; from 1840 the Royal Society for the Prevention of Cruelty to Animals) and the Society for the Protection of Birds (1891, from 1904 the Royal Society for the Protection of Birds), which absorbed the Fur, Fin and Feather Folk (1889) and Plumage League (1889), arose from deeply felt concerns about the environment, the destruction of species and cruelty to animals. Women were at the forefront of public campaigns for land preservation, the protection of domestic animals such as horses, and the control of blood sports, vivisection and the fur and feather trades. They included the social reformer Octavia Hill (1838–1912); Baroness Burdett-Coutts (1814–1906), President of the RSPCA; the art historian and author Vernon Lee (1856–1935); the journalist and feminist campaigner Frances Power Cobbe (1822–1904); Eliza Phillips (1822/3–1916), Vice-President and publications editor of the SPB; and the society's secretary Mrs Frank (Margaretta) Lemon.[41]

The Sea Birds Preservation Act was the first legislation controlling the slaughter of birds to reach the British Statute Book, in June 1869. It provided protection for 33 species by introducing a closed season running annually from 1 April to 1 August when the birds were breeding. Although sea birds' feathers were employed for fashion, birds were equally at risk from egg collectors, the practice of shooting birds for sport, the demand for taxidermy specimens and the use of their eggs as food. Although the law, like other subsequent legislation devised to protect Britain's wild birds, was well-intentioned it was largely in-effective, being difficult to police and limited to the breeding season.

The activities of the RSPB focused on raising awareness about the slaughter of birds for the plumage trade and its ecological consequences and lobbying for measures for the protection of birds. 'Lady-members' were required to set an example by refraining 'from wearing the feathers of any bird not killed for the purposes of food, the ostrich only excep-ted'. (Ostriches were farmed in South Africa for their feathers whose correct removal caused

the bird no harm.) The society published pamphlets, leaflets and postcards and some-times devised imaginative ways of drawing attention to their cause, for instance by staging a protest of placard-carrying men highlighting the devastating consequences for egrets of the fashion for wearing their plumes. The RSPB was supported by naturalists such as William Henry Hudson (1841–1922), the satirical magazine *Punch* (pls 61 and 62) and the artist George Frederick Watts (1817–1904) (pl. 60), as well as writers like John Ruskin (1819–1900). Although the campaign to control the trade in feathers suffered many setbacks, in 1921 the Plumage (Prohibition) Act passed through parliament. It was restricted to imports and subject to evasion but given the vested trade interests it was an achievement.

The drive to raise awareness of the cruelty of the fur trade was promoted mainly by groups concerned with animal rights and protection such as the RSPCA and the Humanitarian League (1891–1919). It particularly targeted the trade in sealskin. Seals, like birds such as egrets that were killed for their breeding plumage, were hunted with no regard for the breeding season. They were shot, clubbed and sometimes skinned while still alive. Joseph Collinson's distressing exposure of the brutal-ity of the trade, *The Cost of a Seal-skin Cloak*, was published by the Humanitarian League in 1899. Between the 1890s and 1911, when Canadian seal-hunting in the North Pacific was particularly intensive, the population of north-ern fur seals was reduced from around 4.5 to 5 million to some 300,000. In 1911 the North Pacific Fur Seal Convention, signed by the USA, Britain (for Canada), Russia and Japan, intro-duced stringent conservation legislation.[42] This internationally binding agreement was an important advance in animal protection.

While pressure groups formed to counter cruelty and protect bird and animal popula-tions, the continuing industrialization of Britain caused significant air and water pollution. This was exacerbated in centres with a high density of people and industrial activity that used fossil fuels to produce heat, light and power. The air and water pollution in Manchester and the surrounding towns was notorious. Dr Robert Angus Smith (1817–1884), an applied chemist, one-time Manchester resident and government inspector overseeing the Alkali and Rivers

59 / PREVIOUS PAGE Caroline Reboux (possibly) (1837–1927), hat. Pine marten fur and grosgrain ribbon. Paris, c.1893–7. Given by Sybil, Marchioness of Cholmondeley, V&A: T.374–1974

60 / LEFT George Frederic Watts (1817–1904), *A Dedication*, 'To all who love the beautiful and mourn over the senseless and cruel destruction of bird life and beauty' (G.F. Watts). Oil on canvas. Britain, 1898–9. Watts Gallery: COMWG.157

61 / RIGHT Edward Linley Sambourne (1844–1910), 'A Bird of Prey', *Punch*, London (14 May 1892). V&A: National Art Library

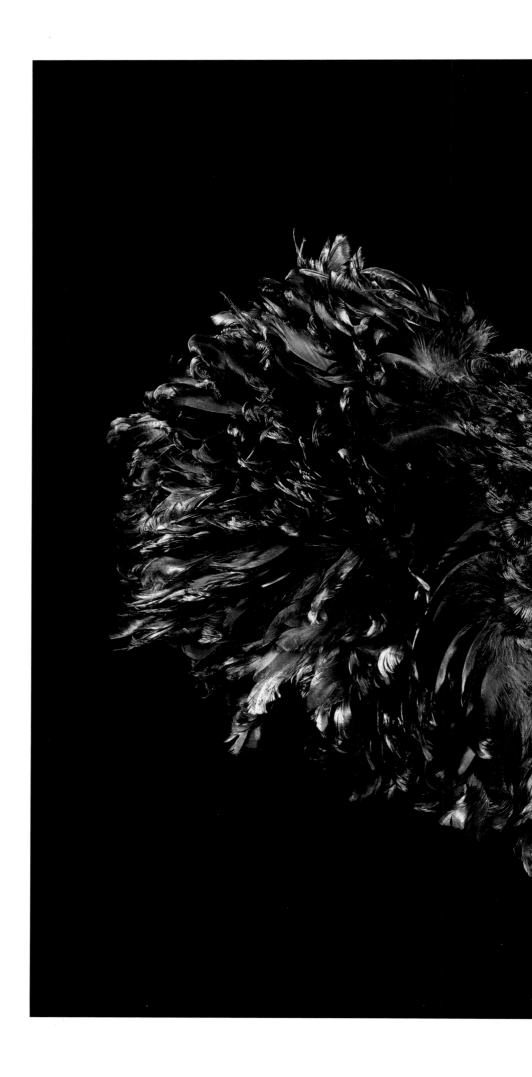

62 / RIGHT Auguste Champot,
cape. Cock feathers. Paris,
c.1895. Given by Mrs Mailin,
V&A: T.84–1968

63 / NEXT PAGE View of Bradford.
The Illustrated London News,
London (20 September 1873).
V&A: National Art Library

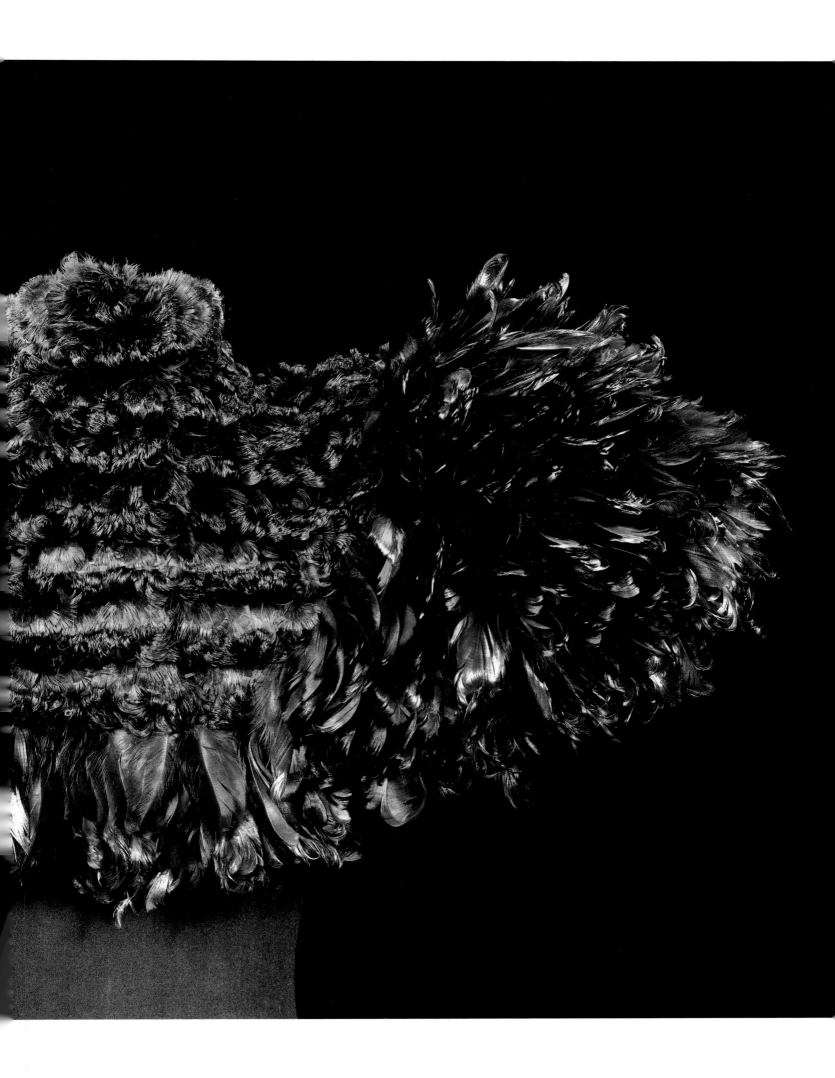

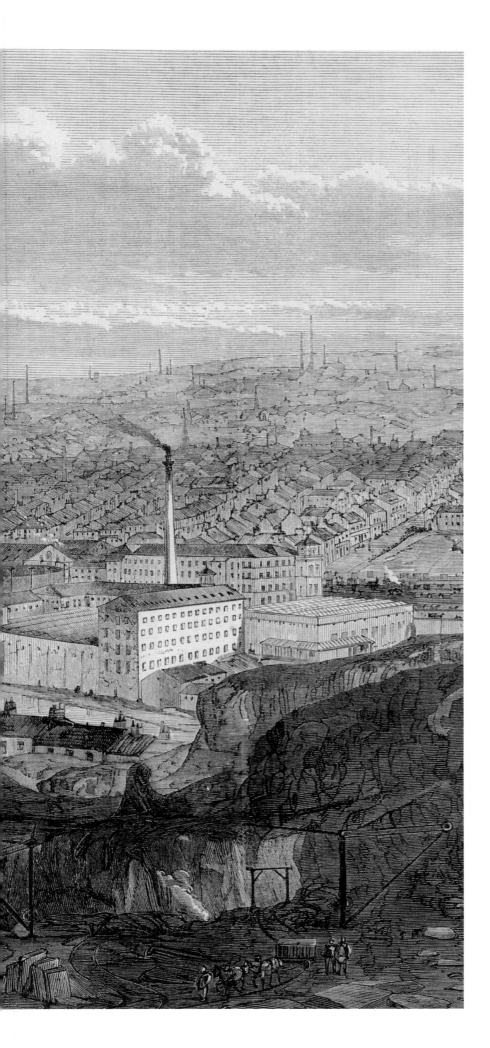

Pollution Prevention Acts (1863 and 1876), conducted research into the composition of the urban industrial atmosphere, its potential long-term effect on health and ways to combat it. Now regarded as a proto-environmental expert, he coined the term 'acid rain' in 1859. Coal containing high levels of sulphur generated sulphur dioxide emissions and made the rain acidic, gradually corroding stone and harming vegetation.[43] The dependence on coal also caused significant problems with waste. Slag heaps arose alongside collieries, and huge mountains of ash and clinker accumulated in cities. Foul-smelling water, sulphur compounds and oily tar, created by distilling coal for gas, were dumped in rivers, killing fish as well as affecting the health of the local community.[44]

The Third Report by the Royal Commission for Inquiring into the Pollution of Rivers (1867) focused on the pollution caused by textile manufacturing in the West Riding of Yorkshire. There were 491 worsted manufacturers, 2,050 woollen manufacturers and 222 cotton manufacturers situated along the Aire and Calder rivers. Other local industries included chemical works, breweries, mines and tanneries. The rivers, which were so polluted in some parts that the 'fluid looks more like ink than water', were fouled by a mixture of liquid and solid waste that affected the entire length of the river system from the polluting source, becoming more concentrated as the stream narrowed. Flooding was common. Washing, scouring, fulling and milling wool and woollen goods introduced oil, grease, soap, suspended matter and dirt; effluents from dyeworks were tainted with chemicals and colouring matter; and ash added to the solid waste.[45] The Commissioners' reports led to The Rivers Pollution Prevention Act (1876), which prohibited the disposal of solid matter, sewage and pollutants into rivers and streams. The Act was pioneering in its ambition but its flaws made it too easy for manufacturers to evade the regulations. It was also shortsighted to give local authorities the responsibility for enforcing the legislation as they often contributed to the problem.[46] Although the link between poor health, environmental damage and pollution was recognized by the industry, it tended to be accepted as a necessary price of industrial development and manufacturers were reluctant to spend more than strictly necessary on pollution controls.[47]

Walking in Flora and Fauna:
A Nineteenth-Century Dress and Hat

BY
Veronica Isaac

This walking dress and hat testify to the significant shifts occurring in the scale and speed of fashion production during the nineteenth century.[1] The former was made to measure by Madame Tridou, a dressmaker who was in business between 1880 and 1895 at 78 rue de Rome in the eighth arrondissement of Paris (pl. 64). The hat was probably purchased at Les Grands Magasins du Louvre in the Place du Palais-Royal, as its lining is printed with a gold lion entwined with a capital 'L' and the accompanying text, 'Modes du Louvre, Paris'. Founded in 1855, this major department store expanded rapidly, establishing a reputation for 'stylish and expensive' ready-to-wear items. By 1875 it had at least 52 different departments over several floors, including a specialist millinery department.[2]

Department stores represented the latest innovation in retail practices and established shopping as a pleasurable pastime. These 'cathedrals of consumption' dominated the retail landscape in the late nineteenth century.[3] Their bold advertisements, lavish window displays and sumptuous interiors deliberately targeted bourgeois consumers, promising them an approximation of the elegance and luxury associated with the couturiers' salons, but at a price they could afford.[4] Their grand scale, together with the vast range of goods they stocked, suggests the significant expansion occurring in clothing production and consumption. New machinery and scientific innovations resulted in cheaper materials and introduced synthetically produced colours to the fashionable wardrobe, while improved communication and transport networks fuelled acceleration in the dissemination of fashions.

Although many department stores had both dressmaking and ready-to-wear departments, independent dressmakers, such as Tridou, offered their clients a personal and exclusive service. Her garments were probably expensive and beyond the budget of the majority of consumers, but priced below the level of the 'great dressmakers' and couturiers, who charged between 500 and 2,000 francs for their most extravagant creations.[5] These prices were extremely high as comparison with the wages of Denise, the heroine of Émile Zola's (1840–1902) novel *Au Bonheur des Dames*

(The Ladies' Paradise) of 1883, reveals. She was a shop assistant in the department store on which the novel focuses, and expected to earn 1,200 francs a year, perhaps up to 2,000 as she gained experience.[6]

Consisting of a separate bodice and skirt, this outfit follows the fashionable silhouette, which demanded a narrow waist and favoured a flat-fronted skirt with an exaggerated projection at the rear. Plate 65 reveals the complex internal structure required to achieve this shape: the bodice is stiffened with 11 channels of baleen that follow the lines of the corset, which, together with a corset cover and/or chemise, would have been worn beneath it. The rear of the skirt would have been supported on a bustle. Further shaping is present in the internal structure, which includes semi-circular hoops held in place with elastic tape. Petticoats would also have been worn underneath to create the required volume. A removable horsehair bustle pad has been added at the centre back waist. The draped overskirt and tailored waistcoat-style bodice demanded a large quantity of material, much of which was cut to shape.

The base of the skirt and the waistcoat-style panels on the bodice are made from silk velvet woven with a plain satin ground, with two heights of uncut pile forming an interconnected pattern of stylized flowers and leaves. This pattern replicates the motifs, stitches and structure of raised Venetian needlelace, with the two heights of pile echoing the characteristic raised elements and 'linking bars' of the lace.[7] There was a revival of interest in this type of seventeenth-century lace in the mid-nineteenth century, and the invention of chemical lace in the 1880s established a profitable industry in both remodelled originals and modern imitations. The pattern of the silk velvet consciously references this trend.[8]

This fabric was expensive and was probably sourced from Lyon, then the primary supplier of silks to the Paris dressmaking trades.[9] Approximately 16 metres of cloth would have been required for the outfit, which would have taken between four and six weeks to weave.[10] The dress itself is likely to have been made in a much shorter time period. Indeed, dressmakers were frequently under pressure to produce garments in the least time possible, sometimes in as little as 24 hours.[11]

64 / LEFT Madame Tridou, bodice and skirt. Silk and wool. Paris, 1885. V&A: T.715:1&2–1997

silk

wool

*walking dress with
two attached petticoats
right side layers*

front of st

Walki

65 / RIGHT Illustration showing
the construction of a bodice
and skirt V&A T.715–1997.
Eileen Budd. London, 2017

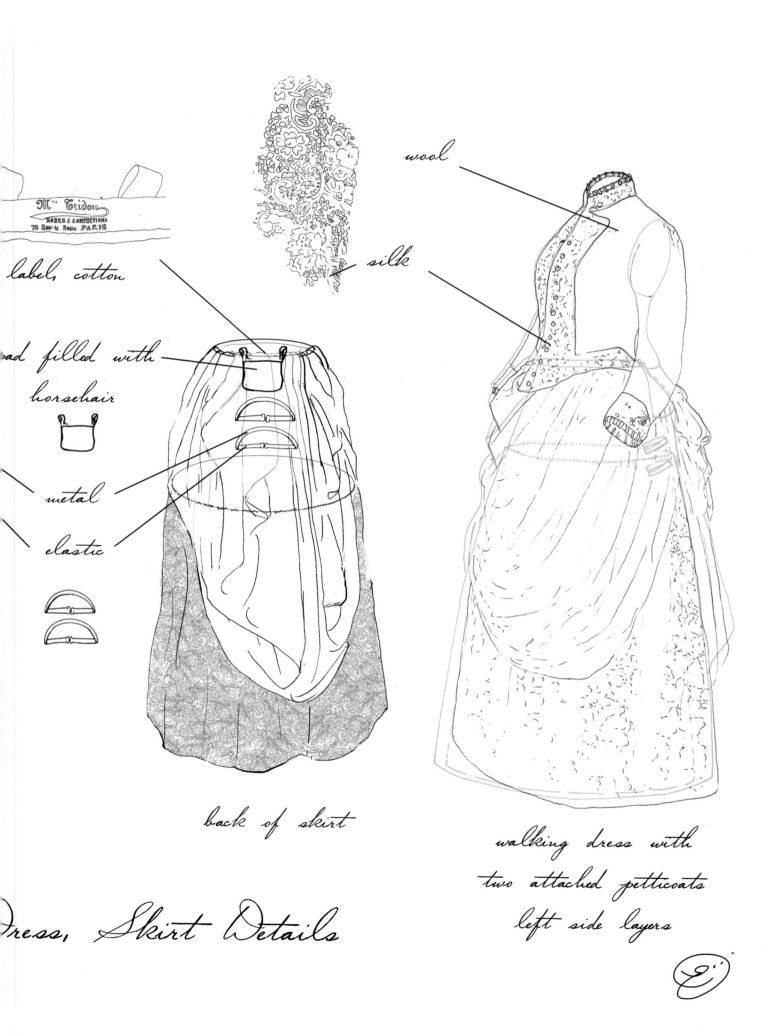

wool

silk

label, cotton

...ad filled with
horsehair

metal

elastic

back of skirt

...ress, Skirt Details

walking dress with
two attached petticoats
left side layers

Dye analysis of threads from the walking dress revealed the presence of both natural and synthetic dyes. The yarn of the draped wool twill overskirt was dyed with a combination of natural turmeric (obtained from the stem of the southern Asian plant, *Curcuma longa*) and a synthetic dye, possibly from the Acid Orange azo dye group (created using synthetic alizarin) (see p. 79).[12] The tan tones of the silk of the skirt and bodice are likely to have been achieved from a combination of synthetic dyes, magenta, probably malachite green and an unknown orange, or dye mixture.[13]

Like the dress, the wool felt hat (pls 66 and 67) includes a range of elaborate decorative effects. Its crown is encircled with a bronze silk ribbon, and lines of sycamore beads and silk chenille braid border the brim.[14] The dominant feature of the hat is the stuffed starling (*Sturnus vulgaris*), its feathers bleached and dyed in tones of pink and orange. The bird has been positioned in mid-flight at the front of the hat, against a backdrop of larger upright feathers from a goose or swan.[15] These have also been dyed, and decorated in metallic paint with bronze and gold thistles (*Cirsium vulgare*).

Escalation in the use of feathers and, as in this case, entire birds within millinery in the nineteenth century provoked alarm and criticism. By the mid-1880s pressure groups were being formed in Britain and beyond to campaign against the destruction of both native and exotic birds, and to promote their protection. The production of accessories like this hat posed a threat not only to the creatures used to decorate them, but also to their makers. Throughout this period, it was common practice to employ mercury nitrate to soften fur and wool during the felting process.[16] Unaware of the dangers to their health, many hatters suffered from mercury poisoning, which in severe cases proved fatal.[17]

This ensemble demonstrates the quantity and types of materials used for the construction of complex garments, which could not be recycled easily into new styles. They belong to a period in which evermore clothing was produced faster and on a greater scale. Nature continued to provide inspiration for designers but their use of it went beyond fur and feather trimmings to creations embellished with entire animals, insects and birds, although such excesses were increasingly controversial.

66 / ABOVE Nick Veasey, X-ray of hat. Britain, 2016. V&A: T.715:3–1997

67 / RIGHT Modes du Louvre, hat. Wool, silk, stuffed starling and goose or swan feathers. Paris, 1885. V&A: T.715:3–1997

Engaging with Nature: The Fern Craze

BY

Edwina Ehrman

Ferns fascinated the nineteenth-century public: they learned about their history through fossils, collected them to create indoor and outdoor fern gardens, dried and pressed their fronds, and embroidered them on fire screens, footstools and cushions. Ferns grow in many climates and habitats and range in size from tree ferns to spleenworts, which thrive in rock clefts.

In the early 1800s ferns were particularly interesting to geologists and botanists because of their extraordinary age, predating flowering plants by 200 million years. Geology was a relatively new and exciting science: the history of the earth's evolution stimulated impassioned debate. In the 1820s fossil finds, such as Mary Anning's (1799–1847) discovery of a nearly complete skeleton of a Plesiosaurus, spurred research into the plants and creatures that had once inhabited the earth. Fossils provided the primary evidence and in 1822 the term palaeontology was coined to describe their study. The botanist Adolphe-Théodore Brongniart (1801–1876) argued that the earliest tree ferns, which were 12 to 15 metres high, came from the 'oldest of the vegetable kingdoms', from the first period of the earth's existence before the formation of coal.[1] Living tree ferns offered an intriguing link to these long-dead giants.

Europeans encountered tree ferns in countries such as Australia, which Captain James Cook (1728–1779) claimed for Britain in 1770. Allan Cunningham (1791–1839), a botanist and explorer who wrote about the flora of New South Wales in the early 1820s, described tree ferns and the parasitical plants they hosted as 'swing[ing] in the violent winds of these elevated lands'.[2] His vivid account gives credence to the unusual depiction of tree ferns embroidered on an evening dress of about 1829 (pl. 68), which swirl around the skirt as if battered by a gale. A trailing plant with six-petalled flowers winds sinuously around them. The tentative identification of the flower with *Wahlenbergia angustifolia*, a trailing five-petalled bellflower growing on the island of St Helena in the South Atlantic, suggests that the tree fern could be a stylized representation of *Dicksonia arborescens*, which is indigenous to the island. In 1822 Brigadier John Pine Coffin (1778–1830), the island's Lieutenant Governor, donated a healthy 4-foot specimen to Kew Gardens.[3] Although we know nothing of the

dress's original owner and whether the embroidery had personal significance, the motif reflects the period's interest in the flora of the world.

Ferns and geology were among the many interests of Paulina ('Pauline') Jermyn Trevelyan (1816–1866). She met her future husband, Walter Calverley Trevelyan (1797–1879), at the 1833 meeting of the British Association for the Advancement of Science, which she attended with her father, the Reverend Dr George Jermyn (1789–1857). Trevelyan was a member of the Geology and Geography Committee. Following the meeting, he was invited to the vicarage to look at ferns and after a courtship that included fossil hunting and the gift of a box of fossils, the couple married in 1835.

In the mid-1850s the Trevelyans contributed financially to Oxford University's new Natural History Museum. Pauline, who was a talented amateur artist, friend of John Ruskin (1819–1900) and an active patron of the Pre-Raphaelites, advised on the plants that were to be carved on the capitals decorating the museum's interior. Perhaps unsurprisingly, the selection included ferns. Indeed, ornament derived from nature was integral to the Gothic style in which the museum was built and wholly appropriate to its contents and purpose.[4]

After Trevelyan succeeded to his father's baronetcy and estates in 1846, the Trevelyans spent time at Seaton in Devon. There Pauline became involved in improving the designs worked by the local Honiton lace industry. Too many patterns had no understanding of the technical constraints of lacemaking and she addressed this in her own exquisite design of British ferns for a handkerchief (pl. 71). The rendering of the ferns is sufficiently accurate to enable four to be identified as a hart's tongue fern (*Asplenium scolopendrium*), a rusty-back fern (*Asplenium ceterach*), a male fern (*Dryopteris filix-mas*) and a hard fern (*Blechnum spicant*).[5] In 1881 Queen Victoria gave Princess Stéphanie of Belgium (1864–1945) a Honiton lace dress in 'Her Majesty's favourite fern pattern' as a wedding present, suggesting that the design, or one similar, was still in use.[6]

The public's interest in ferns is widely attributed to the 'Wardian case' (pl. 69): a miniature greenhouse designed by the amateur naturalist Dr Nathaniel Bagshaw Ward (1791–1868) in which to grow and transport plants. Living in east London, Ward was all too familiar with

68 / LEFT Evening dress. Silk embroidered with a pattern of tree ferns. Britain, c.1829. Given by Messrs Harrods Ltd, V&A: T.744-1913

69 / LEFT Joseph Nash (1809–1878), 'Turkey:
No. 1'. Lithograph (detail showing a Wardian
case). *Dickinsons' Comprehensive Pictures of
the Great Exhibition of 1851* (London 1852).
V&A: National Art Library

70 / RIGHT Wardian case containing ferns used
as a window decoration, *Cassell's Household
Guide* (London c.1869–71), vol. 4

71 / OPPOSITE Lady Paulina ('Pauline') Trevelyan
(1816–1866) (designer), Miss S. Sanson (maker),
handkerchief (detail). Linen bobbin lace in a
pattern of ferns. Honiton, 1864. V&A: 785–1864

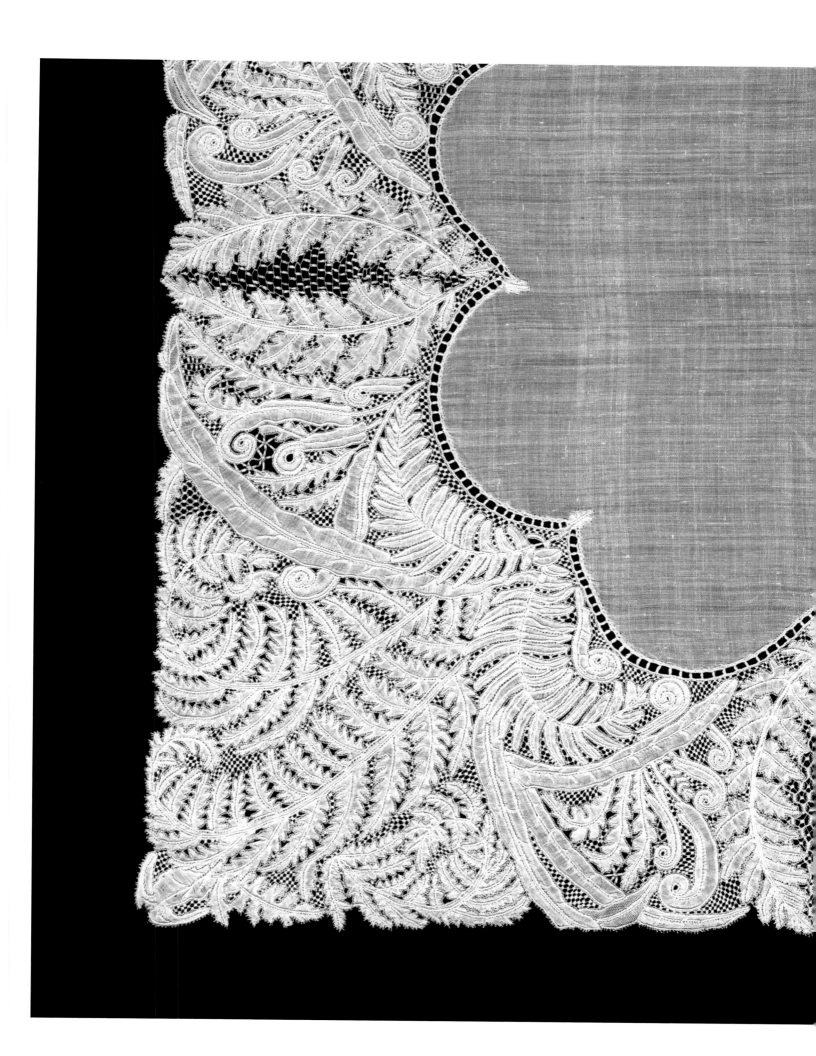

72 / RIGHT H. Paterson, 'Gathering Ferns',
The Illustrated London News, London
(1 July 1871). V&A: National Art Library

garden plants failing because of the appalling levels of smoke pollution that afflicted
British towns and cities. By the mid-nineteenth
century, over half the population lived in towns
that relied almost entirely on coal to provide
power and heat. Ward's case created a pollu-
tion-free, light-filled microclimate watered
by condensation created by the plants' evapo-
ration. By 1833 he had managed to grow 30
different ferns. After Ward published *On the
Growth of Plants in Closely Glazed Cases*
(1842), alternative designs proliferated (pl. 70)
and 'fern cases' quickly became fashionable in
middle-class homes.[7]

The craze for collecting and growing ferns
was supported by numerous publications, from
pocket handbooks to lavish folios, and for
those unable or unwilling to find their own
specimens, specialist nurseries were happy to
oblige. Ferns had several attractions as indoor
plants. They are not seasonal, need less light
than flowering plants and their many variants
encompass a fascinating range of forms and
textures. Sadly, although fern collecting found
approval as a healthy, educational and useful
recreation where the sexes could safely meet
(pl. 72), it led to widespread damage of fern
habitats, spoiling and upsetting the natural
balance of the countryside.[8] Collecting the
fronds to dry and press, an activity enjoyed by
Charlotte Brontë (1816–1855) on her honey-
moon, was a more sustainable alternative to
uprooting the entire plant.[9] Publishers were
quick to produce special fern collectors' albums
with handsome covers, and some professional
collectors, such as Joseph (1796–1860) and
James (1826–1877) Flintoft of Keswick, made
a business of creating ready-made albums of
pressed ferns as drawing room souvenirs.

Chapter 3
1900 — 1990

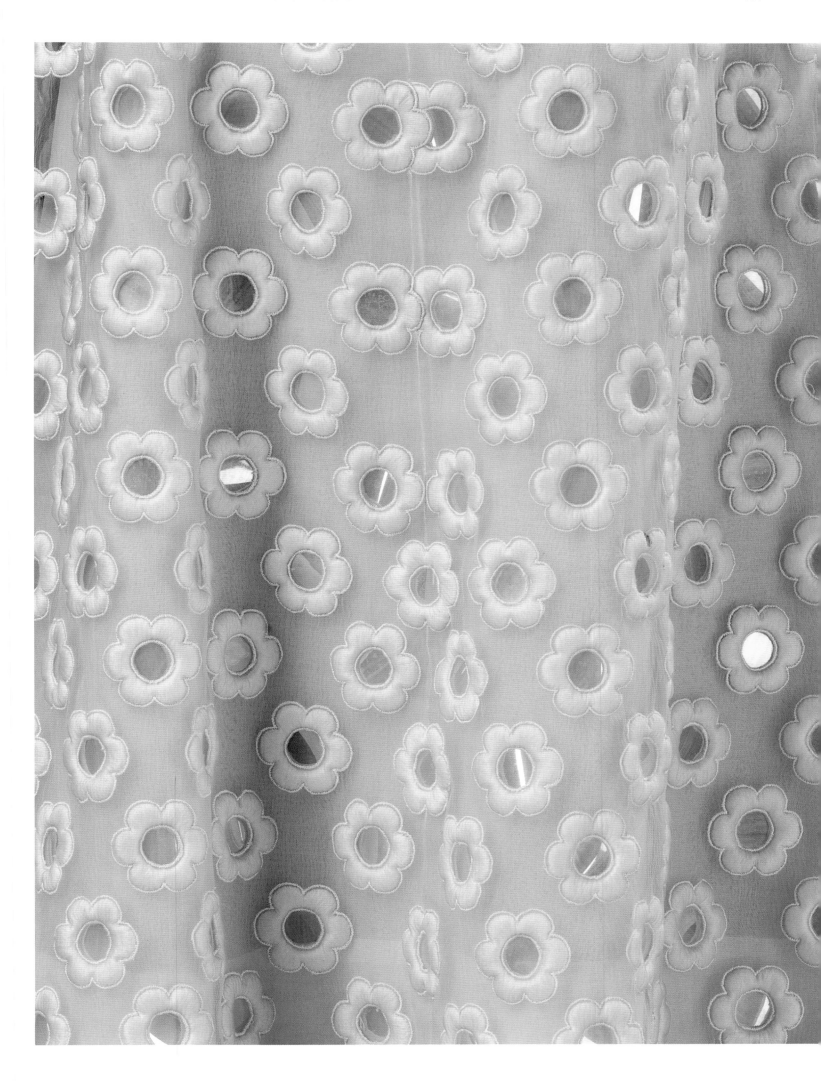

During the twentieth century technological and scientific advances revolutionized transport and communication creating new, faster methods of travel for goods and people, and enabling more immediate forms of commercial interaction, access to information and entertainment. In the textile industry, the expansion of the man-made fibre industry allied chemistry with textiles creating a great variety of new fibres with different characters, qualities and uses, which dramatically added to the potential of all the available fibres.

BY

Edwina Ehrman

The inventions that underpinned these technologies date to the last decades of the nineteenth century, but their full impact was realized only later. In all spheres the two World Wars (1914–18, 1939–45) accelerated technological progress, the need to equip the military and protect civilians driving research and innovation in motor and air transport, communication systems and improved methods of mass production.

Encountering Nature

The 1938 Holidays with Pay Act was a breakthrough in social legislation. It recognized the importance of leisure and travel for all social classes and the economic value of domestic tourism at a time when about a third of the population in Britain, some 15 million people, took one annual holiday away from home.[1] Workers' associations and charitable organizations founded on socialist ideals actively promoted the health and educational value of experiencing different environments, breathing fresh clean air and taking physical exercise. The Youth Hostels Association (YHA, 1930), which had 80,000 members by 1939, aimed 'to help all, especially young people of limited means to a greater knowledge, love and care of the countryside … and thus to promote their rest and education'.[2] Concerns about the countryside led to the formation of other groups such as the Council for the Preservation of Rural England (CPRE, 1926) and the Ramblers Association (1931, renamed 1935), which campaigned for its protection and regeneration while upholding the ambition to create the greatest possible access for all.[3] In 1949 the National Parks and Access to the Countryside Act led to the establishment of National Nature Reserves intended to protect the most important habitats and a national network of Sites of Special Scientific Interest.

Road transport of different varieties made rural tourism more possible in the 1920s and '30s, with motorbuses, coaches and cars affording access to the countryside: many of the former were converted from surplus army trucks after the First World War, while private car ownership rose to around two million people by 1939.[4] Although most car owners were wealthy, the mass-produced Austin Seven

(1922) was designed to be affordable for families on average incomes. Car owners were encouraged to explore Britain's monuments and beauty spots by a proliferation of guidebooks, ordnance survey maps of popular destinations (pl. 74) and the many artist-designed posters (pl. 73) commissioned by the oil company Shell (founded 1907). At this time, the car was not yet associated with air pollution. Overseas travel for leisure, whether by sea or air, train or car, was mainly the preserve of the affluent until after the Second World War when military aircraft passed into civilian use and entrepreneurs in the tourist industry developed package tours to European holiday destinations from 1950.

Radio and television also played a role in encouraging public interest in the British countryside and natural history in general. BBC broadcasters such as Desmond Hawkins (1908–1999), the ornithologist Sir Peter Scott (1909–1989) and Sir David Attenborough (b.1926), and Desmond Morris (b.1928) for Grenada TV, used the spoken word, sound and film to bring nature into their audiences' homes, with radio programmes like *The Naturalist* (1946) and *Out of Doors*, and from the 1950s on television. David Attenborough's first programme for the BBC, *The Pattern of Animals* (1953), led to *Zoo Quest* in 1954, which was based on an expedition to Africa with London Zoo. The initial series was set in Sierra Leone, where the team succeeded in finding the rare *Picathartes* bird, which has lived in the Congo for 44 million years. In 1956 the corporation broadcast *Diving to Adventure* produced by the award-winning film-maker Hans Hass (1919–2013). Presented by his wife Lotte (1928–2015), it was the first television programme to enable viewers to see life under the sea. The following year the BBC established a Natural History Unit at its Bristol studio. By the end of the 1950s there were over 10 million television-owning households. Programmes were available in colour from the late 1960s.[5]

During the inter-war period and into the 1950s, at an imaginary level, in writing on the countryside and the visual arts, the rural landscape was mythologized as the antithesis of the modern urban environment, imbuing it with spiritual and patriotic values. The regularity of the seasons and traditions of the land were interpreted as symbols of stability, offering a

73 / ABOVE John Armstrong (1893–1973),
*Newlands Corner: Everywhere You Go You Can Be
Sure of Shell*. Britain, 1932. Gift of the American
Friends of the V&A; Gift to the American Friends
by Leslie, Judith and Gabri Schreyer and Alice
Schreyer Batko, V&A: E.993-2004

74 / RIGHT Ordnance Survey, *Tourist Map
of the Lake District*, 'Derwentwater to
Skiddaw', illustration by Ellis Martin.
England, *c*.1925. British Library: CC.5.b.31

refuge from the political upheavals and economic uncertainties of the period as well as an
antidote to the perceived Americanization of
British culture. In this process rural life became
equated with 'Englishness' or what being
English meant, rather than with the nation's
political identity.[6] In fashion this was reflected
in the British predilection for 'country'
fabrics such as tweed (pls 75 and 76), and
garments like knitted sweaters and waterproofs, which are still associated with British
style and have been successfully reinterpreted,
and sometimes subverted, for a modern
audience by designers like Dame Vivienne
Westwood (b.1941).

Fashion:
System and Practices

Paris retained its international influence on
women's fashions throughout the first half of
the twentieth century and any hopes that the
privations of the Second World War might have
eroded its authority were dashed by Christian
Dior's (1905–1957) triumphant debut haute
couture collection in 1947. The origination of
new fashions remained firmly within couture's
control and the old hierarchies were main-
tained. Yet within 20 years a swathe of young
designers in Britain, France, Italy and North
America were challenging the role of French
couture as the sole source of creative fashion,
and by the 1980s Japan, too, was entering the
fray. These fresh talents worked in a different
idiom, often influenced by the street and its
subcultures, to fabricate clothes that reflected
the lifestyle, politics and interests of their
peers. Their success led to the rise of other
fashion centres with their own identities in
London, Milan and New York, and the organization of a tight schedule of fashion weeks that
depended on air transport to take its many
participants, from fashion editors and buyers
to models and photographers, from city to city.

   In Britain tastes in fashion were increasingly set by an amalgam of celebrities from the
worlds of entertainment, art and fashion, stylish
members of the social elite and wealthy jet-
setters. Royal fashions continued to be covered
in the press but were of relatively minor
interest until Lady Diana Spencer's (1961–1997)
engagement and marriage to the Prince of

75 / ABOVE Montague Burton Ltd, suit.
Harris tweed. Leeds, 1935. Worn with a
waistcoat by Arthur Shepherd. Knitted
wool. Cambridge and Oxford, 1940s.
Given by Mr Raymond Burton CBE,
V&A: T.13&1 to 3–2006

76 / RIGHT Norman Parkinson
(1913–1990), 'You Take the
High Road', Harper's Bazaar
(September 1937)

Wales (b.1948) in 1981. The princess quickly attracted a loyal following and her clothing choices from her early appearances as a shy young bride to her metamorphosis into an icon of glamour and style inspired many imitations.[7] Society magazines such as *The Tatler* (founded in 1901) and *Queen* (1958, originally *The Queen*, founded 1861), the celebrity lifestyle magazine *Hello!* (launched in 1988), and the gossip and fashion columns in the daily press documented the lifestyle and wardrobes of the influential globe-trotting set.

As the fashion industry grew in importance and size the different sectors formed trade organizations to manage and promote their interests. Until 1910 Paris had one body representing couture and ready-to-wear. As couture became more prominent its leaders decided to set up a separate organization, the *Chambre Syndicale de la Couture Parisienne* (Association of Parisian Couture), to improve its management and reinforce its status as the wellspring of creative fashion. From 1929 the ready-to-wear industry was overseen by the *Fédération du Prêt-à-Porter Féminin* (French Women's Wear Trade Association). British fashion's attempts to create similar support systems were less successful and often short-lived. One of the first, the Fashion Group of Great Britain (1935–9), whose members included dress, fabric and accessory designers, textile manufacturers, fashion writers, illustrators and photographers, store buyers and stylists, and public relations and advertising executives, reflected the growing professionalization of the industry. The Incorporated Society of London Fashion Designers (INCSOC/ISLFD; incorporated 1942 but active from April 1941; dissolved 1975) was founded to promote exports and develop London as a fashion centre after the war, but represented only a small, overly exclusive group of London couturiers.[9] Of the many groups supporting ready-to-wear after 1945, among the more notable were the London Model House Group (1950), the Fashion House Group of London (1958–68), which launched London's biannual Fashion Week, and the London Designer Collections (1975–83). The establishment of the British Fashion Council (BFC) in 1983 to promote the fashion industry and run London Fashion Week heralded a period of continuity and stability. The British Clothing Industry Association

(BCIA, 1980; from 2009 the UK Fashion and Textile Association) represents the mass-market clothing manufacturers.

The provision of fashion remained segmented. The nineteenth-century system of court dressmakers survived into the 1920s being a precursor to and overlapping with London's emerging couture houses.[10] Although the couturiers were few in number their success in exporting fashion to North America and the high profile of those who dressed the royal family helped to establish London as a centre for fashion. Their efforts benefited the high-quality ready-to-wear trade and paved the way for the radically different youth-oriented fashions of the 1960s that drew international attention to London and its vibrant, iconoclastic fashion, art and music scene. The development of designer ready-to-wear in London by figures like Mary Quant (b.1934) and Ossie Clark (1942–1996) was crucial to its emergence as a fashion city and the reputation of its fashion colleges for excellence, but the expansion of the mainstream ready-to-wear industry and spread of high-street chains was what really increased the scale of the industry and impacted on the environment.

Writing at the end of the 1920s S.P. Dobbs, author of *The Clothing Workers of Great Britain* (1928), commented, 'Women's garments are now for the first time being made in bulk by factory methods. Very soon it seems as if only the most exclusive men's and women's garments will be made by hand, so dressmaking and tailoring will be purely luxury trades.'[11] Women's ready-to-wear had been made in small tailoring workshops in the East End of London since the second half of the 1800s but the loose-fitting, simple cut of women's fashion in the 1920s facilitated the bulk manufacturing of clothes. Such styles gave the industry the opportunity to establish itself and meet the demand for ready-made clothes from young working women, laying the foundations for an increase in the scale of production.[12]

The most ambitious and enterprising women's ready-to-wear manufacturers drew on American expertise to improve their systems of manufacture, production and sizing. They visited factories in the United States and employed American consultants and technicians. Unlike the men's ready-to-wear sector, most did not develop chains of retail outlets until

77 / ABOVE Next Too, shirt. Mosquito
London, trousers. Cotton (shirt),
rayon (trousers). Britain, 1989.
Private collection

after the Second World War. Their in-house designers took their lead from Paris and, for more popular, cheaper styles, from Hollywood.[13]

The restructuring and regulation of the textile and clothing industries by the government during the war, in order to ensure supply and control prices, set new standards for British manufacturing, benefiting its post-war development. In the 1950s and '60s the large-scale manufacturers, many of whom built sizeable modern factories in areas with low female employment and labour costs such as South Wales, geared their production to uniform standards of styling, sizing and manufacture, and the long runs and efficient delivery that chain stores required. Some, such as Berketex (founded 1936), which opened a huge factory with 7,800 square metres of floor space in Plymouth in 1948, became retailers, setting up a chain of 120 shops within shops, and an extensive network of Berketex and Cresta shops. By 1970 its output was around a million dresses a year.[14]

Multiple stores, first developed in the nineteenth century (p. 69), grew steadily in numbers and scale in the twentieth century. By 1939 there were 595 Montague Burton (founded 1903) stores, including 77 in London alone, and 234 branches of Marks and Spencer (founded 1884), which earned two-thirds of its turnover from textiles.[16] Burton ran its own factories but Marks and Spencer contracted manufacturers to work for them while controlling the products at every stage of their manufacture. After the war the retail sector as a whole benefited from the increased spending power of young working people as the economy recovered in the late 1950s. A 1959 survey calculated that the real spending power of teenagers had almost doubled between 1938 and 1958.[17] Yet in just over a decade, the challenging economic environment of the 1970s coupled with the confusing proliferation of ephemeral fashion trends and an influx of competitively priced garments imported from Asia led many companies to review their operations.

Burton was threatened on several fronts: its core customers were ageing, the sale of suits had declined in favour of casual wear and imports of menswear were rising. It responded by expanding its womenswear division, making Topshop, formerly a boutique selling British designer ready-to-wear within some branches of Peter Robinson, a standalone brand targeting 16–25 year old consumers. Its profitability encouraged Burton to open Top Man in 1978 and by 1985 it had 177 Top Man branches whose ranges drew heavily on sportswear-influenced styles such as hooded tops and tracksuit bottoms. In a further expansion that same year, having identified a 'gap for quality, high design in the context of the high street', it rolled out Principles for Men to complement Principles for Women.[18] In 1985 the Burton group boasted 1,000 stores and sharply rising sales.[19] Burton's rival multiple tailor, Hepworth (founded 1864), also turned to womenswear in 1982 when, guided by its chairman Sir Terence Conran (b.1931) and new chief executive Sir George Davis (b.1941), it opened Next for 'smart, better-off women' aged between 25 and 35. Next's successful formula of offering well-priced, high-quality, stylish clothes presented in small coordinated collections underpinned its meteoric expansion, which was based on dividing the market into segments. Within six years the brand encompassed: Next for Men; Next Too (pl. 77) and Next Collection, which separated womenswear into 'the working woman's wardrobe' and more individual fashion choices; Next Interiors; Next Jewellery; Next for Boys and Girls; and Next Directory, which was a fresh take on the mail-order catalogue. As the historian Frank Mort observed, the company's business model became synonymous with the so-called 'high street revolution' of the 1980s, which focused on selling a lifestyle.[20]

In 1993 Margareta Pagano and Richard Thomson reported in a survey of the British clothing industry for the *Independent* that chain stores collectively accounted for 75 per cent of national clothing retail sales in Britain (compared with 50 per cent in France and Germany, 25 per cent in Italy and 20 per cent in Spain). Britain was a 'Mecca for good quality, resonably priced, mediocre apparel'. Most British consumers were happy with mainstream fashion inspired by the trends emanating from the designer ready-wear sector and they were reluctant, or unable, to spend a lot of money on individual garments. The high street offered choice and value in an unintimidating, inclusive environment and the familiar brand names inspired trust and loyalty.[21]

The Fabric of Fashion

Silk, wool, cotton and linen were used throughout the twentieth centuries on their own and combined with each other and the new man made fibres. The latter expanded the range of fibres available to designers, reduced prices and led to the fabrication of high-performance fabrics that improved fit and comfort and were easy to care for. Of the traditional fibres, wool and cotton had roles as fashion fabrics and as everyday staples, for tailoring and in the form of jeans respectively. Cotton's potential as a high-fashion fabric was promoted in the mid-century and the introduction of knitted outerwear to the fashionable wardrobe in the 1920s drew on wool and silk. During the Second World War silk was so rare that even heavily damaged silk parachutes were salvaged for clothing (pl. 78). Linen's attributes made it popular for summer, particularly in the 1930s in the form of linen tweed. After a period of decline it experienced a revival as a fashion fabric, thanks in part to its use by Japanese designers in the 1980s. Fine leather outerwear and garments crafted from reptile skins, although not entirely novel in the twentieth century, were important trends, although the use of reptile skins and the continuing vogue for fur excited controversy and opposition.

The rebranding of cotton as a high-fashion fabric in the 1930s by designers such as Gabrielle 'Coco' Chanel (1883–1971), who introduced cotton eveningwear into her spring collection in 1931, opened up the possibility of developing Britain's best-quality cottons as fashion fabrics at a time when the cotton industry was in decline and needed new markets.[22] This idea was taken forward by Sir Raymond Streat (1897–1979) when he became Chairman of the Cotton Board (1940) through the Board's public-facing subsidiary, the Colour Design and Style Centre (CD&SC, 1940), which was run by James Cleveland Belle (1910–1983). Belle devised a series of events to promote the use of cotton in high fashion. They included televised fashion shows featuring day and eveningwear made from cotton fabrics designed by British and European couturiers and exhibitions of designs for cotton prints commissioned from established artists, like Paul Nash (1889–1946) and Graham Sutherland (1903–1980), and emerging designers. Several,

78 / RIGHT Esther Ferguson (1919–2014), blouse. German parachute silk. London, 1942. Given by the family in memory of Esther Ferguson, V&A: T.88–2014

79 / LEFT Levi Strauss & Co. (jeans), Lee
(jacket), BVD (T-shirt). Cotton. USA, 1970–1.
Worn and given by Mr Robert LaVine,
V&A: T.715–1974

80 / RIGHT Horrockses Fashions, dress and
jacket. Cotton. Britain, 1955. Given by Corinne
Dawson, V&A: T.11:1 to 3–1997

including Sutherland, contributed designs to Horrockses Fashions, which was established in London in 1946 as a subsidiary of the Preston-based cotton manufacturer Horrockses, Crewdson & Company Ltd (founded 1791). Horrockses's attractive and wearable designs (pl. 80) made from its parent company's high-quality cottons gained the royal seal of approval when the young Queen Elizabeth II (b.1926) and her sister Princess Margaret (1930–2002) selected off-the-peg dresses for their respective royal tours of Australia and New Zealand (1953–4) and British East Africa (1956). Copies of the dresses worn by the Queen were subsequently offered for sale to the public at a relatively modest £4. 14s. 6d.[23]

In contrast with high-class, fine-printed cotton, cotton denim, dyed with synthetic indigo, became the most ubiquitous cotton fabric after the war. Marlon Brando's (1924–2004) portrayal of Johnny Strabler, the leader of the The Black Rebels Motorcycle Club, clad in jeans, T-shirt and leather biker jacket, in the 1953 film *The Wild One*, made jeans, and leather jackets, potent symbols of masculinity and youthful rebellion. Fashionable for young men in the 1960s, (pl. 79) in the following decade jeans were worn without regard for class, sex or age, although usually styled to fit male or female figures. Jeans varied greatly in their cut, construction, colour and fabric treatment, and had different cultural connotations according to their label, and the way they were worn and customized. In the 1960s and '70s well-worn, faded and frayed jeans had kudos. Achieving this effect took time and patience on the part of the owner, as the denim softened and the dye faded only through wearing and successive washings. A decade later, in an era when consumers were beginning to expect instant gratification, jeans could be bought ready-aged: bleached, patched and literally 'stone-washed' to pre-fade the fabric.[24] This deliberate pre-consumer ageing of a clothing staple reflected a significant change in the value of clothing, which placed fashion over durability and longevity.

Denim's mass appeal also led to its adoption by high fashion. In 1978 the advent of 'designer' jeans widened the market and raised prices. Gloria Vanderbilt (b.1924) promoted jeans branded with her signature on television infusing them with the aura of her glamorous lifestyle and personal elegance. The jeans were snug, with a tailored fit, and cost four times the price of Levis. In the first year sales soared six-fold to $150 million.[25] The Calvin Klein jeans advertised by the 15-year-old Brooke Shields (b.1965) in 1980 were even tighter. The campaign, shot by Richard Avedon (1923–2004), was a resounding commercial success. In one advertisement Shields asked, 'You want to know what comes between me and my Calvins? Nothing.' ABC and CBS in New York immediately banned the commercial for insinuating that Shields was not wearing underwear, providing an invaluable flash of publicity. The following year, at the height of the designer jeans boom, sales of denim jeans in the USA alone peaked at 502 million pairs.[26]

After the First World War the fashion for knitted outerwear created a welcome area of growth for the British textiles industry. The knitting industry, which drew on wool, silk, cotton and man-made fibres, was based mainly in the East Midlands and Scotland. British knitwear was noted for the high quality of its colours and design and the UK was a leader in the field until it lost its dominance to the Italian knitwear industry in the 1960s.[27] Prominent companies included the renowned Scottish knitwear company Pringle (founded 1815), whose designer Otto Weisz (1897–1975) is said to have introduced the tailored twinset to fashion in the 1930s, and Jaeger (founded 1884), which has utilized wool and many other animal fibres since it started making fashionable clothes after the First World War. Jaeger's advertising frequently called attention to the fibres it drew on, their animal source and special qualities. *Jaeger's Natural History* (c.1933) placed humorous verses alongside quirky drawings of animals in their natural habitats:

> The Cashmere goat,
> aloof, remote, is apt to be elusive ...
> he little knows
> how far that goes
> to making him exclusive.

Jaeger's light-touch educational approach encouraged its customers to make informed material choices while enhancing the brand as a purveyor of natural luxury. The company often cited Dr Gustav Jaeger (1832–1917), whose belief in the health-giving properties of wool informed its foundation. His simple observation that 'Nature hath clothed the animal, man clothes himself' drew attention to human responsibility and the wisdom of learning from nature.[28]

During the 1970s and '80s British knitwear designers came to the fore once again when hand-knitting returned to fashion as part of a general revival of interest in craft. The designers, who included Kaffe Fassett (b.1937), working at first with Bill Gibb (1943–1988), and Patricia Roberts (b.1945), drew on traditional styles, patterns and stitches but transformed them with vibrant colours, contrasting yarns, three-dimensional effects and witty styling. The resulting sweaters were often multi-textured, complex and costly because of the high price of materials and labour. Their popularity inspired mass-produced sweaters with more intricate designs frequently made from acrylic. For those able to knit, several designers, such as Susan Duckworth, Sasha Kagan and Sandy Black (pl. 81), developed kits with instructions and yarns supplied by Rowan Yarns of Washpit Mills in Holmfirth, encouraging the revival of a neglected skill.[29] The kits, which were mainly worked in wool with some mercerized cotton, offered hand-knitters a greater range of colours, in the lengths determined by the pattern, than local yarn shops could provide.

The British predilection for wool tweed laid the way for the introduction of linen tweed as a fashion fabric in the 1930s. The fabric was made from pure linen yarns, usually in 'fancy twists' and from linen mixed with wool. The all-linen fabrics were made in a range of weaves in the soft colours favoured at the time for summer, such as natural, off-white, 'porridge', 'bloom pink' and turquoise. The wool and linen tweeds combined coloured woollen and natural linen yarns. Fashion writers enthused about the fabric, which was used for tailored suits, skirts and dresses, describing it as 'the ideal material for the English summer; warm yet not weighty, cool yet practically uncrushable, severe enough for suits yet elegant enough for frocks ... a gem of a material'.[30]

Linen's tendency to crease made it less desirable than woven cotton as a fashion fabric but its use in Japanese fashion, which had a profound influence on European design in the 1980s, led to renewed interest in it, overriding concerns about its perceived fault. The arrival of Japanese designers in Paris at the beginning of the decade introduced a new concept of fashion. Their designs, which were often influenced by traditional Japanese workwear fabricated from linen and cotton, were led by the fabric whose properties dictated a garment's construction and relationship to the body. As a result, the clothes were frequently cut in asymmetrical shapes and their drape altered depending on how they fell over the body. The interaction between European and Japanese designers stimulated a very productive exchange of ideas.[31]

In Britain the designer most associated with linen is Margaret Howell (b.1946), who has always been drawn to the integrity of workwear, artists' clothing and country dress and the traditional British fabrics from which they are made.[32] Howell, who describes herself as a maker-designer rather than a fashion designer, likes the way linen creases, its ease and comfort.[33] For summer 1983 she used dark-coloured, lightweight fabrics, juxtaposing the texture of cotton and linen through layering. One outfit (pl. 82) includes a 'granddad' T-shirt with a three-button opening, produced from Sea Island cotton knitted to Howell's specifications by John Smedley (founded 1784). The vest worn over it is Irish linen, whose feel and irregular slub contrast with the soft, smooth cotton. The skirt is also linen. In 2013 Howell described how her design aesthetic accords with her principles:

Good quality rides over everything ... It can be apparent in something like a cotton T-shirt that has faded well – it doesn't have to be expensive. I prefer clothes that get better with age – cotton raincoats that get softer, moleskin that wears in well. We should respect what it takes to produce something that is of a quality to last, and I feel that we should be thinking about that now, especially in terms of protecting the environment. We should be more careful with our water, with everything.[34]

Leather is also a durable fabric that ages well if appropriately cared for. Leather coats began to be worn in the early 1900s with the advent

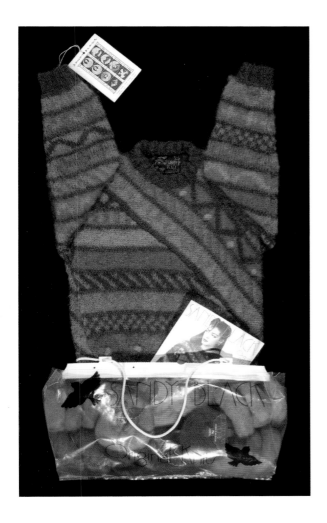

81 / LEFT Sandy Black, jumper and knitting
kit. Mohair and wool. Britain, 1982, 1983.
Given by the designer, V&A: T.64 & 65–1999

82 / RIGHT Margaret Howell (b.1946), day
outfit. Cotton and linen. London, 1983.
Given by the designer, V&A: T.136 to C–1983

of the motor car. Initially designed to be practical and roomy, by the second half of the 1920s they were cut close to the figure following the fashionable silhouette. Chrome-tanned, nappa leather coats were advertised in many shades: red, grey, green, dark and light brown, beige, blue, pale blue, navy and black. In 1926 a vivid scarlet leather coat worn by the British actress Gladys Cooper (1888–1971) ensured she stood out 'among the almost universal black' at a private view of an art exhibition.[35] Chrome tanning was favoured for its speed and ability to produce supple, flexible hides in a wide range of colours but the process creates toxic chromium waste. Today it is considered an environmental hazard.

Reptile skins were used for leather goods in the 1800s but the first London-based broker for reptile skins was set up in 1928. Within six years the vogue for handbags (pl. 85), purses, shoes and other accessories made from crocodile, alligator, lizard and snake skin had reached such proportions that one commentator speculated on the reptiles' survival. Another drew attention to the damage caused to ecosystems and human communities by the wholesale slaughter of pest-eating snakes like pythons.[36] At the same time the widespread use of fur in fashion (pl. 84) continued to be condemned for the cruel ways in which fur-bearing animals died (pl. 83). Fur farming was considered more humane. Mink was successfully 'ranch-bred' in the USA by the mid-1930s and skunk, foxes and mink were farmed in Britain. Farming and cross-breeding from mutations enabled the development of 'new' colours of mink such as platinum and 'silver-blu'. The novel palette boosted sales into the 1960s, despite the high cost of the garments and accessories.[37]

The 1960s and '70s saw revivals of many inter-war fashions. They included the vogue for fur, reptile skins (pl. 86) and leather. Both periods valued the materials for their perceived glamour, eye-catching ostentation and erotic connotations as well as their texture and markings. But whereas most wearers in the past understood fur as a symbol of wealth and status, and an investment and heirloom that required appropriate care, a fur coat in the 1960s, at least for the young and well-to-do, was a fashion garment with a lifespan as short as the trend it reflected.

83 / BELOW 'Cruel furs and others'. Advertisement in *Vogue* (UK) (13 November 1935), vol. 86, no. 10, p. 113

84 / RIGHT Evening cape. Colobus monkey fur and silk. Britain (probably), *c*.1920–30. V&A: T.226–1967

CRUEL FURS AND OTHERS

Furs obtained by torture are :— Broadtail, as above, baby seals, ermine, sable, beaver, red fox, marten, mink, skunk, musquash, monkey, etc.

Write for WHITE LIST of Fur Crusade & Humane Trapping Campaign which names furs you need not be ashamed to wear. Funds needed for more Advts.

MAJOR C. VAN DER BYL, WAPPENHAM, TOWCESTER

Writing in *Nova* in 1967, Molly Parkin (b.1932) reflected that mink was possibly the only fur that could still be considered a status symbol. For 'prestige value' with 'added points' she recommended a full-length crocodile coat. Parkin's article was illustrated with a python trouser suit, a couple wearing near-identical python bomber jackets and several garments featuring water snake designed by Ossie Clark (1942–1996).[38] Clark found a stock of snake skin in a London leather warehouse and crafted it into skilfully cut body-skimming unisex jackets and coats. The clothes were quickly purchased by celebrities like the actress Sharon Tate (1943–1969), Jimi Hendrix's (1942–1970) girlfriend Linda Keith and the models Veruschka (b.1939) and Twiggy (b.1949). Clark's cutter, Tony Costello, thought the skins owed their appeal to their exotic origins and patterns, and ingrained human ideas about snakes whose attributes – their power, stealth and steely grace – humans admire and fear.[39]

The unisex trend extended to leathers of all kinds, and to real and fake fur. Flamboyant, bohemian, long-haired furs such as lynx, wolf, racoon, badger and fox, which merged with their wearer's shoulder-length hair, were popular for men. 'Afghan' sheepskin coats and unruly uncombed Mongolian lamb reflected the prevalent hippy aesthetic and culture of dressing in motley outfits sourced in charity shops and markets. Fur, both real and fake, animal leather and reptile skins –patched, embroidered, printed, bespangled, beaded and fringed – were ubiquitous.[40] The taste for fur created opportunities for the man-made fibres industry. Fake fur is often made from acrylic fibre, which became available in the 1950s.

Acrylic is soft, lightweight and warm and was developed to handle like wool. It is an example of a man-made fibre modelled to simulate the properties of a traditional fibre; other man-made fibres are designed to create textiles with new attributes and applications. The first man-made fibres and plastics were invented in the nineteenth century but apart from a few materials such as celluloid their commercial use dates to the twentieth century. The fibres fall into two groups: those made from chemically treated natural cellulose obtained from organic materials like wood pulp, and those derived from oil and coal products, which are engineered in the laboratory.

85 / BELOW Handbag. Crocodile skin, leather, silk and brass. France, 1938. Given from the Everts-Comnene-Logan Collection, V&A: T.16:1–2003

86 / RIGHT Jacket. Suede and snake skin. Britain, 1972. Given by Clive Mason-Pope, V&A: T.116–1983

The commercial production of cuprammonium viscose (cupra), viscose rayon and cellulose acetate,[41] which derive from cellulose, began in the early 1900s (pl. 87). Viscose rayon was marketed initially as 'art (artificial) silk' because of its lustre and soft draping qualities. Today viscose staple (short lengths of filaments that can be carded and spun into yarn) is used as a cotton substitute and often blended with other fibres, particularly polyester. Viscose filament (long continuous threads that are woven and knitted into fabric) is employed for clothing and lining materials. Cellulose acetate (p. 137) has a more silk-like appearance, which made it a popular choice for lingerie in the 1920s and '30s. Cupra, which is more expensive than viscose and acetate, has a silky drape, high lustre and excellent handle.[42]

In Britain, Samuel Courtauld & Company started manufacturing viscose rayon in 1905. Its raw materials – wood pulp, caustic soda, carbon disulphide and sulphuric acid – were relatively cheap and readily available and the business rapidly became profitable. British Celanese (The British Cellulose and Chemical Manufacturing Co. Ltd) manufactured cellulose acetate selling it under the brand name Celanese from about 1923. The company had its own weaving, knitting and garment-making operations and a well-organized marketing department. Companies in other countries were also quick to recognize the potential of the new fibres and by 1925 Britain, France, Germany, Holland, Italy, Japan and the USA were all significant producers of artificial fibres.[43] The falling cost of rayon between 1921 and 1939, its suitability for blending with other fibres and its continually improving performance made it attractive to the ready-to-wear industry and it offered men and women on modest incomes an opportunity to enjoy mainstream fashions at affordable prices.[44] Magazines advertised pretty, simply cut dresses, blouses, knitwear, underwear and hosiery. In Britain the production of man-made fibres increased by 114 per cent between 1924 and 1928, a statistic that gave manufacturers grounds for optimism.[45]

Although the high sheen of rayon was popular it did not appeal to the Paris couture. DuPont, the leading American producer of rayon, determined to rebrand rayon as a high-fashion fabric, tasked its chemists with de-lustring the fibres.[46] Their success, and a bold plan to secure the support of the leading couturiers for rayon in order to establish it as a high-fashion fabric, led to a series of advertisements published by New York's Rayon Institute in 1928, which incorporated letters of endorsement for the fibre signed by several fashion houses including Callot, Drecoll, Jenny, Lanvin and Poiret. Paul Poiret (1879–1944), who was introduced as an innovator, wrote of the 'novel effects' that rayon offered designers. He worked with it himself and recommended it.[47] The couture designer best known for her use of rayon was Elsa Schiaparelli (1890–1973). She particularly liked materials with interesting textures, such as a rayon crêpe with a crinkled effect called 'tree-bark'.[48] Around the same time the London house of Busvine created an evening dress from textured rayon featuring a fashionable leopard print (pl. 88). The fabric, which is cut on the cross, moulds itself to the body like a second skin. The dress was worn by Emilie Grigsby (1876–1964), a wealthy, free-spirited American living in London whose home was frequented by artists, writers and senior officers in the military.

The development of man-made plastics went in tandem with advances in fibre technology. In 1999 John Brydson, a polymer scientist, defined plastics as materials that 'can be moulded or shaped into different forms under pressure and/or heat'. Horn, turtle shell, rubber and amber are all natural plastics.[49] The first generation of man-made plastics was produced from chemically modified materials found in nature: vulcanite and ebonite from rubber (1843); celluloid from cellulose, exhibited by Alexander Parkes (1813–1890) as 'Parkesine' at the International Exhibition in 1862 and improved by John Hyatt's (1837–1920) 1870 US patent; and casein from milk curds or skimmed milk, patented in 1899.

To begin with, the new plastics, particularly celluloid, were seen largely as affordable substitutes for costly and increasingly rare natural materials such as turtle shell and ivory. Celluloid was made into toilet sets, trinket boxes, jewellery (especially hair combs) and used as a film to coat cotton collars and cuffs that could be cleaned by scrubbing with soap and water without losing their shape and stiffness. Well-laundered, starched collars were a mark of respectability, particularly among

87 / PREVIOUS LEFT Paul Poiret (1879–1944), 'Samovar' evening dress. Probably cuprammonium, gilt metal thread and machine-made lace. France, winter 1921–2. Given by Mr Vern Lambert, V&A: T.338–1974

88 / PREVIOUS RIGHT Busvine, dress. Viscose rayon. Britain, 1933–4. V&A: T.147–1967

89 / BELOW Handbag. Etched Perspex.
France, 1950s. Given by Peggy
Marchant, V&A: T.632:1–1996

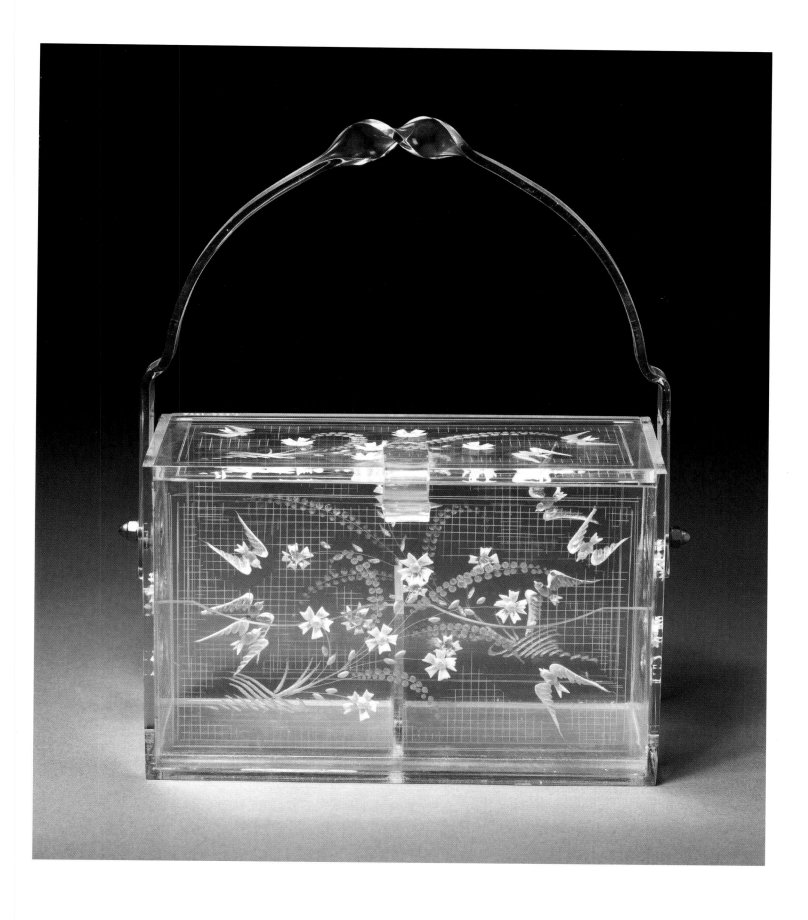

conservative dressers. Their celluloid alternatives preserved outward appearances and saved on labour and laundry bills. In the 1920s and '30s, evening shoes with celluloid heels studded with brilliants twinkled on the dance floor emulating more costly examples made from leather with satin-covered heels.[50] Buttons and beads were produced from casein, marketed under the name 'Erinoid' in Britain.

However, there is a negative side to celluloid. It is made of cellulose nitrate, which is extremely combustible, and releases toxic gases when it is burning. Cellulose acetate and the next generation of plastics offered safer alternatives. The former melts but does not spontaneously combust, and the latter were produced in the laboratory and once hardened were no longer soluble and less responsive to heat.[51] The latter include phenol-formaldehyde resins (Bakelite, invented and patented in 1907 by Dr L.H. Baekeland (1863–1944)) and urea-formaldehyde resins (1919–28), which could be created in light, bright colours and swirling patterns to imitate alabaster and onyx. In 1934 ICI produced a hard form of acrylic, which it called 'Perspex'. It went into commercial production in 1936.

The versatility of plastics was realized in fashion accessories, particularly handbags. In the 1920s elaborately moulded vanity cases, bag and purse frames, chain handles and decorative side panels were fashioned from plastic. In the following decade, when modernity was expressed in sleek, uncluttered designs, smooth sheets of plastic encased bags and purses. A plain Chanel clutch bag in modest faux ivory exemplifies this trend and the designer's belief that ostentation killed luxury.[52] After the Second World War plastic was used in increasingly imaginative ways: multicoloured beads, tiles and plastic-coated wire created novel textures and fun, ephemeral fashions. Rigid, box-shaped bags made of Perspex were especially popular in the 1950s. A transparent example in the V&A's collection, etched to suggest its transformation into a miniature portable aviary housing swooping birds, brought movement and life, albeit caged for human pleasure, into a stiff, laboratory-made geometric form (pl. 89).

The discovery of nylon, the first truly synthetic fibre, by Wallace Carothers (1896–1937), announced by DuPont in 1938, paved the way for the second generation of man-made fibres. Synthetic fibres are polymers made from oil and coal products. Nylon has many qualities in its favour. It is light, strong and keeps its shape; it is unaffected by mould and moths; and it can be permanently 'set', for example in pleats. It is also labour-saving as it is quick to wash and dry, needing only minimal ironing. The new fibre was launched for hosiery in 1939 and its rapturous reception is captured in Erwin Blumenfeld's (1897–1969) photograph of two women (pl. 90), seen in silhouette, gazing in wonder at a nylon stocking radiating light. The image's composition and vibrant colour palette reflect DuPont's marketing strategy, which played on the magic of chemistry and the triumphant march of science that promised a bright new dawn. The photograph's title, Stockings (SOS #39), is ambiguous but could be read to suggest the women's frustration at being unable to buy them, as 'nylons' did not go on sale until May 1940. British women had to wait even longer, until 1948. In Britain, British Nylon Spinners, founded by ICI and Courtaulds in 1940, manufactured the fibre.

Polyesters were first produced by Carothers during his research for DuPont but Terylene, the first polyester to come to the market, was developed in Britain by scientists working at the Calico Printers Association in Manchester. It was announced in the media in 1946 but did not become available to the public until 1952. Made from oil refinery byproducts, polyester is usually blended and became the most important synthetic fibre in terms of volume and garment production.[53] It is as strong as nylon, can be heat-set, is resistant to creasing, does not 'yellow' or 'grey' with age and combines well with wool, cotton and flax. However, it is prone to static.[54]

PVC, or polyvinyl chloride, is a product of the petrochemical industry and can be manufactured in textures from very soft to very hard. It was identified in the nineteenth century but not manufactured in the USA until 1928 and in Britain until 1939. Its high gloss and smooth, almost greasy texture make it exciting to use and in the 1960s, when it first appeared in fashion, it worked equally well for designs influenced by Pop Art and the Space Race. The British fashion designer Mary Quant (b.1934) was the first to experiment with PVC, for rainwear, when she launched her 'wet look'

90 / RIGHT Erwin Blumenfeld (1897–1969), Stockings (SOS #39). Colour print. USA, c.1949. V&A: PH.33–1986

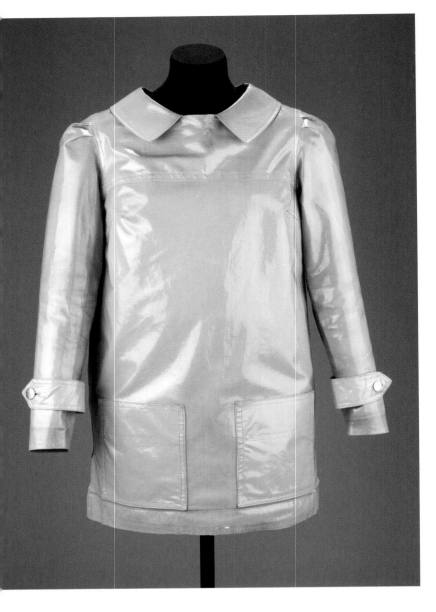

91 / LEFT Mary Quant (b.1934), raincoat.
PVC and cotton. Britain, c.1963. Given
by Dinny Pagan, V&A: T.3–2013

92 / RIGHT André Courrèges (1923–2016),
dress. Nylon, cotton and Perspex. Paris,
1967. Given by Mrs G. Sacher,
V&A: T.348–1975

93 / BELOW Helen Storey (b.1959), top and
trousers. Cotton, Lycra® and Tencel®.
Britain, 1993. Given by the designer,
V&A T.212–1993 and T.228–1993

collection in 1963. Under the headline 'Swing-ing in the Rain', the *Observer* hailed her revolutionary approach to rainwear and 'wild' designs, which included a putty-coloured rain smock (pl. 91).[55] Quant described how she loved PVC: 'this super shiny man-made stuff and its striking colours, vivid cobalt, scarlet and yellow, gleaming liquorice black, white and ginger.'[56] In Paris, in 1968, Pierre Cardin (b.1922) chose black PVC to create sexy thigh-high boots and over-the-elbow gloves. They were modelled by tunic-clad space warriors with hands on hips and legs astride. André Courrèges (1923–2016) is also associated with the Space Age look, but later in the 1960s he worked in an equally contemporary but more feminine aesthetic. His 1967 collection included a mini-length shift dress made of feather-light nylon organza, decorated with 3-D daisies with machine-embroidered petals encased with organza (pl. 92). Each circle of petals frames a plastic disc, which has a faint iridescent sheen resembling petrol spilled on water.

Lycra® (Spandex or elastane), an elasto-meric fibre, was launched by DuPont in 1959. Made out of polyurethane, it has outstanding stretch and recovery properties. It was designed to replace rubber in foundation gar-ments but was rapidly adopted for other forms of underwear, swimwear and sportswear. In the 1980s it proved ideal for the sexy, skin-tight body-conscious garments made fashionable by designers such Azzedine Alaïa (1940–2017). In the same decade fine deniers of Lycra® were developed to add stretch to garments like denim jeans.

As public concern about pollution increased in the 1970s and '80s the textile industry took note. In 1992, after many years of development, Courtaulds launched Tencel®, a cellulosic fibre made from plantation-grown sustainable softwoods, whose manufacture drew on an innovative and environmentally friendly organic solvent spinning process. The manufacturing process is designed to recover over 99 per cent of the solvent, which is non-toxic. The fashion designer Helen Storey (b.1959), who was the first British fashion designer to be invited to trial the fabric, created the first com-mercial examples of its use (pl. 93). These groundbreaking pieces form an important part of the V&A's collection.

Environmental Impact

The growth of the fashion industry between 1900 and 1990 and its increasing reliance on non-renewable fossil fuels and chemicals to provide energy for transport and machinery, and the raw materials for manufacturing fibres, dyes and other finishing effects, had a corresponding impact on the environment, flora, fauna and human communities. Air pollution from private dwellings was exacerbated by the use of motor transport for haulage, the rise in ownership of private cars, and fossil fuel emissions from power stations and factories that had not converted to generated power. The 1956 Clean Air Act introduced smoke control areas but relied on local authorities to designate them. Its limited success was evidenced by a report compiled 10 years later, which revealed that in heavily industrialized areas more than 1,000 tons of grit and dust were deposited over each square mile during the year.[57] A further Act, which *required* local authorities to designate smoke control areas, was introduced in 1968.

Pollution from chemical emissions continued to be an issue. Regulations governing the minimum height for chimney stacks reduced local acidification but increased long-distance air pollution and acid rain. The discharge of chemicals also contributed to water pollution. In 1929 long-running public complaints and concerns about the potential damage to health from the noxious smells, air and water pollution caused by rayon manufacturing at Courtaulds' Coventry factory were summarily dismissed by the Alkali Acts Chief Inspector, albeit with the grudging acknowledgement that 'the amenities of everyday life may have been ... interfered with'. The principal culprit of the pollution and of severe occupational health problems that were endemic in the rayon industry was carbon disulphide.[58] Rivers were also polluted by detergents employed for scouring, which could not be broken down by bacteria in the rivers or in the filter beds of sewage plants. The resulting build-up of foam on the surface of the water reduced the oxygen content of the river killing fish stocks and slowing its flow but by 1967 new 'soft' detergents were being trialled in Germany.[59]

The dependence on oil and its transport around the world led to a corresponding rise in oil pollution in the sea and on beaches from oil-fired ships and oil tankers. In 1952 the Royal Society for the Protection of Birds (RSPB) and British branch of the International Committee for Bird Preservation calculated that between 50,000 and 250,000 sea birds were harmed by oil pollution in the winter of 1951–2. Most died from starvation, cold, oil poisoning or, unable to fly, were battered to death by waves.[60] Disasters like the grounding of the Torrey Canyon tanker on the Seven Stones Reef in Cornwall in 1967 had a significant impact on marine life and birds. It resulted in around 36,000 tonnes of raw oil being released into the sea (pls 94 and 96).

Other similar ecological tragedies and increasing public awareness of the chemical pollution caused by the manufacture of chemically made and modified fibres damaged their reputation in the 1970s. This and economic factors, which reduced the price differential between man-made and natural fibres, and a swing back to fashion of wool and cotton, dramatically reduced consumer demand for synthetics. The little growth there was, however, was met by a flood of imports from low-cost producers in South-East Asia.[61]

Concerns about threats to the environment, flora and fauna, and the treatment of animals led to the establishment of many campaign groups. They include the World Wildlife Fund (founded 1961) (pl. 95), Friends of the Earth (1971), Greenpeace (1971) and People for the Ethical Treatment of Animals (PETA, 1980). Lynx (1985–92) focused on the fur trade, running a slick, shocking, controversial advertising campaign with graphic images photographed by David Bailey (b.1938) and Linda McCartney (1941–1998). The Washington Convention, which came into effect on 1 July 1975, reflected raised awareness of the threat to wildlife caused by human behaviour. This international treaty was a landmark in the history of conservation. It was signed by 80 nations including Britain and accords varying degrees of protection to more than 35,000 species.

Although initiatives like the Washington Convention gave grounds for optimism, the impact of human activity on the planet continued unabated in scale and momentum, affecting an ever wider geographical area, over the following decades.

94 / ABOVE LEFT Marine Conservation
Society, *I Can Only Live in a Clean
Sea*. Colour offset lithograph.
Britain, 1990. Given by the
Marine Conservation Society,
V&A: E.3062–1991

95 / ABOVE RIGHT Tom Eckersley
(1914–1997), *Help Save Our World*.
Colour offset lithograph. Britain,
1981. Accepted by HM Government
in lieu of Inheritance Tax and allocated
to the Victoria and Albert Museum,
2007, V&A: E.2715–2007

96 / RIGHT Bird coated in oil after
a spill on the Seven Stones Reef.
Cornwall, 1967

Cellulose in Couture:
An Evening Coat

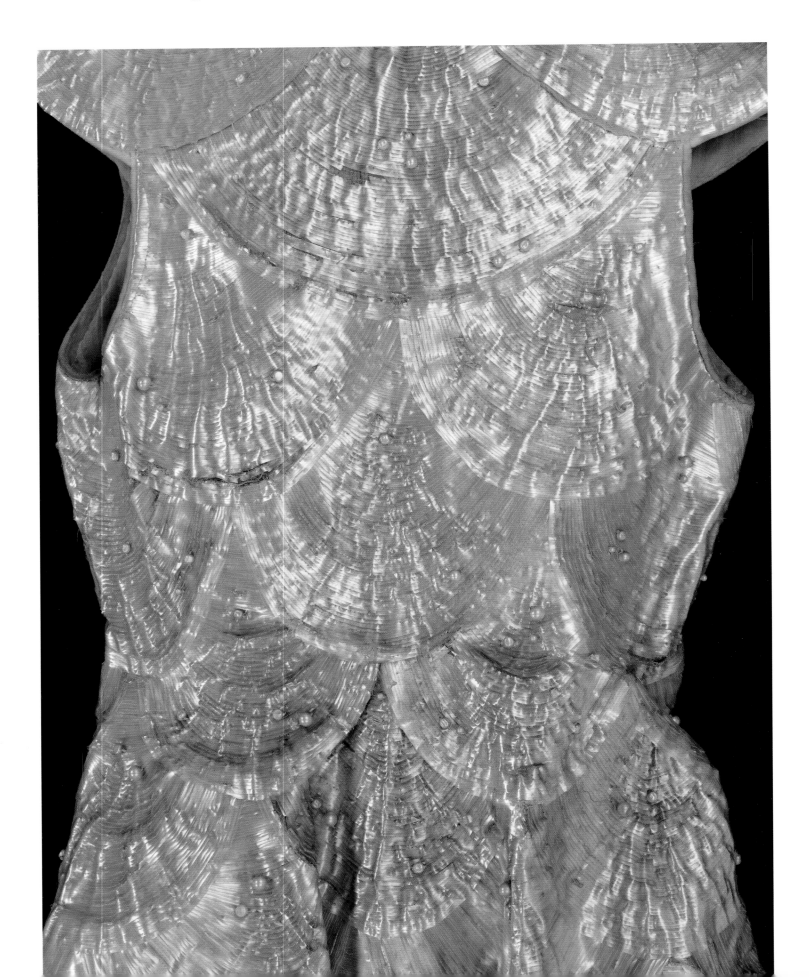

BY
Sarah Glenn

This Alix (Madame Grès, 1903–1993) evening coat (pls 97 and 98) is an important textile document in the history of semi-synthetic materials, perfectly exemplifying 'the dawn of synthetic splendour'.[1]

Made in France in 1936, it represents the relatively early use of cellulosic-based materials in the Parisian couture houses of the time. The coat is covered in 6-millimetre strips of cellulose acetate and imitation pearl beads, which have been stitched onto a plain weave silk ground to form a motif reminiscent of the interior of a shell (see pl. 99). It is lined with silk chiffon.

The growing use of semi-synthetic cellulosic material during the 1920s and '30s was well documented in contemporary literature. Cellulose acetate fabric was desirable for clothes manufacture for several reasons: it is low cost, has excellent draping qualities, does not usually shrink when wet and is resistant to mould. However, acetate has a low melting point and will disintegrate when heated.

In 1934 Harper's Bazaar reported on the new materials and featured a design by Alix of a white rubber coat 'embroidered with black cellophane straw butterflies and multi-coloured synthetic jewels'. Illustrated in the same editorial were a square-cut bodice and jacket by Lucien Lelong (1889–1958), 'embroidered with cellophane which glistens and flashes as it catches the light'.[2] The use of cellulosic material as an appliqué finish or as an addition to the fabric weave on garments appears to have been common in the pre-war period. Woven strips of cellophane could be employed like straw or horsehair, making it also popular for millinery.[3]

By 1936, it was common for whole garments to be made of 'cellophane' fabric, with designers such as Elsa Schiaparelli (1890–1973) and Nina Ricci (1883–1970) producing dresses, coats and jackets in these new materials.[4]

Created in 1865, cellulose acetate was one of the first semi-synthetic fibres. British chemists Charles F. Cross (1855–1935) and Edward J. Bevan (1856–1921) worked on its development in 1894, leading eventually to a commercially viable product in the early twentieth century.[5] The Celanese Corporation, USA, began producing acetate fibres by 1923, alongside the British Cellulose and Chemical Manufacturing Company, which operated factories in both the UK and the USA.[6] It is most likely, however, that the Parisian couture houses of the 1930s used semi-synthetic fibres made by the French textile company Colcombet.[7]

Although commonly referred to as synthetic or semi-synthetic fibres, the raw material that goes into their manufacture is obtained from nature: cellulose is derived from cotton or tree pulp. A variety of differing materials can be manufactured from purified cellulose, such as Parkesine (cellulose nitrate, 1862), viscose rayon (1890s) and 'cellophane' (invented in 1920). However, these cellulosic derivatives were not commonly used until the early twentieth century. Cellulose acetate is the acetate ester of cellulose. Cellulose is mixed with carbon disulphide, acetic acid and acetic anhydride to form a highly viscous liquid, and is then submerged in sulphuric acid, and forced through tiny nozzles (to make filaments) or a thin slit (to create a film).[8] Partial hydrolysis to remove sulphate and a number of acetate groups produces the desired properties of cellulose acetate.[9]

Analysis of cellulosic-based materials using Fourier Transform Infrared Spectroscopy (FTIR) usually reveals the specific kind of cellulose fibres in historic collections. A survey of the V&A collection showed a number of references to cellophane in garments from the 1930s, '40s and '50s.[10] Scientific analysis identified the exact composition of the cellulose fibres in the garments. Alongside testing of the Alix coat, a Charles James (1906–1978) padded evening jacket, of 1937 (pl. 100), for example, was found to be made entirely from cellulose acetate fibre, showcasing the smooth surface of the fabric in its structural quilted design.

Semi-synthetic fabrics are often generically referred to as 'cellophane', that is, a thin, transparent sheet made of regenerated cellulose. Cellophane is a registered trademark now belonging to Futamura (formerly registered to Innovia Films Ltd, UK), however the name has passed into common usage to describe regenerated cellulose films. It is often used incorrectly to describe similar materials, when in fact chemically they are different.[11]

Despite the generic references to cellophane, differing forms of cellulosic-based material used by French couturiers are occasionally referred to in contemporary fashion editorials in order to highlight the progressive

97 / LEFT Alix (Madame Grès) (1903–1993), evening coat (detail). Cellulose acetate, silk and imitation pearl. France, 1936. Given by Mrs B. Gurschner, V&A: T.234–1976

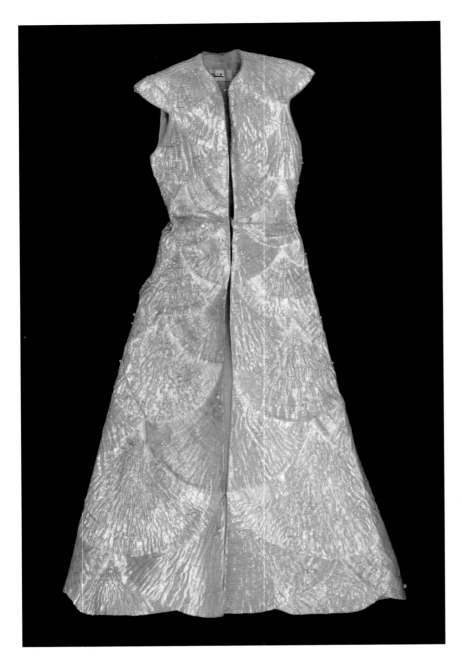

98 / ABOVE LEFT Alix (Madame Grès) (1903–1993), evening coat. Cellulose acetate, silk and imitation pearl. France, 1936. Given by Mrs B. Gurschner, V&A: T.234–1976

99 / BELOW LEFT Mollusc shell

100 / RIGHT Charles James (1906–1978), evening jacket. Cellulose acetate. Paris, 1937. V&A: T.385–1977

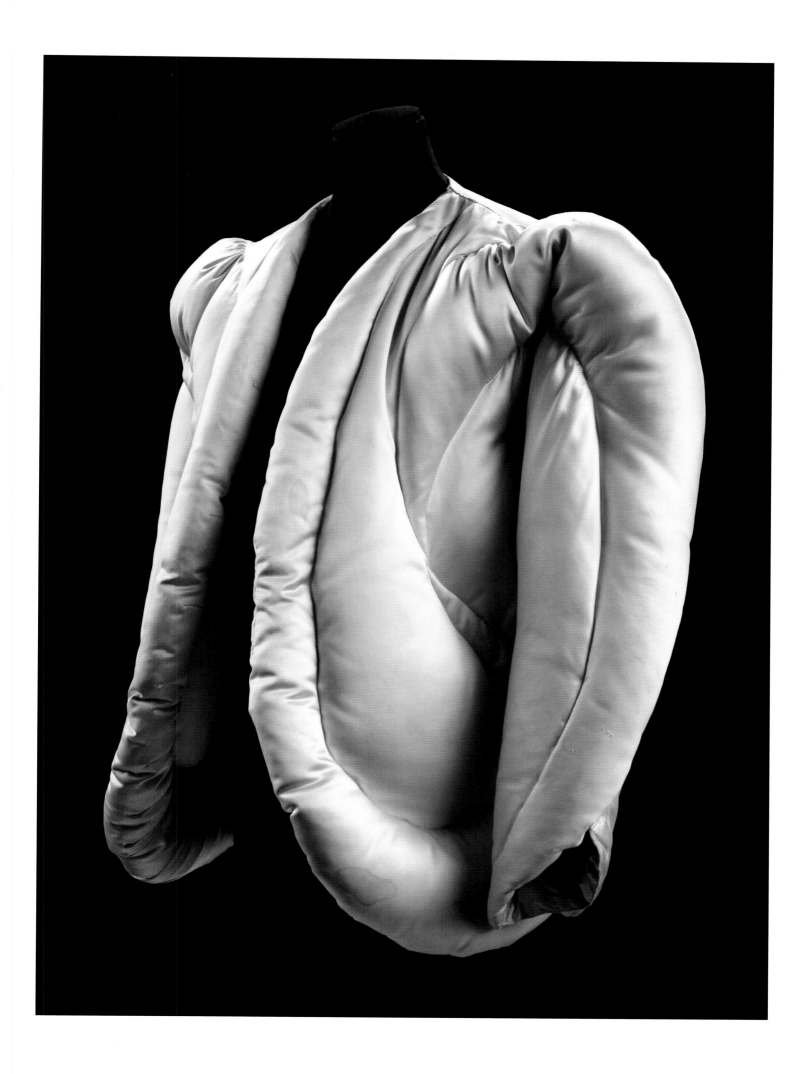

101 / LEFT Christian Dior (1905–1957),
'Zemire' evening ensemble ('La Ligne H').
Cellulose acetate and silk. France, Autumn
/Winter 1954. V&A: T.24:1 to 5–2007

work of textile manufacturers. Schiaparelli's innovative 'glass fibre cape' was made from 'Rhodophane', a mixture of cellophane and other synthetics, which was developed by Colcombet in the 1930s.[12] The Christian Dior 'Zemire' dress (pl. 101), made from cellulose acetate and lined in silk, was commissioned by Agota Sekers (1917–2001), using the fabric manufactured in England by her husband, the Hungarian textile manufacturer Miki Sekers (1910–1972).[13]

Research into the conservation of early polymeric materials is relatively new in the conservation profession. There are few references to the conservation of cellophane or cellulosic-based fibres because on the whole it is stable in comparison with many early plastics.[14] Preventive conservation techniques are key to preserving such materials, and the environmental conditions – relative humidity, temperature and lux levels – within which the Alix evening coat is stored and displayed are carefully considered. The chemical degradation of cellulose acetate is an acid hydrolysis process known as deacetylation, during which acetyl groups are lost from the side chains and react with water to form acetic acid.[15] Often hydrolysis occurs before signs of deterioration are visible, but can be detected by measuring the pH and the distinctive vinegar odour given off by degrading cellulose acetate.[16] This process can catalyse degradation of other nearby materials; however, the impact can be reduced through correct storage.

The environmental impact of producing semi-synthetic fibres should not be underestimated. While the resulting material may be considered safe and stable in the long-term, the manufacturing process releases toxic chemicals (carbon disulphide) into the environment, and can have an adverse effect on those working on the production line.[17] While reflecting the chemical and manufacturing developments of the twentieth century and the modernity of fashion designers like Alix, it nevertheless appears that 'synthetic splendour' may come at a cost.

Imagining Nature: 1952—2010

BY

Oriole Cullen

In the canon of twentieth-century fashion two towering figures, Christian Dior (1905–1957) and Alexander McQueen (1969–2010), were directly inspired and often obsessed by the natural world. Although on the surface it would seem that the mild-mannered French bourgeois and the radical working-class Londoner would have little in common, both were transfixed by nature to such an extent that it permeated all their respective collections and designs. Yet despite this interest, the natural human body was not what they celebrated, rather using it as an armature around which to mould their otherworldly creations: Dior's 'flower women' and McQueen's splendid hybridized creatures are prime examples.

For both designers, nature was an interest cultivated from their earliest years. Childhood friends remembered Dior as 'a pink, plump, shy boy interested in growing flowers'.[1] Dior recalled how his mother instilled a love of gardens in him and he was never happier than 'amongst plants and flower-beds' with his 'chief delight … to learn by heart the names and descriptions of flowers in the coloured catalogues of the firm Vilmorin and Andrieu'.[2] In his 1952 Spring/Summer *Sireneuse* line Dior would create the 'Vilmorin' dress in tribute, hand-embroidered by the house of Rébé with thousands of tiny daisies (pl. 102).

Although intricate decoration played a key role in Dior's expressions of flora, he went much further with his attempt to cultivate nature in fashion, turning his models and clients into living embodiments of flowers. He spoke of designing 'clothes for flower-like women, with rounded shoulders, full feminine busts, and hand-span waists above enormous spreading skirts'.[3] In 1947 his first collection, a sensational success and dubbed the 'New Look' by the press, was shown among large floral arrangements by the famed Parisian florist Lachaume.[4] It featured the *En huit* and *Corolle* lines.

Corolle used the botanical language of flowers to describe what would become Dior's signature look: the narrow stem-like torso, which burst into exceptionally full and blooming skirts like the corolla of a flower. These 'flower women' were no bare-footed natural beauties. Instead, Dior evoked the cultivated sophistication of the hothouse flower. Carefully constrained with corseted waists, padded hips and low décolletage enhanced by the sensual swish of abundant skirts, the Dior woman in actuality personified the natural adapted to the artificial. These were not benign, decorative figures; they yielded a powerful sexuality recalling the archly seductive nature of the 'Parisienne' of the nineteenth century.

As a gardener, Dior's approach to plants and nature was highly controlled. In 1951 American *Vogue* reported on his garden outside Fontainebleu, in northern France: 'unconventional plantings – fat pink roses next to the dark red pompon dahlias – which Dior is forever redesigning. His ideas are carried out by a big silent gardener who raises plants in the kitchen garden and transplants them as they bloom, so that the colour is always breath-taking.'[5] Journalist Bettina Ballard wrote of her visits to Dior's home at Milly-la-Forêt, 'No one has ever had a garden like this: rich, thick-coated herbaceous borders, impressionist in feeling, but with the combination of colours and surprise variation in the sizes and textures of the flowers that made the beds a pure Dior composition'.[6]

In 1953 his Spring/Summer collection was titled the *Tulipe* line with skirt lines echoing the shape of this most famous of cultivated flowers. It featured the 'Mexico' dress with its chiffon skirt falling in soft petals of fabric and a large fabric rose placed at the waist to emphasize the floral. Successive designers at the house of Dior have referenced the New Look silhouette but none more dramatically than John Galliano's (b.1960) 2010 Autumn/Winter haute couture collection for the House of Dior, which returned to this obsession and the famous silhouette in the form of billowing petal skirts against the backdrop of giant tulip-flower sculptures. Lest anyone miss the reference to floristry and the commerce of flowers, the dresses were accompanied by colourful, transparent Perspex hats by Stephen Jones (b.1957) evoking the cellophane used to wrap bunches of flowers (pl. 103). Referencing Dior, the models exuded a sophisticated sexuality, emphasized by highly exaggerated make-up.

While Dior observed the fine cultivation of nature, Alexander McQueen was drawn to the wild and animalistic. McQueen sought nature in his urban environment and was a keen swimmer. As a childhood member of the Young Ornithologists Club (a junior wing of the RSPB) he was fascinated by kestrels he observed from

102 / LEFT Christian Dior (1905–1957), 'Vilmorin' dress. Silk and nylon. France, Spring/Summer 1952. Metropolitan Museum of Art: C.I.55.76.20a–g, Gift of Mrs Byron C. Foy

the roof of a tower block near his London home. He was also captivated by the images in *National Geographic* magazine and attracted to the raw, untamed world documented by television nature programmes.

McQueen's ecological awareness was referenced time and again in his collections, highlighting the darker side of nature, often mixing human and animal traits to turn his models into extraordinary creatures with a signature elongated torso. Materially, he loved to plunder and fabricate from nature, most notably in his use of feathers. From the swaying ostrich feather skirts and taxidermied birds in one of his most noted shows, *Voss* (S/S 2001, named after the Norwegian wildlife habitat of Voss), to the intricately embroidered sheaths of tiny feathers in the *Widows of Culloden* (A/W 2006) and *La Dame Bleue* (S/S 2008), to the monstrous bird women of *The Horn of Plenty* (A/W 2009), feathers played a vital role in his work.

McQueen also incorporated unorthodox materials. His *It's a Jungle Out There* collection (A/W 1997) was inspired by the Thomson's gazelle (*Eudorcas thomsonii*) and featured a pony-skin jacket with impala horns bursting out of the shoulders. *Eshu* (A/W 2000) included skin, fur and hair. Even seashells (*Voss* S/S 2001) were considered viable, with garments made directly from mussel and polished oyster shells and razor clams. Rigid, sharp and unmalleable, each one was painstakingly pierced and individually applied by hand. McQueen's collaborator, milliner Philip Treacy (b.1967), contributed to this strange beauty with enchanting hats and headdresses fashioned from materials such as antlers and coral.

McQueen's final fully realized collection, *Plato's Atlantis* (S/S 2010), imagined a world of melting ice caps and climate change, where land was submerged and humans evolve to survive beneath the water. As an eerie reminder to his audience that the future was already in motion, McQueen completed this dystopian vision with the latest technology, using complex digital prints of amphibious skin on his garments and, in a first for the fashion industry, choosing to live-stream the show online with cameras fitted to giant mechanical arms. Otherworldly elongated models walked in giant 'armadillo' shoes, hair in dramatic vertical horns and amphibious protuberances on their faces as though ready to embrace underwater life (pl. 104).

Yet alongside his love of unrestrained nature McQueen could also appreciate the romantic lure of the garden. His *The Girl Who Lived in a Tree* collection (A/W 2008) was a fairy tale inspired by an ancient elm tree in the garden of his East Sussex country home. His *Sarabande* collection (S/S 2007) celebrated beauty and decay in nature, one of the references being English country garden flowers (pl. 105). The finale piece was a dramatic gown with a high neck and floor-sweeping hemline, entirely covered with frozen flowers, inspired by an image of the flower-strewn corpse of Sarah Bernhardt (1844–1923).[7] However, in shape, embellishment and colour it closely resembles Dior's 'Miss Dior' dress of 1949, with its tightly fitted bodice and flared skirt decorated with a carpet of delicate embroidered flowers bursting out from the ground fabric.[8] These two dresses perhaps provide the ultimate comparison between the designers: Dior abundant yet controlled like his carefully tended garden; McQueen a moment of impossible beauty that dies away, signifying the brutal exhilarating life of the wilderness.

103 / PREVIOUS LEFT John Galliano (b.1960) for Dior Couture, dress. Autumn/Winter 2010

104 / PREVIOUS RIGHT Alexander McQueen (1969–2010), *Plato's Atlantis*, Spring/Summer 2010

105 / RIGHT Alexander McQueen (1969–2010), *Sarabande*, Spring/Summer 2007

Chapter 4
1990 — Present

Fashion, as a verb, comes from the Latin *facere*,[1] to make, so fashion at its root means to give shape or form to something. The title of this book and the associated exhibition,

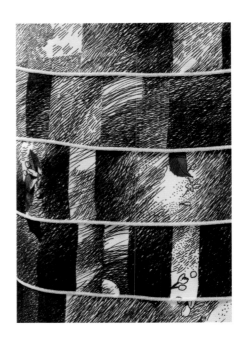

Fashioned from Nature, presents a simple but profound truth that fashion is made from nature. Nature provides the source for each garment that we choose to wear as our second skin. Fashion is made from nature and is dependent on it. Land, water, air and people form fashion's supply chain,

from growing to manufacturing, transportation and delivery into our hands and our everyday lives.

BY

Dilys Williams

Through these interactions, fashion is taking from nature at a rate that cannot be sustained.

Fashion is much more than static items of clothing. We use clothes to weave a dynamic commentary to express who we are as individuals: our personal world is described, implicitly or explicitly, through our clothes. At a broader level, fashion serves as a barometer of our times.[2] From a cursory perspective this is perhaps why fashion is accused of being fickle, transitory or superficial. It is subject to apparently notional ideas: silhouettes shift; colour palettes alter; styles are applauded, then often dismissed with a flick of the pejorative *so last season*. Through fashion, however, we can observe shifts in the environmental, social, political, economic and cultural climates that permeate our lives: at the level of the individual, the local community and on a global scale. Fashion invites us to notice these movements and may offer us alternatives, shaping change itself.

It might be useful at this point to consider what we mean by nature in the context of fashion. We humans are, of course, part of nature. We are one of many species living on earth, but our actions imply that we see nature as separate from us because we act on it with apparent impunity. With this in mind, the question now becomes: what is fashion saying about us and the world we live in, right now? We must therefore reflect on what is happening in the world around us and, by extension, what is happening to nature.

Pushing Planetary Boundaries

Prior to the mid-twentieth century, the earth experienced approximately 12,000 years of stable climate during which human civilization developed. Since then the effects of the Industrial Revolution, the striking acceleration since the mid-twentieth century of carbon dioxide emissions, rising sea levels, global extinction of species, and the transformation of land by deforestation have led experts to assert that we are now in the age of the 'Anthropocene'.[3] This is the era in which human activity has been identified as the main driver of profound environmental changes to the earth. In 1988 the United Nations set up the Intergovernmental Panel on Climate Change (IPCC) to assess the risk of human-induced climate change. At the Paris climate conference (COP21) in 2015, 195 nations committed to act together to ensure the earth remains as hospitable a place to live in the future as it has been in recent centuries past. The withdrawal from this collective agreement by US President Donald Trump in 2017 reduced this number by one.

The Stockholm Resilience Centre and the Australian National University have identified nature's limits in quantifiable terms. In naming the earth's nine planetary boundaries, their research shows that we are already moving beyond a safe operating space for humanity in terms of climate change, species extinction, waste pollution, land use and biochemical usage (pl. 106). Having crossed four of the nine boundaries, action is needed on a worldwide scale.[4]

In 2011, the World Economic Forum identified storms and cyclones, flooding, biodiversity loss, and climate change as four of the top five global risks in terms of likelihood.[5] They had been absent from this list in the previous five years. By 2017, extreme weather conditions and major natural disasters fell within this risk register and also among the top five risks in terms of impact. The future of climate change mitigation and adaptation is also in this highest risk of impact category.[6] We might surmise from this that the world's economists, like its scientists, are deeply concerned.

But what does all this have to do with fashion, with the clothes in our wardrobe and those that we are wearing right now? Fashion is, in fact, a significant contributor to climate change. The uncomfortable truth is that because fashion is indeed *made from nature*, its current industrial practices gobble up staggering quantities of water, chemicals and fossil fuels, degrading the land and the diversity of nature's species while belching out 1.9 billion tonnes of waste per year. Resources are stressed to the extent that if we continue on our current path, demand for water by 2030 will outweigh supply.[7] The question then becomes: should we use available water for growing fashion, or for drinking? Land poses a similar question: should it be for food or fashion? These questions require a radical reconsideration of the making, acquiring, wearing and valuing of our attire.

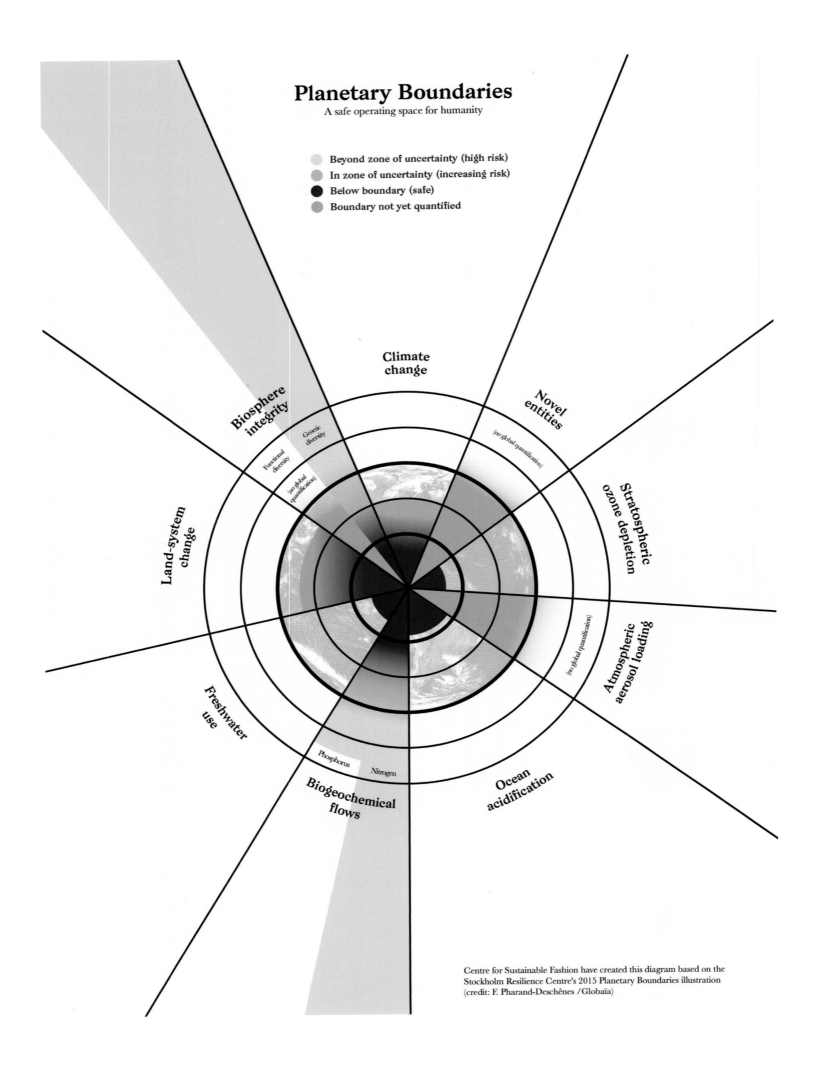

Planetary Boundaries

A safe operating space for humanity

Beyond zone of uncertainty (high risk)

In zone of uncertainty (increasing risk)

Below boundary (safe)

Boundary not yet quantified

Climate change

Biosphere integrity

Genetic diversity

Functional diversity

(no global quantification)

Novel entities

(no global quantification)

Stratospheric ozone depletion

Land-system change

Atmospheric aerosol loading

(no global quantification)

Freshwater use

Phosphorus

Nitrogen

Biogeochemical flows

Ocean acidification

Centre for Sustainable Fashion have created this diagram based on the Stockholm Resilience Centre's 2015 Planetary Boundaries illustration (credit: F. Pharand-Deschênes /Globaïa)

WATER<LESS™
EVERY DROP COUNTS, SO WE GOT SERIOUS ABOUT SAVING WATER. OUR DESIGNERS CAME UP WITH NEW, INNOVATIVE WAYS TO GET THE DENIM FINISHES YOU LOVE, USING A LOT LESS WATER. WE CALL IT LEVI'S® WATER<LESS™.
WE'VE SAVED OVER
1 BILLION
LITERS OF WATER
AND RECYCLED
30 MILLION
LITERS SO FAR
WE CAN REDUCE
UP TO 96%
OF THE WATER NORMALLY USED IN DENIM FINISHING
MADE OF PROGRESS
Levi's®
JOIN US ON OUR JOURNEY TO SAVE WATER.
LEARN MORE AT LEVI.COM

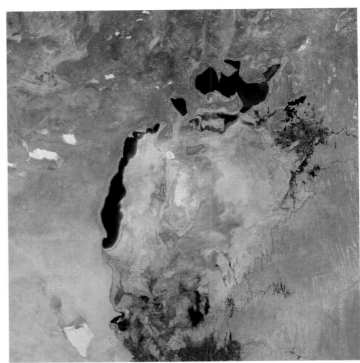

106 / PREVIOUS LEFT After
F. Pharand-Deschênes/Globaïa,
Planetary Boundaries.
Stockholm, 2015

107 / PREVIOUS RIGHT Advertisement
for Levis, *Water<less*, 2011

The Consequences of 'Fashioned from Nature'

It is important to map out the principal ways in which today's fashion system impacts on the world. In establishing the Centre for Sustainable Fashion (CSF) in 2008, we did just that, as a call to all who value fashion and nature and to begin to understand how fashion, which can be such a magnificent manifestation of being human, has deviated from the fundamental human goal of thriving.

Biodiversity loss and ecosystem degradation are an even bigger risk than terrorism according to the World Economic Forum (2010). Fashion contributes to this risk in several ways. To take one example, approximately 120 million trees are cut down annually to make cellulosic fabric, about one third of which are ancient or endangered trees and forests.[8]

Water is essential to life and integral to fashion (pl. 107). Fashion draws on water for cotton growing, fabric dyeing and garment production in places that are already in water crisis. The shrinking of the Aral Sea is a stark reminder of this fact (pl. 108).[9] At garment level, an average of 8,183 litres of water is needed to grow enough cotton to create one pair of jeans and 6 trillion litres are employed in dyeing textiles annually. One cotton mill can use 200 tons of water for every ton of fabric during the dyeing process, which can release up to 72 chemicals into local water supplies (pl. 109).[10]

Domestic water use, while not always in places of water crisis, is a cultural problem in western habits of 'over washing'. Concerns have been heightened by growing evidence of microfibre pollution in oceans, caused by fibres shed by synthetic clothing while being laundered.[11]

Toxic chemicals and pesticides are employed in creating both raw and finished materials in contemporary fashion. More chemicals are used in the growing of cotton than in any other crop,[12] and the disastrous effects of this on communities and environments are well documented. It might sound quite unlikely, but there are, in fact, up to 8,000 chemicals in a single piece of clothing.[13]

Oil-based synthetic fibres such as polyester, from which approximately 60 per cent of all garments are made, add significantly to fashion's environmental tab. Polyester emits

almost three times more carbon dioxide in its life cycle than most other materials. The energy used in manufacturing, transport and retail is also predominantly from fossil fuel, rather than from renewable resources.

In broadcaster and naturalist Sir David Attenborough's (b.1926) words, 'anyone who believes in indefinite growth on a physically finite planet is either mad, or an economist'.[14] Between 2000 and 2014, clothing production doubled. The average western customer now buys 60 per cent more clothes a year and keeps them for about half as long as 15 years ago.[15] With the world's population expected to reach nearly 9 billion by 2030,[16] fashion consumption is projected to increase a further 63 per cent by that point unless we change our habits.[17] In Europe 8.4 million tonnes of textile waste is landfilled or incinerated each year, equating to 18 kilograms of clothes per person, per year.[18] Elsewhere almost half of Chinese customers buy more than they can afford, with around 40 per cent qualifying as excessive shoppers.[19]

Around 60 million people work in fashion's industries worldwide. In some cases this offers fulfilling and creative livelihoods, yet within fashion's manufacturing, which is usually performed by female workers, many are paid less than half the amount considered to be a living wage.[20] Gender-based pay inequality is prevalent in many fashion-manufacturing countries.[21] The extent to which modern-day slavery is endemic in the fashion industry is well documented, with over 70 per cent of fashion businesses suspecting that slavery might be taking place in their supply chains.[22] Human inequality is not limited to fashion. An estimated 21 million people live in modern slavery worldwide.[23] Fashion businesses are, however, culpable of stimulating the industrialized world's craving for an endless supply of ever-cheaper clothes, seeking out rock-bottom cheap places to make them. Corners are cut with, at times, catastrophic human consequences. Indeed, the human impact of fashion cannot be underestimated, but a more detailed discussion is outside the scope of this chapter.

Taken together these statistics show how many of fashion's practices are contributing to the destabilizing of the planet. It is essential that the campaign against climate change involves highlighting these issues.

108 / ABOVE LEFT Satellite images
from 2000 and 2014 showing the
shrinking Aral Sea, caused by
the Amu Darya and Syr Darya
rivers being diverted in order
to provide irrigation for cotton
production in Uzbekistan and
Turkmenistan. Jesse Allen,
NASA Earth Observatory

109 / BELOW LEFT Water pollution
caused by the textile industry
in Tirupur, India, 23 March 1997

Fashion and Mindsets for Change

'Deviation from nature is a deviation from happiness.' Samuel Johnson (1709–1784)

If fashion is a barometer of change and a commentary on the way we live, echoing the words of Samuel Johnson, the industry has deviated from nature and in so doing brought much unhappiness to the planet and many of its most vulnerable people. If fashion is to contribute to our happiness, we need to find ways in which we can harmonize with nature through fashion.

Fashion, and its industry, responds swiftly and, at times, boldly to reflect and respond to cultural, economic, environmental, technological and political dynamics. In reviewing the last three decades of fashion, a picture begins to emerge of artistic, business and social practices that have altered in some places for better and in others for worse. In the words of Herbert Simon (1916–2001), an American scientist and recipient of a Nobel Prize in Economics, 'to design is to devise courses of action aimed at changing existing situations into preferred ones'.[24] This speaks to the core of thoughtful and thought-provoking design – to create better than that which currently exists – and captures succinctly the design intent that drives the work of many fashion practitioners. Some recognize that necessity is indeed the mother of all invention, and that the need to innovate around how fashion is designed and made is reaching a critical point. These fashion practitioners are notable for the keen creative pragmatism they apply to their work with the intention of honouring nature and people. Their design practices reveal diverse approaches to creativity and how it can be fashioned with nature in mind.

There are those who approach their fashion practice with an eminently resourceful mindset: working only with what is already available or can be found in abundance. Given the amount of fabric waste generated by the fashion industry in production and from discarded purchases, some practitioners choose to work with these existing materials, bypassing the need to take more from nature. A radically resourceful student at the Centre for Sustainable Fashion, Shibin Vasudevan, has taken fluff found in washing machines and cotton threads swept up from the workroom floor to exemplify this approach, creating beautiful and striking pieces in the process.

Others strive for equity for everyone related to the fashion industry. Individuals and organizations are actively working towards fairness for all involved. Baroness Lola Young (b.1951), a member of the UK House of Lords, is shining a light on fashion-industry practices in championing an amendment to enhance the Modern Slavery Act 2015.

In an industry known for its competitiveness, we are beginning to see a marked change in practice. By sharing sources of materials and production, costs, margins and expertise, success and failure are pooled. Even direct competitors such as Nike, Puma and Adidas are working together towards a collective goal of ensuring that their business does not contribute to the degradation of nature (pl. 110). Collaboration and cooperation are at the heart of social enterprises and collectives such as Here Today Here Tomorrow, which exemplify wonderfully the idea of mutual benefit.[25]

The call for fashion companies to share the history and origins of their products with customers is getting louder. Openness in relationships and practice requires 'transparency', and to verify the provenance of a piece, 'traceability'. Legislation has a place here, in demanding that such data is available and several emerging technologies now offer the potential to trace each stage in a garment's often global journey through production. Other companies make long-term commitments to localities and people in non-technical ways. Authenticity in this case is about honest relationships, which cannot be measured as easily as auditing geographic locations or production methods.

Some are taking a bold stance to bring fashion's unpalatable realities to our attention and to activate reform. In these instances, fashion is a platform for exposing normalized and accepted practices as neither normal nor acceptable, stimulating cultural and business responses. The pink 'pussy hat', seen in 2017 in marches across the world, symbolizes such activities, connecting related causes for concern: climate change, gender inequality, racism and social injustice.

Still others choose to create fashion that has resilience. This means not only designing pieces able to withstand the test of time and stress, but also building social resilience, connecting communities and encouraging conversations where divisions are rife. Recent events in Europe, the USA and elsewhere show a need to find new ways to overcome a growing disconnection. Fashion's social practices are personal and professional: its sharing economies exchange skills, garments and knowledge, connecting through making, as Amy Twigger Holroyd's (b.1979) 'Keep & Share', the Craftivists and Prick Your Finger all do to great effect.

Alexander McQueen stated, 'Everything I do is connected to nature in one way or another'.[26] These words chime with the approach of designers who are weaving ecological thinking into their design practice, whether through drawing on biomimicry to find nature-designed solutions to our complex problems or through taking a place-based perspective to create fashion grounded in the assets, both human and natural, that thrive within a particular location.

Fashion is about change and about challenging the status quo, which, at present, is about 'more stuff'. In asking how much is enough and looking at the elements of fashion that offer greatest delight, citizens and fashion professionals alike are questioning the quantitative approach to fashion and exploring ways in which its qualitative aspects can be brought to the fore.[27]

Fashion Movements

Two distinct, but not mutually exclusive, business strategies have evolved over the past three decades. One reflects on and reacts to increasingly urgent concerns about environmental change and the precarious welfare of some of the world's most vulnerable people. The other responds swiftly to market forces and capitalizes on changes in the economic, technological and political landscape.

1990–2000: A Quickening

The 1992 Rio Earth Summit and the formation of the United Nations Framework Convention on Climate Change (UNFCCC) evidenced an urgent rallying cry to stabilize greenhouse gas concentrations at a level that would prevent humans from endangering the earth's climate.

Simultaneously, the global fashion industry was developing rapidly, responding to economic, political and technological change. Export-led growth became a key strategy of China's economic reforms initiated by Deng Xiaoping (1904–1997), opening China to foreign investment and entrepreneurship.

Less proclaimed, but a hugely significant influence on globalization, is the modern shipping container. Possibly a bigger contributor to globalization than all free-trade agreements put together, with 94 per cent of countries having ports that could receive them by the late 1980s, a massive rise from 1 per cent in the late 1950s when they were first introduced. By 2015 the cost to ship cargo had dropped by 90 per cent in 60 years; around 90 per cent of every purchased item was shipped inside a container; and a simple sweater could travel 3,000 miles by sea for a few pence.[28]

In 1989 the *New York Times* coined the term 'fast fashion' to describe Zara's 'Quick Response' model.[29] This model was initially introduced in Japan for car manufacturing, the US clothing industry adopting it in the late 1980s to improve efficiencies in manufacturing and supply chains. 'Quick Response' coincided with outsourcing being formally identified as a fashion business strategy, spurred on by free-trade agreements that facilitated easy movement of fashion's raw materials from one place to another.

The pace of fashion also accelerated via the internet. The nascent e-brands of eBay, Amazon and Zappos collectively primed us for future-comfort with online, one-click shopping. By the close of the millennium, a perfect storm was brewing for the fashion industry to become a huge contributor to the environmental crisis that currently swells around us.

A different ethos prevailed elsewhere, led by a group of established and emerging designers. By the early 1990s, the Paris-based artist and fashion designer, Lucy Orta (b.1966), was already known for creating 'symbolic clothing' that dealt with poverty, exclusion, dislocation and homelessness in contemporary urban life. Responding to fashion's blatant consumerism and apparent inattention to what was going on in the world, Orta created *Refuge*

110 / NEXT PAGE Nike, 'Flyknit Racer' trainers. USA, 2012

Wear, a range of distinctive, multifunctional prototype clothes that could be reconfigured according to an individual's immediate needs (pl. 111). Presented outside the Musée du Louvre during Paris Fashion Week in 1994 Orta's collection stood in stark contrast to the spectacle of other shows taking place.

Katharine Hamnett (b.1947) is known for her attention to social and environmental injustice. Since the early 1980s, she has been translating her remarks onto the catwalk, actively questioning the fashion industry status quo. Her standing in the industry means that she has spoken directly to industry luminaries and press, taking her messages to an audience of cultural shapers and responders. Hamnett's iconic shows give fashion meaning both to and beyond the clothes themselves. An early collection, to the accompaniment of the 'acid rain rap', included billowing and sculpted white, khaki, navy and black silk and cotton dresses, before voluminous parkas blazed out a finale in bright yellow, blue and red. While stunning in themselves, the most memorable pieces were the provocative 'SAVE THE WORLD' T-shirts and those emblazoned with the words 'WORLD WIDE NUCLEAR BAN NOW'.

By the 1990s, Hamnett was focusing her sights on the multinational companies selling pesticides and, by the early 2000s, GMO (Genetically Modified Organism) seeds to Indian cotton farmers on credit. The stark facts that she highlighted were not only of the environmental degradation caused by fashion, but also the 270,000 farmer suicides between 1995 and 2013, caused by desperation due to the spiraling repayment costs of pesticides and seeds sold on credit.[30] Knowing that conventional cotton production was polluting rivers, killing wildlife, harming communities that relied on these natural resources and leading to mass suicide, the Katharine Hamnett collection committed to using only organic cotton. Incensed by the direct impacts of her own industry and the lack of widespread knowledge about what was going on, Hamnett's *Clean Up or Die* collection (pl. 112) called out these companies and raised awareness of the true victims of fashion.

Across the Atlantic, on the west coast of America, Lynda Grose (b.1959) and her team at Esprit were applying ecological thinking in the making of fashion at scale. The *ecollection*

was a bold first move by a high-street retailer. It showed – through the creation of an organic cotton collection – that focus on environmental alongside financial prosperity is possible.

In Japan, Safia Minney (b.1964), through her company People Tree, was pioneering the first model for fair-trade fashion, with an integrated supply chain from farm to product. Now a well-known British brand, People Tree was launched in Japan with the intent of championing equity and dignity for all involved in fashion's making. While Minney began to pave a road towards a fair fashion system for others to follow, that road is as yet incomplete.

In London, Sarah Ratty's (b.1964) first collection, *Conscious Earthwear*, created a new fashion aesthetic, implementing a strong belief in eco-consciousness (pl. 113). Lucille Lewin (b.1948), the eagle-eyed owner of Whistles, spotted *Conscious Earthwear* and bought it to sit alongside the Whistles label. Lewin was not alone in identifying Ratty's visionary first collection. The V&A also showcased pieces in its 1994–5 *Streetstyle* exhibition.

Moving from London to Tokyo, where Christopher Nemeth (1959–2010) set up a studio in 1986, the principle of resourcefulness became manifest in a unique aesthetic, which he developed over the following decade. An artist by training, Nemeth taught himself pattern cutting and sewing in order to create a collection using mailbags and canvas from his paintings as his fabric of choice. In establishing The House of Beauty and Culture in 1986, Nemeth and fellow collaborators, Judy Blame (b.1960), Mark Lebon (b.1957) and John Moore (d.1988/89), were at the forefront of a design technique that has been developed by others into a now recognized field of fashion upcycling. This is a subject for the Textiles, Environment, Design (TED) research group at Chelsea College of Arts, University of the Arts, London.

2000–2010: Momentum

By the start of the new century, these two distinct, and distinctly different, fashion movements were each making strides. ASOS and Net-a-Porter both opened their virtual doors in 2000, evidencing the gold-rush effect of fashion's rapid-response model and the rise of online shopping.

111 / RIGHT Lucy Orta (b.1966),
Refuge Wear. Britain, 1998

112 / BELOW LEFT Katharine Hamnett (b.1947),
Clean Up or Die outfit. Leather, cotton
and metal. Britain, 1989–90. Given by
the designer, V&A: T.208–1990

113 / BELOW RIGHT Sarah Ratty (b.1964)
for *Conscious Earthwear*, 'Architects
of the Future, Part II'. OEKO–TEX® certified
polyester by Schoeller Switzerland (skirt),
recycled polymer fleece by Dyersburg
Corporation (gilet), OEKO–TEX® certified
polyester by Chadwick Textiles UK (gilet
and top), cotton and bamboo (sandals).
Britain, 1998/9. Photo: Naneen Rossi.
Styled by Ashley Elliot Fowles.

114 / LEFT Christopher Raeburn (b.1982),
dress, bag, jacket and hat. Royal Air Force
1950s silk maps (dress, hat and bag) and
parachute nylon (jacket). Worn with Clarks
and Christopher Raeburn 'ZARYA SOLO'
sandals. London, 2017

115 / RIGHT Donated clothes cover a
building for the launch of Marks & Spencer
and Oxfam's 'Shwopping' campaign at the
Old Truman Brewery, London, 2012

In September 2006, Estethica, a showcase of sustainability led designers was established by Orsola de Castro (b.1966), Filippo Ricci (b.1966) and Anna Orsini (b.1953) as part of London Fashion Week. The first fashion capital to house such designers within its fashion week, it built on the pioneering efforts of The Paris Ethical Fashion Show launched in 2004, sitting outside Paris Fashion Week.

Galahad Clark (b.1975) was featured in Estethica in February 2008, showing a collection based on his Eco Design Matrix, which combined efficiency, aesthetics, functionality, environmental consideration and recyclability. One of the distinctive qualities of his early footwear collections was a vibrant style achieved by using colourful Saami quilts, sourced from a co-operative in Pakistan, for the upper material, while recycled leather and recycled rice husks formed the sole.

Christopher Raeburn (b.1982), drawing on a design code of resourcefulness, started his Re-Made in the UK label in 2008. It included carefully cut garments using repurposed escape maps printed onto silk and rayon from the Second World War, transforming them into exquisite, collectible items (pl. 114). Raeburn went on to win the British Fashion Award for Emerging Designer in 2011 and the GQ Breakthrough Designer of the Year Award in 2015.

Designers such as William Kroll (b.1983) of Tender Co. named his company with a dual purpose: after the coal truck of a steam engine, and in the hope that owners of his pieces might treat them with tender thought and hand. Kroll's woad-dyed denim collection was designed for resilience. His intention is for the garments to document the life and times of the people wearing them as denim shows the patina of daily life, and his designs and materials are selected for longevity.

Change was afoot on a mass scale too. Marks & Spencer (M&S), one of the UK's most well-known retailers, set out 100 bold, measurable commitments in 2007 in its 'Plan A', so named because, in the words of then CEO Stuart Rose (b. 1949), 'there is no Plan B'. Heralded as the most progressive project of its kind by a mainstream retailer,[31] fashion actions covered: limiting the impact of climate change through the use of renewable energy and more efficient production processes; extending a commitment to fair-trade cotton;

supporting farmers; and encouraging energy conservation in the care of clothes by customers through the introduction of a 'wash at 30 degrees' label.[32] This responsibility for post-purchase energy reduction began to recognize our critical role as wearers in achieving sustainability habits through the way we buy, look after and discard our clothes (pl. 115).

M&S formed strategic alliances with Non-Governmental Organizations (NGOs), including the World Wildlife Fund (WWF), which provided the company with expertise to help it achieve its goals. The UK government, meanwhile, understood the value of the fashion industry to the UK and the growing environmental and social implications of some of its practices. The Department of Environment, Food and Rural Affairs (Defra) convened businesses, research institutions and NGOs to create an agreed roadmap of actions towards more environmentally and socially positive business practices.[33]

The Dow Jones Sustainability Index was first published in 1999 and in 2009 something astounding happened: Walmart, the biggest retailer in the USA, and Patagonia, a particularly progressive brand, collaborated on a radical mission. They connected peers and competitors from across the clothing, footwear and textile sectors to collectively develop a universal approach to measuring sustainability performance. This groundbreaking collaboration became the Sustainable Apparel Coalition (SAC), which has grown into a global consortium of brands, retailers, manufacturers, academia and NGOs. Through the SAC, environmental and social impacts can now be measured and areas for improvement highlighted in an iterative development process.

The problems endemic in unsustainable consumption were also exposed. A report published in 2015 by the United Nations Environment Programme (UNEP) made this crystal clear. The report outlines how 'the continued poverty of the majority of the planet's inhabitants and excessive consumption by the minority are the two major causes of environmental degradation. Our present course is unsustainable and postponing action is no longer an option'.[34] This foreshadowed the growing interrogation of the social and environmental credentials of brands. A potential market need and opportunity for

sustainability was identified, linking the goals of business to the goals of sustaining nature. In the words of François-Henri Pinault (b. 1962), 'sustainable business is good business'.[35]

While the pace was quickening to address the urgent need for a sustainable approach to fashion, ever-cheaper fashion was also accelerating, feeding an apparently insatiable western appetite. This was hastened by rapid developments in technology and through outsourcing to economically poor countries with weak government regulation. A vivid example of the fast-fashion model was seen during the launch of Primark UK stores in 2007, when shoppers were seen trampling each other to get in.

Each fashion movement, market and ethically led, increased their momentum. The early 2000s saw the US Environmental Protection Agency confirming a link between global warming and waste. Awareness of the global environmental challenges we face arguably reached a pivotal point in the collective consciousness in 2006 when Al Gore (b.1948) released his critically acclaimed documentary, *An Inconvenient Truth*, communicating his deeply held concerns about climate change and its consequences for nature and, by extension, for humankind.

2010 Onwards: What Has Really Changed?

By 2010, the call for the fashion industry to address sustainability was rising in volume. Increasing numbers of mainstream fashion businesses were taking action to address their damaging practices.

Echoing Katharine Hamnett's iconic collections, the 2011 Greenpeace 'Detox Campaign' challenged some of the world's most popular fashion companies to eliminate the release of all hazardous chemicals from their production processes (pl. 116).[36] Many brands responded, making commitments that they had to meet verifiably. Detoxing fashion continues to be problematic for companies whose outsourced rapid-response model has great customer appeal and financial profitability. The dialogue for them is more about maintaining the model while decoupling growth from the degradation of nature. But how far can we go with existing models of fashion business?

Businesses are looking at transparency and traceability from two angles. Some are doing so with the intention of reducing risk and ensuring reputation; others are opening up their businesses to public scrutiny to learn from what they see and others say, to create sustainability in their business practice. An early and beautiful conceptualization of traceability for sustainability, *Mirror Africa*, by the artist Nicole Hahn (b.1972), brought Radio-Frequency Identification (RFID) data to life through film, connecting fashion customers to real stories and people behind their purchase.[37] Other iterations of this model are currently being explored. The recent collaboration between Provenance technology, CSF graduate Neliana Fuenmayor's (b.1986) Transparent Company consultancy and designer Martine Jarlgaard uses blockchain technology to tell the story of a product's journey from raw material through the supply chain to the finished garment, creating a detailed digital history.

Bruno Pieters (b.1975) is a designer who has created his own Honest By label, openly sharing information about his collection's sources, costs and environmental impacts. This demonstrates that openness and commercial success in fashion are not an impossible task. It may, as yet, lack perfection and will develop and improve over time, but its intent is clear (pl. 117).

Brilliant in its profound simplicity, Fashion Revolution's 'Who Made My Clothes?' campaign is a response to the catastrophic and fatal collapse of the Rana Plaza factory, in Bangladesh, in 2013. Not the first, or last, work-related death of a garment worker, the negligence exposed by the atrocity and its scale created a groundswell of shocked concern. The simple question behind Fashion Revolution's now worldwide campaign is one that nobody in fashion can continue to ignore (pl. 119).

Stella McCartney's (b.1971) ethos of integrity and stewardship combines a unique sense of culture, knowledge and personal values (pl. 118). She is also a member of a group of fashion businesses, under the helm of Kering, whose stance includes sharing knowledge and findings and also investing in creating open-source tools. Kering's Environmental Profit and Loss (E, P&L) tool costs garments, revealing ways to reduce cost-to-nature in financial terms and devising nature-positive solutions for business. Through CSF's partnership with

116 / LEFT Models wear eco fashion apparel designed by Indonesian designers Felicia Budi, Indita Karina and Lenny Agustin during 'Detox Catwalk' organized by Greenpeace in a polluted paddy field in Rancaekek, West Java province. The event aimed to highlight the toxic pollution caused by the clothing industry. Greenpeace, 2015

117 / LEFT Honest By by
Bruno Pieters (b.1975), jacket
and skirt. Polyester and
cotton. Belgium, 2016.
V&A: T.1702:1&2–2017

118 / RIGHT Stella McCartney (b.1971)
at the launch of her menswear
collection, November 2016

119 / BELOW Staff at the Iris Textiles
garment factory pose for Fashion
Revolution, Guatemala, 2017

Kering, it has been able to introduce student designers to this new way of knowing, encouraging them to innovate creatively around fashion and sustainability. Collaborating with Kering's team, new iterations of the tool, including socially positive measures, are being developed. The E, P&L has democratic intent: it can be downloaded as an app to inform decision-making across the fashion industry.

In 2012 CSF students explored the idea of better decision-making through collaborating with Nike to create 'Making', a tool designed to collate a vast amount of data relating to the environmental impacts of a range of materials. In effect designing a way to design, the Nike 'Making' app is being used by other designers and is freely available as an open source tool.

Some fashion businesses are looking towards co-creating pieces by opening up dialogues between the public, designers and manufacturers. Unmade, showcased in Selfridges, which has itself created 'Better Buying' practices with all of its teams, vividly exemplifies co-creation (pl. 120). Its model enables customers to co-design a piece, then watch it being made on knitting machines before their eyes. The IOU Project was established in 2010 to enable potential customers to decide what they would like to buy based on dialogues with fabric and garment makers across the world.[38] Everybody's World and Away to Mars, both set up more recently, develop collections born out of their potential customers' ideas and values, using social media to gather and vote for designs before they are put into production.

Reclaiming and reusing discarded fashion has likewise been evolving in aesthetics, innovation and technique. Since 2010, Michelle Lowe-Holder (b.1959) has been making exquisite pieces from found materials with a creative resourcefulness far closer to Robert Rauschenberg (1925–2008) and his life-affirming creative ethos of 'work with what you have', than to the 'make do and mend' code of austerity (pl. 121).[39] Meanwhile, H&M (pl. 122) has been working with CSF students to explore resourcefulness, based on ideas such as wabi-sabi, creating collections sourced solely from its take-back recycling scheme. A range of dynamic repurposing ideas are taking hold: outliers include Eileen Fisher and Filippa K, building on the work of From Somewhere, Re-Made in Leeds, the Goodone and others.

120 / ABOVE LEFT Unmade and Opening Ceremony,
jumper. Customized by Lou Stoppard prior to
manufacture and machine-knitted to order.
Merino wool. London, 2017. V&A: T.1711-2017

121 / BELOW LEFT Michelle Lowe-Holder (b.1959),
'Sunset Petal' cuff. Laser-cut birchwood. Britain, 2017

122 / BELOW H&M Conscious Exclusive,
'Serpentine' dress. Recycled ocean plastic
(BIONIC® yarn). Sweden, Spring/Summer 2017.
Image courtesy of H&M Hennes & Mauritz Ltd

123 / ABOVE Mayya Saliba (b.1983), bag.
Piñatex™ (pineapple fibre). Germany, 2015

124 / RIGHT Salvatore Ferragamo S.p.A.,
'Flying Zagara' tunic and skirt. Orange
Fiber (citrus waste and silk). Italy, 2017.
Given by Salvatore Ferragamo, S.p.A.,
V&A: T.1710:1&2–2017

DON'T BUY THIS JACKET

COMMON THREADS INITIATIVE

It's Black Friday, the day in the year retail turns from red to black and starts to make real money. But Black Friday, and the culture of consumption it reflects, puts the economy of natural systems that support all life firmly in the red. We're now using the resources of one-and-a-half planets on our one and only planet.

Because Patagonia wants to be in business for a good long time – and leave a world inhabitable for our kids – we want to do the opposite of every other business today. We ask you to buy less and to reflect before you spend a dime on this jacket or anything else.

Environmental bankruptcy, as with corporate bankruptcy, can happen very slowly, then all of a sudden. This is what we face unless we slow down, then reverse the damage. We're running short on fresh water, topsoil, fisheries, wetlands – all our planet's natural systems and resources that support business, and life, including our own.

The environmental cost of everything we make is astonishing. Consider the R2® Jacket shown, one of our best sellers. To make it required 135 liters of

REDUCE
WE make useful gear that lasts a long time
YOU don't buy what you don't need

REPAIR
WE help you repair your Patagonia gear
YOU pledge to fix what's broken

REUSE
WE help find a home for Patagonia gear you no longer need
YOU sell or pass it on*

RECYCLE
WE will take back your Patagonia gear that is worn out
YOU pledge to keep your stuff out of the landfill and incinerator

REIMAGINE
TOGETHER we reimagine a world where we take only what nature can replace

water, enough to meet the daily needs (three glasses a day) of 45 people. Its journey from its origin as 60% recycled polyester to our Reno warehouse generated nearly 20 pounds of carbon dioxide, 24 times the weight of the finished product. This jacket left behind, on its way to Reno, two-thirds its weight in waste.

And this is a 60% recycled polyester jacket, knit and sewn to a high standard; it is exceptionally durable, so you won't have to replace it as often. And when it comes to the end of its useful life we'll take it back to recycle into a product of equal value. But, as is true of all the things we can make and you can buy, this jacket comes with an environmental cost higher than its price.

There is much to be done and plenty for us all to do. Don't buy what you don't need. Think twice before you buy anything. Go to patagonia.com/CommonThreads or scan the QR code below. Take the Common Threads Initiative pledge, and join us in the fifth "R," to reimagine a world where we take only what nature can replace.

patagonia®
patagonia.com

TAKE THE PLEDGE

*If you sell your used Patagonia product on eBay® and take the Common Threads Initiative pledge, we will co-list your product on patagonia.com for no additional charge.
© 2011 Patagonia, Inc.

125 / LEFT An advertisement for Patagonia, published in the *New York Times* on 'Black Friday', 25 November 2011. The advertisement encouraged shoppers to think about the environmental impact of garments, and urged them to repair and recycle their clothing instead of buying something new

Designers and students are taking radical approaches to resourcefulness, from turning orange peel or pineapple leaves, food-industry discards, into fibre (pls 123 and 124), to producing fabrics from mycelium (mushrooms) and algae, and creating biomaterials, including bio-fur. These examples and others evidence the emergence of a new definition of designer: one that considers success in multiple, interconnected terms, with capabilities that are technical, philosophical, commercial and critical in thought and action.

The fundamental issue of infinite growth from a finite planet, however, remains. Recognizing this, Patagonia made a uniquely bold move in the US on 'Black Friday' in November 2011. It ran an advertisement in the *New York Times*. Accompanying an image of its 'best seller', the R2 jacket, it read: 'Don't Buy This Jacket' (pl. 125). While it has long been recognized for its nature-respecting practices, this was a remarkable move on the day of proclaimed hyper-consumption. It suggests that what you have might be sufficient.

Vast quantities of fashion are discarded to landfill or incinerators: some still with tags on, never having been worn. If, as Shakespeare said, 'apparel oft proclaims the man', what does this amount of profligate waste say about us as designers, producers and customers? As a designer, if pieces I create head to landfill, worn briefly or not at all, I have not designed 'better'. If, as a customer, I am buying clothes and soon discarding them, what do these pieces proclaim about me?

Fashion is an indicator of change; fashion colleges are incubators for its future. Since its inception in 2008, the MA in Fashion and the Environment (renamed MA Fashion Futures in 2015) at London College of Fashion (LCF) has been offering the study of social, environmental, cultural and economic perspectives on fashion. The ecological thinking of Tara Mooney, one of its students, led to her creating a moss collar: a metaphorical call to slow down (moss grows incredibly slowly) and take care (moss needs careful attention, while being extremely resilient). By putting nature and human equity at the foundation of fashion design, its practice changes radically in intention and appearance.

While much of this chapter has been devoted to fashion-industry practitioners designing actions aimed at changing existing situations into preferred ones, we, as citizens, wearers, buyers and communities of fashion, have a critical role to play. What we choose to wear and how we care for our clothes, or 'tend' them, depends on interconnecting factors of knowledge, culture and personal values. 'Tending' is part of the language of the *Craft of Use*,[40] CSF Professor, Dr Kate Fletcher's (b.1971) insightful and industry-challenging publication, which questions some of the deep underlying political, economic and cultural issues at the heart of fashion's current unsustainability.

Where Are We Now?

In 2017, US President Barack Obama (b.1961) referenced Martin Luther King's (1929–1968) belief that there was such a thing as too little too late. To paraphrase his words, with regard to climate change, the hour is upon us, but if we act swiftly and boldly we can leave a world to future generations marked not by the suffering of nature and some of its people, but a world marked by human progress.[41] Fashion is known for its creativity; it is defined by and defines change. It has contributed to some of the problems we are facing in the world today but it can use its inherent creativity and skills to fashion a safe operating space for us in nature. So, the question now becomes: can fashion help us to find ways to reconnect to nature, the life force that sustains us all?

For those in the fashion industry and each of us as citizens, relationships involve intangible, emotional, experiential as well as measurable, transactional elements. The direction of change is dependent on intent. By taking one or more of the mindsets outlined in this chapter, we contribute to a new culture. This is, in the words of the environmental activist Joanna Macy (b.1929), 'a time of great turning', from an era of self-destruction to a life-sustaining society.[42] It involves being honest about our intentions and our actions. Equipped with a strong idea of our values and with the knowledge to make informed decisions, understanding that all things come from nature, each of us can take action. For fashion, this means diverse, personal, splendid ways of moving towards a goal of protecting ourselves, each other and our shared home in nature.

Traceability and Responsibility:
A Twenty-First Century T-Shirt

BY
Connie Karol Burks

This unremarkable, mass-produced, cotton T-shirt may not have been created by an eminent designer, nor is it an example of rare artisanal skill, but it highlights one of the overarching concerns within sustainable fashion: the importance of traceability. What distinguishes this apparently ubiquitous T-shirt is that we know everything about how and where it was made (pl. 126).

In 2013 the 'Planet Money' radio programme (broadcast on NPR, USA) set about making a run of just over 25,000 T-shirts in two batches (men's and women's), documenting the full journey of their creation from 'seed to shirt'.[1] Funded by a Kickstarter campaign and aided by the large apparel producer Jockey International, the project posed the question: do we really know where our clothes come from? This simple query proved surprisingly hard to answer by even those closely involved with producing the T-shirts. When asked where the cotton that made the T-shirts came from, the director of textile sourcing at Jockey admitted 'that's a tough one'. This response is not unusual; given the complex global supply chains, companies often have no idea where elements in the clothes they produce originate, particularly parts such as buttons, zips and other trimmings. In contrast, staff at the spinning plant in Indonesia could provide the origin of the cotton fibre: the USA (pl. 128).

Once the cotton was grown, processed and packed in America, the batch for the men's T-shirts was shipped to Indonesia to be spun into yarn. Next, the yarn was transported to Bangladesh to be knitted, dyed, cut and sewn into a T-shirt. The women's shirts were also made from American cotton, but spun, knitted, dyed, cut and sewn in Columbia.[2] In both cases, the cotton that began life in the USA was then shipped back, albeit in a rather different form, to the printing factory in New York. The simple garments had already travelled back and forth across the world before they were ever worn (pl. 127).

Despite the multiple stages of production across several continents and involving dozens of people, the labels on the T-shirts simply give the locations in which they were sewn: 'Made in Bangladesh' or 'Made in Columbia'. This labelling hides the garments' complex journeys, and makes invisible the other stages of production and the numerous pairs of skilled hands involved in their creation. In Bangladesh, for instance, Planet Money reporters found that a total of 32 people along the production line had a part in sewing the T-shirt: 32 individuals whose skills and labour usually remain unseen.

The reaction and debate prompted by the radio series among listeners worldwide revealed a widespread desire to know more about the production of our clothing, fuelled not only by curiosity, but also by ethics. Recent studies have revealed that an increasing number of people are more likely to buy from brands that demonstrate environmental and social responsibility.[3] A study by Nielsen UK in 2015 found that 66 per cent of people surveyed were willing to pay more for sustainably and ethically produced products, up from 50 per cent in 2013.[4]

Traceable products and transparent supply chains are a primary issue for groups promoting sustainable fashion. Fashion Revolution, established in reaction to the Rana Plaza factory collapse of 2013, highlights the issue with the #whomademyclothes hashtag and an annual Transparency report, in which co-founder Carry Somers (b.1966) argues 'lack of transparency and accountability [is] costing lives'.[5] Similarly, Greenpeace's Detox campaign, first launched in 2011 with the aim of eradicating harmful chemicals from fashion supply chains, also puts transparency at the forefront of its mission, stating that consumers have a 'right to know'.[6] The 2017 Pulse report compiled by the Global Fashion Agenda and The Boston Consulting Group for the Copenhagen Fashion Summit 2017 stated that transparency was a vital component for a sustainable fashion industry.[7]

The conclusion of the Planet Money series asked, once we are made aware of the global supply chain, what is our responsibility? Advocates of transparency argue that we cannot change what we do not know. Greater transparency not only forces brands to take responsibility for the conditions in their full supply chain, but also alerts consumers about the social and environmental impact of the clothes on offer, and allows them to make informed decisions about what to buy.

The Environmental Justice Campaign underlines the importance of traceability for cotton particularly, stressing concerns around the use of child labour in cotton picking in

126 / LEFT T-shirt produced for the 'Planet Money' radio programme, broadcast on National Public Radio, USA, 2013. Illustration by Bob Bianchini. Given by National Public Radio's Planet Money Project, V&A: T.203–2016

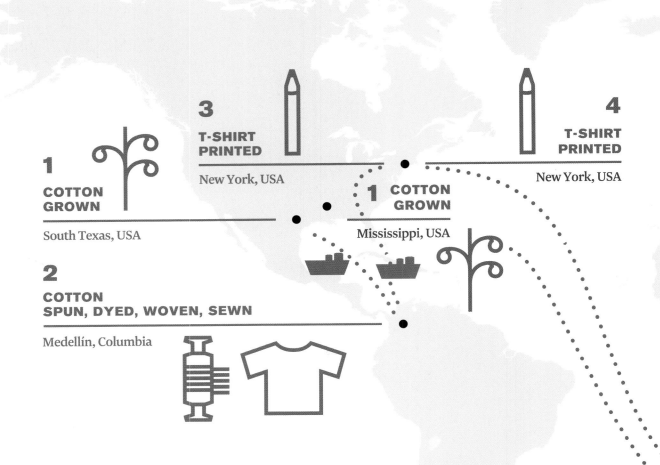

1
COTTON GROWN

South Texas, USA

2
COTTON SPUN, DYED, WOVEN, SEWN

Medellín, Columbia

3
T-SHIRT PRINTED

New York, USA

1
COTTON GROWN

Mississippi, USA

4
T-SHIRT PRINTED

New York, USA

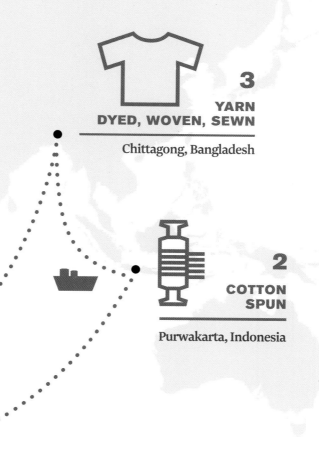

3
YARN
DYED, WOVEN, SEWN

Chittagong, Bangladesh

2
COTTON
SPUN

Purwakarta, Indonesia

127 / PREVIOUS PAGE The global
journey of the Planet Money
T-shirts. Judith Brugger, 2017

128 / RIGHT A field of harvest-
stage cotton, Mississippi, USA

Uzbekistan.[8] Cotton from multiple sources is often blended before being spun, which makes tracing the provenance of the cotton in one single T-shirt incredibly difficult. Higher-end suppliers have begun implementing new technologies in an attempt to certify their crops. Cotton LEADS™, used in Australia and the USA, assigns a unique identification number to each bale of cotton to enable easy tracking through the supply chain. PimaCott®, part of one of the largest cotton producers in the world, is developing DNA tagging to allow buyers and consumers to discover exactly where the cotton was grown.

Former art director at Hugo Boss, Bruno Pieters, made a pioneering step in 2012 by launching Honest By, presented as the world's first 100 per cent transparent company. Pieters publishes everything from mark-ups and the supplier details of each element, down to the thread used to sew the garments.

An increasing number of brands are implementing new technology to make a garment's complete production history and impact visible to the consumer. In May 2017, London-based designer Martine Jarlgaard and technology company Provenance launched a pilot collection to provide completely traceable products. Shoppers scan a 'smart label' to view the garment's entire journey from farm to shop.[9] Software company EVRYTHING and label producers Avery Dennison are creating similar 'smart labels' to enable shoppers to compare each garment's individual green credentials by presenting data from the Sustainable Apparel Coalition's Higg index, which rates the environmental and social impact of a product throughout its supply chain.[10]

Such tracking technologies will allow us to have the same level of knowledge and understanding about the origin and production of our clothes that the Planet Money radio show provided for these T-shirts. It may well soon be possible to know the complex and compelling stories behind every item in our wardrobe.

ENDNOTES

INTRODUCTION

1. *The Tariff of Conscience: Free Trade in Slave Produce, Considered and Condemned: a Dialogue* (1850). Wilson Anti-Slavery Collection, The University of Manchester, John Rylands University Library, http://www.jstor.org/stable/60238486 (accessed 18 April 2017).
2. Webster 2017, p. 25.
3. Collections of 'vegetable products' and 'mineral products' drawn from the exhibits at the Great Exhibition were donated by the Commissioners of the Exhibition to the Museum of Economic Botany, which had opened at Kew in 1847, and the Museum of Practical Geology in Jermyn Street, London, established in 1837.
4. Christie 2011a, p. 4.
5. Desrochers 2011, pp. 1–2. The Waste Product Collection was eventually destroyed.
6. Evans 2016, p. 294.
7. Anonymous, [Inscription concernant la représentation ... et Le Macaque], embroidery pattern, tracing paper and gouache, 1780. Musée des Tissus, Lyon: A 334.1.40.
8. Buffon 1785, pp. 132 and 140.
9. 'New Books', *London Chronicle* (17 June 1766), n.p.; 'The Following Valuable Books', *The Morning Herald and Daily Advertiser* (London) (16 June 1781), n.p.; 'Classified Advertisements', *Public Advertiser* (London) (7 January 1788), n.p.
10. Spary 2000, pp. 16 and 27.
11. North 2008, pp. 92–104.

CHAPTER ONE: 1600–1800

1. 'Cheap, useful and instructive Ornaments for Rooms', *Flying Post or the Post Master* (London) (3–5 February 1713).
2. Blanning 2002.
3. Allen 1994, p. 39; for the interest of London's Spitalfields weavers in botany, floriculture and entomology, see Mayhew (1849) 1972, pp. 105–6.
4. 'There is come to this town ...', *Manchester Mercury* (11 May 1762), Classified Advertisements.
5. 'London June 8', *Stamford Mercury* (13 June 1765); 'Friday's Post, E. London, &c. Thursday, June 18', *The Ipswich Journal* (20 June 1767); Rothstein 1961.
6. Allen 1994, p.24. My thanks to Blanca Huertas and Paul Cooper at the Natural History Museum, London, for their assistance in researching the source of the *Lepidoptera* painted on the silk.
7. Thépaut-Cabasset 2010.
8. Styles 2017, pp. 37–40, 41–4, 48–51.
9. Snodin and Styles 2001, p. 178.
10. Styles 2007, pp. 156–8, pp. 161–4.
11. Clifford 1999, p. 154.
12. Riello 2014, p. 93.
13. V&A: T.219–1973; Rothstein 1987, pp. 29–35.
14. Rothstein 1990b.
15. Home (1889) 1970, pp. 115 and 119.
16. Jenkins and Ponting 1987, pp. 1–8.
17. Ribeiro 2005, pp. 297–8.
18. Kvavadze et al. 2010.
19. Levey 1983, pp. 52–3.
20. Stone-Ferrier 1985, pp. 125–6.
21. Lemire 2009, pp. 212–14 and 217–18.
22. Riello 2013, pp. 54–5.

23. J.F. 1696, p. 7.
24. Lemire 1991, p. 19.
25. Hudson 2009, p.338, citing Joseph E. Inikori, *Africans and the Industrial Revolution in England* (Cambridge 2002), p. 432.
26. Lemire 1991, p. 33.
27. 'London', *Derby Mercury* (27 January 1736).
28. Simon Barnes, at the Black Bull, 'next Greyhound Inn, Southwark', 'maker of the best cane and whalebone hooping', advertised regularly in the *London Journal* in 1725; Samuel Sparks, Haberdasher, Whale-bone Cutter and Cane Merchant, placed an advertisement in 1768 advising his customers that he had opened a warehouse at 46 St Paul's Churchyard, London (*Manchester Mercury*, 19 July 1768); see also Sorge-English 2005, pp. 26–31, for Billiers and Poston, a London company of haberdashers, trading in 'Whalebone and Rattan' from 1719 to 1754.
29. Staniland 2003, p. 45.
30. Wimmler 2017, pp. 56–8.
31. Richardson 1943, p. 7.
32. 'Publicola', *Leeds Intelligencer* (30 December 1760), p. 3; Porter 2000, p. 316.
33. Kean 1998, pp. 15–23.
34. 'Manner of Hunting Elephants at the Cape of Good Hope (From Spearman's Voyages lately published)', *Saunders's Newsletter* (29 December 1785), p. 4.
35. 'To the Printer of the Leeds Intelligencer', signed 'Veritas, Leeds, Jan. 23rd, 1783', *Leeds Intelligencer* (28 January 1783), p. 4.

FROM COCOON TO COURT: AN EIGTEENTH-CENTURY MANTUA

1. Museum no. T.252–1959. On court dress, see Arch and Marschner 1987, pp. 26–42; Arizzoli-Clémentel and Ballesteros 2009, especially pp. 22–54, 72–89, 186–211, 222–5. French court dress worn in most other parts of Europe was quite different.
2. Greig 2011, pp. 67–89; Greig 2009, pp. 80–93. A note in the Accession register documents that according to family tradition this mantua belonged to Catherine Villiers (m.1727; d.1772), wife of John Craster (d.1764) of Craster, Northumberland. He was MP for Weobley, Herefordshire, from 1754 to 1761.
3. Philippe Lasalle claimed to have been first to invent a pattern with a tiger skin in 1756; Miller 2006, p. 74.
4. Its width – 53.5 cm – conforms to that stipulated in the regulations of the silk weaving guild. *Arrêt qui ordonne les Statuts et Règlements pour la Fabrique de Lyon*, Lyon (19 June 1744), p. 45ff. English silks were not subject to such rules and were usually narrower, about 48 to 51 centimetres. Rothstein 1990a, p. 27. Smith 1756, pp. 36–7.
5. Mansel 2005, p. 50, citing Mansfield 1980 and Cumming 1989. None offers firm primary evidence. Nathalie Rothstein explains the lack of official evidence of royal protection and the roots of the notion of Queen Charlotte's encouragement in Rothstein 1961, p. 423 (and facing note 3).
6. In the Musée des Tissus, Lyon, a matching set of chasuble (MT 29041.1), stole, maniple and chalice veil in a very similar silk was probably recycled from fashionable dress. It was not

unusual for bequests or gifts to be given to the Catholic Church for vestments or image robes. Durand et al. 2016, p. 32.
7. Cited in Buck 1979, pp. 16–17.
8. Ewing 1981, Chapter 3; Marschner 2009, pp. 146–53.
9. Campbell 1747, p. 222.
10. Savary des Bruslons 1723, 'Argent' and 'Or', vol. I, pp. 136–41 & vol. II, pp. 900–6. On Lyonnais trade with South America, see Garden 1969, especially pp. 91–4; Lamikiz 2013, p. 83.
11. Miller 2014, p. 17, citing the petition of 1751.
12. Lady Mary Coke acquired a similar silk (it looked as if it were embroidered) straight from the loom (so it was English) in 1767, paying about £70 (933 *livres*) for the length: Home (1889) 1970, vol. I, pp. 114–15. In France, this category cost between 36 and 180 *livres* per ell (£2. 14s. to £13. 10s.), and if they entered Britain legally an additional 49 per cent tax was added to the cost. Therefore, a gown made from a 100 *livres* per ell, taking about 17 ells, would cost 1700 *livres* (£127. 10s.) plus 49 per cent import tax, so £190. In 1709 the exchange rate stood at £3 to 40 *livres*. On exchange rates, see *The Marteau Early 18th-Century Currency Converter,* http://www.pierre-marteau.com/currency/converter.html (accessed 20 June 2017). On French incomes in the eighteenth century, see Sgard 1982, pp. 425–33. For an approximation of incomes in England, see Porter 1982; Rule 1992.
13. Languedoc, Provence and Dauphiné. Diderot and d'Alembert 1765, vol. 15, p. 1371.
14. A dress of this type needed up to 17 metres.
15. Lady Mary Coke (1727–1811) recorded the arrival of what sounds like a very similar silk from the loom on Tuesday 13 January 1767 and tried on her court dress for the queen's birthday drawing room at half past ten in the morning on Friday 16 January: Home (1889) 1970, pp. 115 and 117. The sewing together of the 15 parts of a mantua whose bodice was mostly intact (V&A: T.592:1 to 7–1993) took conservator Joanne Hackett 38 hours in 2007. Even though an eighteenth-century mantua maker might have worked more speedily, it seems likely that for the full task of making a mantua in three days she would have worked with one or more assistants. Personal communication, 26 June 2017.
16. '*Teinture de soie*', in Diderot and d'Alembert 1765, vol. 16, pp. 29–30; Cardon 2007.
17. Half a pound of soap per pound of silk. '*Teinture de soie*', in Diderot and d'Alembert 1765, vol. 16, pp. 29–30.
18. Quye and Han 2016. There were also traces of an unknown orange component.
19. Archives municipales de Lyon, HH131 various documents, 1725–72, itemized in Godart (1899) 1976, p. 485.
20. Burning wood emits carbon dioxide into the air; iron and alum in large quantities pollute water.

DRAWN FROM NATURE 1600–1800

1. For example, fragmentary Greek embroidery depicting lions, c.500 BC, V&A: T.220–1953.
2. Bath 2008, ch. 4.
3. Saunders 1995, pp. 17–40.
4. Ibid., pp. 41–64. *Le Jardin du Roy* was updated and reissued for King Louis XIII (1601–43) in 1623.

5. Quoted in Allen 1985, pp. 32–45.
6. Browne 2000.
7. Christie 2011b, pp. 299–314.
8. Smith 1756, vol. II, p. 43.

CHAPTER TWO: 1800–1900

1. Allen 1994, p. 148.
2. Gates 2002, p. 554.
3. Cruchley 1865: in 1865 admission to the zoo
   cost 1s., with a reduction to 6d. on Mondays.
   Children entered for half price.
4. Jackson 1987, pp. 106–7.
5. Davidoff 1973, pp. 15–16 and 49.
6. Breward, Ehrman and Evans 2004, pp. 71–2.
7. Ehrman 2006, pp. 117–19.
8. Haye and Mendes 2014, p. 14.
9. Sharpe 1995, pp. 203–13; Chapman 1993,
   pp. 5–24.
10. Jeffries 2005, pp. 3–4.
11. Snodin and Styles 2001, p. 178.
12. Breward, Ehrman and Evans 2004, pp. 31–5, 45.
13. Evans 2016, p. 133.
14. Ibid., pp. 133–4.
15. Smith and Cothren 1999, pp. 100–5.
16. Blanc 1982, pp. 106–8.
17. Girardin 1843, pp. 268–9. This book is a
    compilation of sketches written for La Presse
    from 1836 to 1839 by Delphine de Girardin
    under the pseudonym Charles de Launay.
18. 'British India', The Illustrated London News
    (2 August 1851), p. 26.
19. Royle 1856; 'Lecture by J. Hill Dickson: On the
    Fibres of India and Their Adaptability to the
    Purposes of Silk, Foreign Flax, Wool and Cotton,
    Before the Council of the Leeds Chamber of
    Commerce'; 'Sales on Tuesday. Corrie and Co.,
    Brokers', Public Ledger and Daily Advertiser (26
    August 1854); Belfast Mercantile Register and
    Weekly Advertiser (11 May 1858), p. 2.
20. 'Exhibition at The Manchester Mechanics'
    Institution', Manchester Guardian (20 May
    1840), p. 3.
21. 'Cloth of glass', Taunton Courier and Western
    Advertiser (23 September 1840), p. 8. This article
    describes specimens of the cloth in crimson and
    amber, and green and silvery white. 'Opening of
    the New and Elegant Saloons in Oxford Street',
    Naval and Military Gazette and Weekly Chronicle
    of the United Service (18 May 1844), p. 16. Silk
    and glass hangings supplied by Williams &
    Sowerby were installed in the Throne Room at
    St James's Palace.
22. 'Ladies Dresses', Morning Post (London)
    (26 May 1840), p. 6.
23. US Patent 232.122A Glass Cloth or Fabric, 14
    September 1880. I am very grateful to Charlotte
    Holzer for her assistance with my research into
    the textile applications of spun glass.
24. Pelouze 1826, plate III, p. 190; Buckland 1863, p. 5;
    'Spun Glass: The Crystal Palace Glass Blower',
    The Times (16 December 1863). Frank Buckland's
    letter was reprinted in many regional newspapers;
    'Woman's Ways and Works' quoting The Lady,
    The Ipswich Journal (4 March 1898).
25. This process, 'hot press vulcanization',
    introduced sulphur into rubber through heat
    and pressure.
26. Levitt 1986, pp. 180–6 and 156–7.
27. The International Exhibition of 1862: The
    Illustrated Catalogue of the Industrial Department
    (London 1862), vol. 2, class XXVII, p. 394.

28. Barbara Leigh Bodichon Smith, Women and
    Work (London 1857), quoted by Hirsch 1999,
    p.146. Advertisements for cooks in The Times
    in January 1857 specified wages of between
    £12 and £16 a year for live-in cooks with tea
    and sugar provided, rising to £20 with no
    allowances in a 'gentleman's' household.
29. Travis 2004.
30. Matthews David 2015, pp. 111–15.
31. 'Chemical Science Section: Meeting of the
    British Association of Science, Leeds', Leeds
    Mercury (10 September 1890), p. 6.
32. Parker 2016, p. 74.
33. Morning Post (London) (24 April 1828), p. 3.
34. Advertisement placed by Culverwell Brooks
    & Co., Brokers, Public Ledger and Daily
    Advertiser (16 October 1867), p. 2.
35. 'Important Trifles', The Washington Post
    (4 July 1886), p. 4; 'Fashion Notes', Fife Herald
    (1 February 1888), p. 2.
36. Holder 1887, pp. 59–60. The author points out
    that this was a common practice in Vera Cruz,
    Mexico; 'In Fashion's Realm: Fads and Fancies
    Which Interest Its Leaders in Other Cities', The
    Washington Post (24 June 1908), p. 7.
37. 'Parisian Fashions for January', Belfast
    Commercial Chronicle (17 January 1829), p. 1;
    'Female Fashions for January', Leamington
    Spa Courier (2 January 1830), p. 3.
38. 'Bird Trimmings from The Ladies Treasury',
    Coventry Times (1 June 1859), p. 4.
39. Carter 1996, pp. 158–61.
40. Froude 1883, vol.iii, p. 70, letter to Mrs
    Russell, dated 31 December 1860; Oliphant
    1866, vol. III, pp. 51 and 61.
41. Gates 2002, p. 174.
42. McTaggart-Cowan and Abra (2006) 2015.
43. Reed 2016, p. 9.
44. 'The Pollution of the Ribble', Preston Herald
    (14 December 1867), p. 5.
45. 'The Third Report by the Royal Commission
    for Inquiring into the Pollution of Rivers',
    The Observer (18 August 1867), p. 6.
46. Hassan 1998, pp. 33–4.
47. Harrison 2006, p. 297.

WALKING IN FLORA AND FAUNA: A
NINETEENTH-CENTURY DRESS AND HAT

1. Purchased by the V&A at auction from
   Christie's in 1997, little is known about the
   original owner of this fashionable ensemble.
   The walking dress and hat formed part of a lot
   that included several garments, all of which
   were believed to have been made for the
   trousseau of a French duchess who married
   and emigrated to America in around 1885.
2. Perrot 1994, p. 67. Its main competitor, Le Bon
   Marché, had been founded three years earlier.
3. Corrigan 1997, p. 56.
4. Groom 2012, pp. 210–14.
5. Perrot 1994, pp. 40–1 and 187.
6. Zola (1883) 1998, p. 89. Zola drew inspiration
   from both Les Grands Magasins du Louvre
   and Le Bon Marché when writing this novel.
   Émile Zola, 'Notes for Au Bonheur des
   Dames', Bibliothèque nationale, NAF10277,
   cited in Miller 1981, p. 5.
7. I am indebted to Clare Browne for bringing this
   connection to my attention.
8. Wardle and de Jong 1985, pp. 143–4.
9. Wilson (1985) 2011, pp. 70–1.

10. Kerry 2017.
11. Walkley 1981, pp. 10–12.
12. Ponting 1980, pp. 2 and 174.
13. Quye and Wertz 2017, p. 1.
14. Morris 2010, n.p.
15. Adams and Grouw 2009.
16. Burgio 2009, n.p.
17. Matthews David 2015, pp. 55–8.

ENGAGING WITH NATURE: THE FERN CRAZE

1. 'Science. Edinburgh Philosophical Journal, No.
   12, Article, 15th Brongiarten (sic) The
   Vegetation of the Earth at Different Epochs',
   The Scotsman (29 April 1829), p. 1.
2. 'Tree Fern', Public Ledger and Daily
   Advertiser (London) (21 July 1826), p. 3,
   quoting Barron Field (ed.), Geographical
   Memoirs on New South Wales (London 1825).
3. 'Saturday and Sunday's Posts, London
   Saturday Nov. 11', The Derby Mercury
   (13 November 1822).
4. Batchelor 2006, pp. 14 and 63–7; Trevelyan
   2004.
5. My thanks to John David, Head of
   Horticultural Taxonomy at the Royal
   Horticultural Society, for his advice on the
   ferns depicted on the handkerchief.
6. 'London Gossip', Hampshire Telegraph and
   Sussex Chronicle (11 May 1881), p. 4; reprinted
   from Society.
7. Horwood 2007, pp. 84–7 and 110–12.
8. 'A Finely Grown Otter …', London Evening
   Standard (10 March 1884), p. 5; 'The Character
   of the Nation', Tamworth Herald (28 June
   1884), p. 5; 'The Disappearing Fern', The
   Inverness Courier (10 March 1899), p. 5.
9. Gates 1998, p. 36.

CHAPTER THREE: 1900–1990

1. Lickorish and Middleton 2005, pp. 4 and 7.
2. Ibid., p. 5.
3. Stevenson 2003, pp. 191–2 and 196–8.
4. Lickorish and Middleton 2005, p. 3.
5. British Television, The British Film and
   Television Industries – Communication
   Committee, www.parliament.uk
   https://publications.parliament.uk/pa/
   ld200910/ldselect/ldcomuni/37/3707/
   htm (accessed 20 September 2017).
6. Stevenson 2003, p. 191.
7. Stemp 2015, p. 304.
9. Ehrman 2015b, pp. 31–43.
10. Haye 2015, pp. 11 and 25–7.
11. See Ewing 1986, p. 120.
12. Breward, Ehrman and Evans 2004, pp. 90–1.
13. Ewing 1986, pp. 126–30 and 146–7.
14. Ewing 1986, pp. 216–17 and 246–56.
16. Horwood 2005, p. 42; Ewing 1986, p. 138.
17. Handley 1999, p. 102, citing Mark Abrams,
    Teenage Consumer Spending in 1959.
18. Nixon 1996, pp. 43–4 and 46.
19. Feltham 1985, p. 17.
20. O'Byrne 2009, pp. 119–20; Mort 1996,
    pp. 122–3.
21. O'Byrne 2009, pp. 8–10.
22. Riello 2013, pp. 269 and 294.
23. Prichard 2015, pp. 261–71; Boydell 2010,
    pp. 133–5. The average weekly wage in 1953
    was £5 2s. 5d., https://www.theguardian.com/
    observer/comment/story/0,,967980,00.html

24. 'Sally Brampton on the Changing Fortunes of the Denim Jean', *Observer* (22 May 1985), p. 29.

25. 'Brand News', *The Economist* (24 October 1987), p. 90; Hilton 1981.

26. 'Faded youth', *The Economist* (19 November 1988), p. 110.

27. Chapman 2003, pp. 1023–43.

28. Clark and Haye 2009, pp. 19 and 24–9.

29. Black 2012, pp. 173–6.

30. 'Scottish Tweeds: New Fabrics Featured', *Wool Record and Textile World* (21 September 1933), vol. 43, no. 1271, p. 26; Lady Muriel Beckwith, 'Clothes for Easter Golf', *Sunday Times* (16 April 1933), p. 14; 'Frocks and Suits', *Manchester Guardian* (25 June 1934), p. 6.

31. McCrum 1996, pp. 54–5.

32. Alistair O'Neill, email to the author, 29 September 2017.

33. Margaret Howell, personal comment, 1 July 2017.

34. Howell 2013.

35. 'Court and Social', *Sunday Times* (17 January 1926); 'Dickins & Jones Ltd', *Sunday Times* (14 October 1928).

36. 'Reptiles in Favour', *Manchester Guardian* (7 February 1934), p.8; Boulenger 1934. The author points out the python's useful role in eating rats, calculating that if the approximately 2,000,000 pythons exported in 1932 from Asia had survived they would have eaten at least 500,000,000 rats a year.

37. Carter 1977, pp. 175–6. In 1954 the department store Debenham & Freebody's advertised a 'Silverblu' mink stole as a special offer during their sale for 585 guineas. Its original price was 910 guineas. Casual coats, usually priced from 21 to 27 guineas, were reduced to 16 guineas. 'Debenham & Freebody's Sale', *Observer* (3 January 1954).

38. Parkin 1967, pp. 81–7.

39. Watt 2003, pp. 62–4, 67 and 71.

40. McCooey 1968, pp. 24–5; Adburgham 1970, p. 13.

41. Cuprammonium was granted a patent in 1890; it was commercially viable by about 1910–14. It was made in Germany by J.P. Bemberg. Viscose rayon was patented in 1892; a patent for an acetate process was taken out in 1894.

42. Owen 2010, pp. 308–9.

43. Ibid., pp. 16 and 22.

44. Coleman 2003, p. 943.

45. 'The Artificial Silk Exhibition', *The Economist* (26 January 1929), p. 3.

46. Hounshell and Smith 1988, p. 167.

47. 'Paul Poiret Employs Rayon to Interpret the Evening Mode', *Good Housekeeping* (USA) (March 1928), pp. 112–13. Poiret's 'letter' reads: 'Les tissues "Rayon" violà un nouvel element qui s'offre aux modélistes et qui permettent de nouveaux effets. J'enai fait plusieurs modèles. 'ensuis satisfait et j'enpréconise l'emploi'. ('Rayon offers designers a new fibre which enables new effects. I have used it to make many models. I am satisfied with it and I recommend its use'.) The advertisements placed by The Rayon Institute benefited the fashion houses, offering them 'reader recognition'. North America was an important market for French and British fashion designers in the 1920s and '30s. Handley 1999, p. 79.

48. Blum 2003, pp. 60 and 64.

49. Mossman 1997, pp. 1 and 3.

50. 'Her Feet Beneath Her Petticoat', *Manchester Guardian* (1 July 1921); Hopkins 2015, pp. 156–7.

51. 'Plastics: An Industrial Newcomer', *The Economist* (24 September 1938), p. 581.

52. Ivo 2001, pp. 194 and 209; Haye and Tobin (1994) 2003, p. 51.

53. Handley 1999, p. 55.

54. Harrop 2003, p. 952.

55. King-Hall 1963.

56. Quant 1966, p. 135.

57. Loftas 1967, p. 16.

58. Blanc 2016, pp. 51 and 172–3.

59. Loftas 1967, p. 16.

60. 'Annual Toll of British Sea-Birds by Oil Pollution: Societies Call for "50-Mile Limit" for Shipping', *Manchester Guardian* (1 September 1952).

61. 'Man-made Fibres: Heading for Losses of $900m', *The Economist* (15 October 1977), p. 93.

CELLULOSE IN COUTURE: AN EVENING COAT

1. 'The Dawn of Synthetic Splendour: On with the Passion for Cellophane', *Harper's Bazaar* (April 1934), p. 94.

2. Ibid.

3. Gordon and Hill 2015.

4. *The Times* 1936, p. 17.

5. Haldane 2007.

6. Cellulose acetate has a number of common trade names including Acele, Avisco, Celanese, Chromspun and Estron.

7. An example of a Colcombet fabric woven from rayon and silk made in 1934 can be found in the V&A collection (T.459–1976).

8. Blanc 2016.

9. Cellulose acetate shares many similarities with rayon, although it differs in the use of acetic acid in manufacture, and is not converted back into cellulose after processing.

10. Haldane 2007.

11. Ibid.

12. Handley 1999.

13. Textile manufacturer Miki Sekers had a particular interest in the production of innovative fabrics. 'Zemire' underwent extensive conservation treatment at the V&A before display in *The Golden Age of Couture* exhibition.

14. Haldane 2017.

15. Mossman and Abel 2008.

16. Shashoua 2008. The silk chiffon lining in the Alix coat is yellowing, indicating that there is some acid hydrolysis occurring in the cellulose acetate strips, which are adversely affecting the silk fibres of the lining. However, no odour can be detected from the coat, suggesting that the cellulose acetate has not yet reached a high level of acid hydrolysis.

17. Blanc 2016.

IMAGINING NATURE: 1952–2010

1. Ballard 1960, p. 233.

2. Dior (1957) 2015, p. 168.

3. Ibid., p. 22.

4. Buck 1987, p. 538.

5. 'People and Ideas: Le Moulin de Coudret', *Vogue* (USA) (1 June 1951), p. 90.

6. Ballard 1960, p. 239.

7. Bethune 2015, p. 318.

8. Chenoune and Hamani 2007, p. 83.

CHAPTER FOUR: 1990–PRESENT

1. Schwarz 1993.

2. Lewis 2013.

3. Clémençon 2012.

4. Rockstrom et al. 2009.

5. *Global Risks 2011: 6th Edition*, World Economic Forum (2011), http://reports. weforum.org/wp-content/blogs.dir/1/mp/ uploads/pages/files/global-risks-2011.pdf (accessed 1 May 2017).

6. *Global Risks 2017: 12th Edition*, World Economic Forum (2017), http://www3. weforum.org/docs/GRR17_Report_web.pdf (accessed 1 May 2017).

7. *High and Dry: Climate Change, Water, and the Economy*, Executive Summary, World Bank, Washington, DC (2016), https:// openknowledge.worldbank.org/bitstream/ handle/10986/23665/K8517%20Executive% 20Summary.pdf (accessed 17 July 2017).

8. *A Snapshot of Change: One Year of Fashion Loved by Forests*, Canopy (2014), http:// canopyplanet.org/wp-content/ uploads/2015/03/Canopy_Snapshot_ Nov2014.pdf (accessed 4 April 2017).

9. *The Aral Sea Crisis*, www.columbia. edu/~tmt2120/introduction.htm (accessed 12 July 2017).

10. *Threading Natural Capital Into Cotton: Doing Business with Nature*, Report by the Natural Capital Leaders Platform, University of Cambridge Institute for Sustainability Leadership (CISL) (Cambridge, 2016), http:// www.cisl.cam.ac.uk/publications/pub lication-pdfs/threading-natural-captal-into- cotton-doing.pdf (accessed 1 May 2017).

11. Bruce et al. 2017.

12. *The Deadly Chemicals in Cotton*, Environmental Justice Foundation in collaboration with Pesticide Action Network UK (London 2007), https://ejfoundation.org/ resources/downloads/the_deadly_chemicals_ in_cotton.pdf (accessed 1 February 2017).

13. Hailes 2007.

14. RSA President's Lecture 2011: People and Planet with Sir David Attenborough. Held on Tuesday 10 March 2011.

15. Remy et al. 2016.

16. *World Population Prospects: The 2017 Revision*, United Nations, Department of Economic and Social Affairs, Population Division (New York 2017), https://www. compassion.com/multimedia/world- population-prospects.pdf (accessed 4 April 2017).

17. Eder-Hansen et al. 2017, p. 10.

18. Hollins 2016.

19. Wahnbaeck and Roloff 2017, p. 5.

20. Clean Clothes Campaign 2014.

21. Huynh 2016.

22. Lake et al., *Corporate approaches to addressing modern slavery in supply chains: A snapshot of current practice*, Ethical Trading Initiative (ETI) (2015) http:// s3-eu-west-1.amazonaws.com/www. ethicaltrade.org.files/shared_resources_ corporate_approaches_to_addressing_ modern_slavery.pdf (accessed 4 April 2017).

(accessed 20 September 2017).

23. *Global Estimate of Forced Labour Report 2012*, International Labour Organisation (ILO) (2012), http://www.ilo.org/wcmsp5/groups/public/---ed_norm/---declaration/documents/publication/wcms_182004.pdf (accessed 3 March 2017). p. 13.

24. Simon 1996, p. 111.

25. Here Today Here Tomorrow is a collective of three designers with backgrounds in the field of sustainable fashion.

26. Armstrong 2004, p. 138.

27. Skidelsky and Skidelsky 2012.

28. 'The Container History. The World in a Box', *The Economist*, 2006, http://www.economist.com/node/5624791 (accessed 24 April 2017); *A Complete History of The Shipping Container*, Container Home Plans 2015, http://www.containerhomeplans.org/2015/03/a-complete-history-of-the-shipping-container/ (accessed 24 April 2017).

29. Christopher and Towill 2001.

30. Stephenson 2013.

31. Bowers 2007.

32. *Your M&S: How We Do Business, 2007 Report*, Marks & Spencer, https://images-na.ssl-images-amazon.com/images/G/02/00/00/00/32/17/82/32178202.pdf (accessed 5 March 2017).

33. 'Sustainable Clothing Roadmap', *Textiles*, Issue 4 (2009), http://www.thesustainablebusinessgroup.com/js/plugins/filemanager/files/Reuse_and_Recycling_of_Clothing_And_Textiles.pdf (accessed 1 May 2017).

34. *Sustainable Consumption and Production: A Handbook for Policymakers*, Global Edition, UNEP (2015) https://sustainabledevelopment.un.org/content/documents/1951Sustainable%20Consumption.pdf (accessed 16 May 2017).

35. François-Henri Pinault during the inaugural Kering Talk at London College of Fashion, UAL, October 2014.

36. *Detox My Fashion*, Greenpeace, 2011, http://www.greenpeace.org/international/en/campaigns/detox/fashion (accessed 1 May 2017).

37. Hahn 2010.

38. *IOU Project* (2010), http://iouproject.com/stories/ (accessed 4 April 2017).

39. Dickerman 2016.

40. Fletcher 2016.

41. Talk given by Barack Obama at the Seeds & Chips Global Food Innovation Summit. See Obama 2017.

42. Macy and Johnstone 2012, pp. 4–5.

TRACEABILITY AND RESPONSIBILITY: A TWENTY-FIRST CENTURY T-SHIRT

1. *Planet Money Makes a T-shirt* (2013) npr.org/shirt (accessed 27 May 2017).

2. McCune 2013.

3. Barton, Koslow and Beauchamp 2017.

4. *The Sustainability Imperative: New Insights on Consumer Expectation*, Nielsen UK (October 2015), http://www.nielsen.com/content/dam/corporate/us/en/reports-downloads/2015-reports/global-sustainability-report-oct-2015.pdf (accessed 14 July 2017).

5. Somers 2017, p. 3.

6. *The Detox Catwalk 2016: Campaign and Criteria Explained*, Greenpeace (July 2016), https://secured-static.greenpeace.org//international/Global/international/code/2016/Catwalk2016/pdf/Detox_Catwalk_Explained_2016.pdf (accessed 27 May 2017).

7. Eder-Hansen et al. 2017, pp. 28 and 46.

8. *Somebody Knows Where Your Cotton Comes From: Unravelling the Cotton Supply Chain*, Environmental Justice Foundation (2009), http://www.cottoncampaign.org/uploads/3/9/4/7/39474145/2009_ejf_sombodyknowswherecottoncomesfrom.pdf (accessed 27 May 2017).

9. Arthur 2017.

10. McManus and Armbrust 2017.

BIBLIOGRAPHY

Adams and Grouw 2009
  Mark Adams and Heln van Grouw, *Specimen Identification, Feather/Bird on Hat* (unpublished report, Natural History Museum, Tring, 24 September 2009)

Adburgham 1970
  Alison Adburgham, 'Adventures in the Skin Trade', *Guardian* (18 November 1970), p. 13

Allen 1985
  David E. Allen, 'Natural History and Visual Taste: Some Parallel Tendencies', in Allan Ellenius (ed.), *The Natural Sciences and the Arts* (Stockholm 1985), pp. 32–45

Allen 1994
  David Elliston Allen, *The Naturalist in Britain. A Social History* (Chichester 1994)

Anderson 2016
  Fiona Anderson, *Tweed* (London 2016)

Arch and Marschner 1987
  Nigel Arch and Joanna Marschner, *Splendour at Court: Dressing for Royal Occasions since 1700* (London 1987)

Arizzoli-Clémentel and Ballesteros 2009
  Pierre Arizzoli-Clémentel and Pascale Gorguet Ballesteros (eds), *Fastes de cour et cérémonies royales: Le costume de cour en Europe, 1650–1800* (Château de Versailles and Réunion des musées nationaux, Paris 2009)

Armstrong 2004
  Lisa Armstrong, 'Diary of a Dress', *Harper's Bazaar* (US), (August 2004), pp. 136-9

Arthur 2017
  Rachel Arthur, *From Farm to Finished Garment* (2017), https://www.forbes.com/sites/rachelarthur/2017/05/10/garment-block-chain-fashion-transparency/#3881536874f3 (accessed 27 May 2017)

Baines 1985
  Patricia Baines, *Flax and Linen* (Princes Risborough 1985)

Ballard 1960
  Bettina Ballard, *In My Fashion* (New York 1960)

Barton, Koslow and Beauchamp 2017
  Christine Barton, Lara Koslow and Christine Beauchamp, *How Millennials are Transforming Marketing: The Reciprocity Principle*, BCG Perspectives (2017), https://www.bcgperspectives.com/content/articles/marketing_center_consumer_customer_insight_how_millennials_changing_marketing_forever/?chapter=3 (accessed 27 May 2017)

Batchelor 2006
  John Batchelor, *Lady Trevelyan and the Pre-Raphaelite Brotherhood* (London 2006)

Bath 2008
  Michael Bath, *Emblems for a Queen: The Needlework of Mary Queen of Scots* (London 2008)

Bethune 2015
  Kate Bethune, 'Encyclopaedia of Collections in Alexander McQueen', in Claire Wilcox (ed.), *Alexander McQueen: Savage Beauty* (London 2015), pp. 303–21

Black 2012
  Sandy Black, *Knitting: Fashion, Industry, Craft* (London 2012)

Blanc 1982
  Paul David Blanc, *How Everyday Products Make People Sick: Toxins at Home and in the Work Place* (Berkeley, Los Angeles and London 1982)

Blanc 2016
  Paul David Blanc, *Fake Silk: The Lethal History of Viscose Rayon* (New Haven and London 2016)

Blanning 2002
  Tim Blanning, *The Culture of Power and the Power of Culture: Old Regime Europe 1660–1789* (Oxford 2002)

Blum 2003
  Dilys Blum, *Shocking! The Art and Fashion of Elsa Schiaparelli* (New Haven and London 2003)

Boulenger 1934
  E.G. Boulenger, 'The Slaughter of Snakes: A Plea for the Python', *Observer* (18 February 1934)

Bowers 2007
  Simon Bowers, 'M&S Promises Radical Change with £200m Environmental Action Plan', *Guardian* (15 January 2007), https://www.theguardian.com/business/2007/jan/15/marksspencer.retail (accessed 5 March 2017)

Boydell 2010
  Christine Boydell, *Horrockses Fashions: Off-the-Peg Style in the '40s and '50s* (London 2010)

Breward, Ehrman and Evans 2004
  Christopher Breward, Edwina Ehrman and Caroline Evans, *The London Look: Fashion from Street to Catwalk* (New Haven and London 2004)

Browne 2000
  Clare Browne, 'The Influence of Botanical Sources on Early 18th-Century English Silk Design', in Regula Schorta et al., *Eighteenth-Century Silks: The Industries of England and Northern Europe* (Switzerland 2000), pp. 925–35

Bruce et al. 2017
  Nicholas Bruce et al., *Microfiber Pollution and the Apparel Industry*, Bren School of Environmental Science & Management (2017), http://brenmicroplastics.weebly.com/uploads/5/1/7/0/51702815/bren-patagonia_final_report_3-7-17.pdf (accessed 20 April 2017)

Buck 1979
  Anne Buck, *Dress in Eighteenth-Century England* (London 1979)

Buck 1987
  Joan Juliet Buck, 'New Look Then and Now', *Vogue* (USA) (1 March 1987), p. 538

Buckland 1863
  Frank Buckland, 'A New Fashion', *The Times* (12 December 1863), p. 5

Buffon 1785
  Georges-Louis Leclerc, Comte de Buffon, *Histoire Naturelle, générale et particulière*, 2nd edition (London 1785)

Burgio 2009
  Dr Lucia Burgio, *Analysis Report 09-110-LB, Hat T.715:3–1997* (Unpublished report, V&A, Science Section, Conservation Department, 23 September 2009)

Campbell 1747
Robert Campbell, *The London Tradesman* (London 1747)

Cardon 2007
Dominique Cardon, *Natural Dyes: Sources, Tradition, Technology and Science* (London 2007)

Carter 1977
Ernestine Carter, *The Changing World of Fashion: 1900 to the Present* (London 1977)

Carter 1996
Michael Carter, *Putting a Face on Things: Studies in Imaginary Materials* (Sydney 1996)

Chapman 1993
Stanley Chapman, 'The Innovating Entrepreneurs in the British Ready-Made Clothing Industry, *Textile History* (1993), 24(1), pp. 5–25

Chapman 2003
Stanley Chapman, 'Hosiery and Knitwear in the Twentieth Century', in D.T. Jenkins (ed.), *The Cambridge History of Western Textiles* (Cambridge 2003), vol. 2, pp. 1023–43

Chenoune and Hamani 2007
Farid Chenoune and Laziz Hamani, *Dior: 60 Years of Style, from Christian Dior to John Galliano* (London 2007)

Christie 2011a
Ann Christie, '"Nothing of Intrinsic Value": The Scientific Collections at the Bethnal Green Museum', *V&A Online Journal* (Spring 2011), no. 3, http://www.vam.ac.uk/content/journals/research-journal/issue-03/nothing of intrinsic-value-the-scientific-collections-at-the-bethnal-green-museum (accessed 1 May 2017)

Christie 2011b
Ann Christie, 'A Taste for Seaweed: William Kilburn's Late Eighteenth-Century Designs for Printed Cottons', *Journal of Design History* (2011), vol. 24, no. 4, pp. 299–314

Christopher and Towill 2001
Martin Christopher and Denis Towill, 'An Integrated Model for the Design of Agile Supply Chains', *International Journal of Physical Distribution & Logistics Management* (2001), vol. 31, issue 4, pp. 235–46

Clark and Haye 2009
Judith Clark and Amy de la Haye, *Jaeger 125* (London 2009)

Clémençon 2012
Raymond Clémençon, 'Welcome to the Anthropocene: Rio+20 and the Meaning of Sustainable Development' *The Journal of Environment and Development* (2012), pp. 311–38

Clifford 1999
Helen Clifford, 'A Commerce with Things: The Value of Precious Metalwork in Early Modern England', in Maxine Berg and Helen Clifford (eds), *Consumers and Luxury: Consumer Culture in Europe 1650–1850* (Manchester 1999), pp. 147–68

Coleman 1989
Elizabeth Ann Coleman, *The Opulent Era: Fashions of Worth, Doucet and Pingat* (New York 1989)

Coleman 2003
Donald Coleman, 'Man-Made Fibres Before 1945', in David Jenkins (ed.), *Cambridge History of Textiles* (Cambridge 2003), vol. 2, pp. 933–47

Corrigan 1997
Peter Corrigan, *The Sociology of Consumption: An Introduction* (London 1997)

Crossick and Jaumain 2002
Geoffrey Crossick and Serge Jaumain, *Cathedrals of Consumption: The European Department Store, 1850–1939* (Aldershot 2002)

Cruchley 1865
G.F. Cruchley, *Cruchley's London in 1865: A Handbook for Strangers* (London 1865)

Cumming 1989
Valerie Cumming, *Royal Dress* (London 1989)

Davidoff 1973
Leonore Davidoff, *The Best Circles: Society Etiquette and the Season* (London 1973)

Desrochers 2011
Pierre Desrochers, 'Promoting Corporate Environmental Sustainability in the Victorian Era: The Bethnal Green Museum Permanent Waste Exhibit (1875–1928)', *V&A Online Journal* (Spring 2011), issue 3

Dickerman et al. 2016
Leah Dickerman et al., *Robert Rauschenberg* (London 2016)

Diderot and d'Alembert 1765
Denis Diderot and Jean Le Rond d'Alembert (eds), *Encyclopédie ou dictionnaire raisonné des sciences, des arts et des métiers* (Paris 1765)

Dior (1957) 2015
Christian Dior, *Dior by Dior* (1957) (London 2015)

Durand et al. 2016
Maximilien Durand et al. (eds) *Du Génie de la Fabrique au Génie 2.0* (Lyon 2016)

Eder-Hansen et al. 2017
Jonas Eder-Hansen et al., *Pulse of the Fashion Industry 2017*, Global Fashion Agenda & The Boston Consulting Group (2017), https://www.copenhagenfashionsummit.com/wp-content/uploads/2017/05/Pulse-of-the-Fashion-Industry_2017.pdf (accessed 27 May 2017)

Ehrman 2006
Edwina Ehrman, 'Frith and Fashion', in Marks Bills and Vivien Knight (eds), *William Powell Frith: Painting the Victorian Age* (New Haven and London 2006), pp. 111–29

Ehrman 2015a
Edwina Ehrman, 'Digby Morton', in Amy De La Haye and Edwina Ehrman (eds), *London Couture 1923–1975: British Luxury* (London 2015) pp. 115–27

Ehrman 2015b
Edwina Ehrman, 'Supporting Couture; The Fashion Group of Great Britain & The Incorporated Society of London Fashion Designers', in Amy de la Haye and Edwina Ehrman (eds), *London Couture 1923–1975: British Luxury* (London 2015), pp. 31–43

Evans 2016
Richard J. Evans, *The Pursuit of Power: Europe 1815–1914* (London 2016)

Ewing 1981
Elizabeth Ewing, *Fur in Dress* (London 1981)

Ewing 1986
Elizabeth Ewing (1974), *History of Twentieth Century Fashion*, 3rd edition (London 1986)

Feltham 1995
Cliff Feltham, 'Sales Rise by a Third at Burton', *The Times* (16 January 1985), p. 17

Fletcher 2016
Kate Fletcher, *Craft of Use* (London and New York 2016)

Froude 1883
James Anthony Froude (ed.), *Letters and Memorials of Jane Welsh Carlyle* (London 1883), 3 vols

Garden 1969
Maurice Garden, 'Le grand négoce Lyonnais au début du XVIIIe siècle. La maison Melchior Philibert: de l'apogée a la disparition', *Colloque Franco-Suisse d'Histoire économique et sociale* (Geneva 1969), pp. 83–99

Gates 1998
Barbara T. Gates, *Kindred Nature: Victorian and Edwardian Women Embrace the Living World* (Chicago and London 1998)

Gates 2002
Barbara T. Gates (ed.), *In Nature's Name: An Anthology of Women's Writing and Illustration, 1780–1930* (Chicago and London 2002)

Gatty 1872
Margaret Gatty, *British Sea-weeds* (London 1872)

Girardin 1843
Mme Émile de Girardin, *Lettres Parisiennes* (Paris 1843)

Godart (1899) 1976
Justin Godart, *L'ouvrier en soie* (1899) (reprint, Geneva 1976)

Gordon and Hill 2015
Jennifer Farley Gordon and Colleen Hill, *Sustainable Fashion: Past Present and Future* (New York 2015)

Greig 2009
Hannah Greig, 'Dressing for Court: Sartorial Politics and Fashion News in the Age of Mary Delany', in M. Laird and A. Weisberg-Roberts (eds), *Mrs Delany and her Circle* (New Haven and London 2009), pp. 80–93

Greig 2011
Hannah Greig, 'Faction and Fiction: The Politics of Court Dress in Eighteenth-Century England', in Natacha Coquery and Isabelle Paresys (eds), *Se Vêtir à la Couren Europe, 1400–1815* (Lille 2011), pp. 67–89

Groom 2012
Gloria L. Groom, *Impressionism, Fashion, & Modernity* (Chicago 2012)

Hahn 2010
Nicole Mackinlay Hahn, 'Out of Africa, Into RFID' (2010), in *New City Reader*, http://reapwhatyousew.org/blog/mirrorafrica/newmuseum-2/ (accessed 5 March 2017)

Hailes 2007
Julia Hailes, *The New Green Consumer Guide* (London 2007)

Haldane 2007
Elizabeth-Anne Haldane, 'Surreal Semi-Synthetics', *V&A Conservation Journal* (Spring 2007), issue 55, pp. 14–18

Haldane 2017
Elizabeth-Anne Haldane, 'Shiny Surfaces: The Conservation of Cellophane and Related Materials', paper given at the North American Textile Conservation Conference, Mexico City, Mexico (6–11 November 2017)

Handley 1999
Susannah Handley, *Nylon: The Manmade Fashion Revolution* (London 1999)

Harrison 2006
R.M. Harrison (ed.), *An Introduction to Pollution Science* (Cambridge 2006)

Harrop 2003
Jeffrey Harrop, 'Man-Made Fibres since 1945', in David Jenkins (ed.), *The Cambridge History of Western Textiles* (Cambridge 2003), vol. 2, pp. 948–71

Hassan 1998
John Hassan, *A History of Water in Modern England and Wales* (Manchester 1998)

Haye 2015
Amy de la Haye, 'Court Dressmaking in Mayfair

from the 1890s to the 1920s', in Amy de la Haye and Edwina Ehrman (eds), *London Couture 1923–1975: British Luxury* (London 2015), pp. 9–27

Haye and Mendes 2014
Amy De La Haye and Valerie D. Mendes, *The House of Worth: Portrait of an Archive* (London 2014)

Haye and Tobin (1994) 2003
Amy De La Haye and Shelly Tobin, *Chanel: The Couturière at Work* (1994) (London 2003)

Hilton 1981
Anthony Hilton, 'How Gloria Put Zip into Jeans', *The Times* (20 May 1981)

Hirsch 1999
Pam Hirsch, *Barbara Leigh Smith Bodichon: Feminist, Artist and Rebel* (London 1999)

Holder 1887
Charles Frederick Holder, *Living Lights: A Popular Account of Phosphorescent Animals and Vegetables* (London 1887)

Hollins 2016
Oakdene Hollins, *Chemical Recycling – A Solution for Europe's Waste Textile Mountain?* (December 2016), http://www.oakdenehollins.com/pdf/news/307rep1.pdf (accessed 4 April 2017)

Home (1889) 1970
J.A. Home (ed.), *The Letters and Journals of Lady Mary Coke* (1889) (Bath 1970), vol. 1

Hopkins 2015
Alan and Vanessa Hopkins, *Footwear: Shoes and Boots from the Hopkins Collection* (London 2015)

Horwood 2005
Catherine Horwood, *Keeping Up Appearances: Fashion and Class Between the Wars* (Stroud 2005)

Horwood 2007
Catherine Horwood, *Potted History: The Story of Plants in the Home* (London 2007)

Hounshell and Smith 1988
David A. Hounshell and John Kenly Smith, *Science and Corporate Strategy: Du Pont R&D, 1902–1980* (Cambridge 1988)

Howell 2013
Margaret Howell, 'Why Good-Quality Clothes Matter', *Guardian* (20 September 2013)

Hudson 2009
Pat Hudson, 'The Limits of Wool and The Potential of Cotton in the Eighteenth and Early Nineteenth Centuries', in Giorgio Riello and Prasannan Parthasarathi, *The Spinning World: A Global History of Cotton Textiles, 1200–1850* (Oxford 2009), pp. 327–50

Huynh 2016
Phu Huynh, 'Gender Pay Gaps Persist in Asia's Garment and Footwear Sector', *Asia-Pacific Garment and Footwear Sector Research Note* (April 2016), issue 4, pp.1–4, http://www.ilo.org/wcmsp5/groups/public/---asia/---ro-bangkok/documents/publication/wcms_467449.pdf (accessed 17 July 2017)

Inikori 2002
Joseph E. Inikori, *Africans and the Industrial Revolution in England* (Cambridge 2002)

Ivo 2001
Sigrid Ivo, *Bags: a Selection from The Museum of Bags and Purses* (Amsterdam 2011)

Jackson 1987
Peter Jackson, *George Scharf's London: Sketches and Watercolours of a Changing City, 1820–50* (London 1987)

Jeffries 2005
Julie Jeffries, 'The UK Population: Past, Present and Future', *Focus on People and Migration, Office for National Statistics* (London 2005)

Jenkins 2003
David Jenkins, 'The Western Wool Textile Industry in the Nineteenth Century', in David Jenkins (ed.), *The Cambridge History of Western Textiles* (Cambridge 2003), vol. 2, pp. 761–89

Jenkins and Ponting 1987
D.T. Jenkins and K.G. Ponting, *The British Wool Textile Industry, 1770–1914*, Pasold Studies in Textile History 3 (Aldershot 1987)

J.F. 1696
J.F., *The Merchant's Ware-house Laid Open Or, The Plain Dealing Linnen-Draper* (London 1696)

Kean 1998
Hilda Kean, *Animal Rights: Political and Social Change in Britain since 1800* (London 1998)

Kerry 2017
Sue Kerry, *Notes and Research for V&A Edwina Ehrman and Connie Karol Burks, March 2017, for Fashion in Nature Exhibition – Weave Identification, T.715:1-2–1997* (Unpublished report, V&A, March 2017)

King-Hall 1963
Ann King-Hall, 'Swinging in the Rain with Mary Quant', *Observer* (26 May 1963)

Kvavadze et al. 2009
Eliso Kvavadze et al. '30,000-Year-Old Wild Flax Fibres', *Science*, vol. 325, issue 5946, p. 1359

Lamikiz 2013
Xabier Lamikiz, *Trade and Trust in the Eighteenth-Century Atlantic World* (London 2013)

Lemire 1991
Beverly Lemire, *Fashion's Favourite: The Cotton Trade and the Consumer in Britain, 1660–1800* (Oxford 1991)

Lemire 2003
Beverly Lemire, 'Domesticating the Exotic: Floral Culture and the East India Calico Trade with England, c.1600–1800', *Textile* (2003), vol. 1, issue 1, pp. 65–85

Lemire 2009
Beverly Lemire, 'Revising the Historical Narrative: India, Europe and the Cotton Trade, c.1300–1800', in Giorgio Riello and Prasannan Parthasarathi, *The Spinning World: A Global History of Cotton Textiles, 1200–1850* (Oxford 2009), pp. 227–46

Levey 1983
Santina M. Levey, *Lace: A History* (London 1983)

Levitt 1986
Sarah Levitt, *Victorians Unbuttoned* (London 1986)

Lewis 2013
R. Lewis, *Modest Fashion: Styling Bodies, Mediating Faith* (London 2013)

Lickorish and Middleton 2005
Leonard J. Lickorish and Victor T.C. Middleton, *British Tourism: The Remarkable Story of Growth* (Oxford 2005)

Loftas 1967
Tony Loftas, 'The Poisoners Among Us', *The Illustrated London News* (9 September 1967)

Macy and Johnstone 2012
Joanna Macy and Chris Johnstone, *Active Hope: How to Face the Mess We're in without Going Crazy* (California 2012)

Mansel 2005
Philip Mansel, *Dressed to Rule* (New Haven and London 2005)

Mansfield 1980
Alan Mansfield, *Ceremonial Costume* (London 1980)

Marschner 2009
Joanna Marschner, 'The Coronation Robe of George III and the Order of the Garter', in Pierre Arizzoli-Clémentel and Pascale Gorguet-Ballesteros (eds), *Fastes de Cour et cérémonies royales: Le costumes de couren Europe (1650–1800)* (Paris 2009), pp. 146–53

Matthews David 2015
Alison Matthews David, *Fashion Victims: The Dangers of Dress Past and Present* (London 2015)

Mayhew (1849) 1973
Henry Mayhew, 'The Spitalfields Silk-Weavers: Cultural Habits of the Weavers', Letter II, 23 October 1849, in Eileen Yeo and E.P. Thompson, *The Unknown Mayhew* (New York 1973), pp. 105–6

McCooey 1968
Meriel McCooey, 'Fur Enough', *Sunday Times* (Design for Living), (8 December 1968), pp. 24–5

McCrum 1996
Elizabeth McCrum, *Fabric and Form: Irish Fashion Since 1950* (Stroud 1996)

McCune 2013
Marianne McCune, 'Our Industry Follows Poverty', *Planet Money* (2013), http://www.npr.org/sections/money/2013/12/04/247360787/our-industry-follows-poverty-success-threatens-a-t-shirt-business (accessed 10 August 2017)

McManus and Armbrust 2017
Rachel McManus and Frederik Armbrust, *Introducing a New Age of Brand Transparency* (11 April 2017), https://evrythng.com/introducing-a-new-age-of-brand-transparency/ (accessed 27 May 2017)

McTaggart-Cowan and Abra (2006) 2015
Ian McTaggart-Cowan with revisions by Erin James Abra, 'Seal', *The Canadian Encyclopaedia* (7 February 2006 [last edited 22 March 2015]), http://www.the canadianencyclopaedia.ca/en/article/seal/ (accessed 10 October 2016)

Merk 2014
Jeroen Merk, *Living Wage in Asia* (2014), https://cleanclothes.org/resources/publications/asia-wage-report (accessed 17 May 2017)

Miller 2006
Lesley Ellis Miller, 'The Marriage of Art and Commerce: Philippe Lasalle's Success in Silks', in Katie Scott and Deborah Cherry (eds), *Between Luxury and the Everyday: The Decorative Arts in Eighteenth Century France* (Oxford 2006) pp. 63–88

Miller 2014
Lesley Ellis Miller, *Selling Silks* (London 2014)

Miller 1981
Michael Barry Miller, *The Bon Marche: Bourgeois Culture and the Department Store, 1869–1920* (Princeton 1981)

Morris 2010
Roisin Morris, *Condition Report*, (Unpublished report, V&A, London 2010)

Mort 1996
Frank Mort, *Cultures of Consumption: Masculinities and Social Space in Late Twentieth-century Britain* (London 1996)

Mossman 1992
Susan Mossman, 'The Problems of Synthetic Fibers, Polymer Preprints', The Division of Polymer Chemistry, Inc., American Chemical Society, Washington, D.C. (August 1992), vol. 33, no. 2, pp. 662–3

Mossman 1997
Susan Mossman (ed.), *Early Plastics: Perspectives, 1850–1950* (London 1997)

Mossman and Abel 2008
Susan Mossman and Marie-Laurie Abel, 'Testing Treatments to Slow Down the Degradation of Cellulose Acetate', in Brenda Keneghan and Egan Louise (eds), *Plastics: Looking at the Future and Learning from the Past* (London 2008), pp. 106–15

Nixon 1996
Sean Nixon, *Hard Looks: Masculinities, Spectatorship and Contemporary Consumption* (London 1996)

North 2008
Susan North, 'The Physical Manifestation of an Abstraction: A Pair of 1750s Waistcoat Shapes', *Textile History* (May 2008), 39 (1), pp. 92–104

Obama 2017
Barack Obama, 'The Long Read: Barack Obama on Food and Climate Change', *Guardian* (26 May 2017), https://www.theguardian.com/global-development/2017/may/26/barack-obama-food-climate-change (accessed 2 June 2017)

O'Byrne 2009
Robert O'Byrne, *Style City: How London Became a Fashion Capital* (London 2009)

Oliphant 1866
Margaret Oliphant, *Chronicles of Carlingford: Miss Marjoriebanks* (Edinburgh and London 1866), 3 vols

Owen 2010
Geoffrey Owen, *The Rise and Fall of Great Companies: Courtaulds and the Reshaping of the Man-Made Fibres Industry* (Oxford 2010)

Parker 2016
Steve Parker, *Colour and Vision through the Eyes of Nature* (London 2016)

Parkin 1967
Molly Parkin, 'Reptiles in Season', *Nova* (September 1967), pp. 81–7

Pelouze 1826
Edmond Pelouze, *Récréations Tirées de l'Art de la Vitrification* (Paris 1826)

Perrot 1994
Philippe Perrot, *Fashioning the Bourgeoisie: A History of Clothing in the Nineteenth Century* (Princeton 1994)

Polan and Tredre 2009
Brenda Polan and Roger Tredre, *The Great Fashion Designers* (Oxford 2009)

Ponting 1980
Kenneth G. Ponting, *A Dictionary of Dyes and Dyeing* (London 1980)

Porter 1982
Roy Porter, *English Society in the Eighteenth Century* (London 1982)

Porter 2000
Roy Porter, *Enlightenment: Britain and the Creation of the Modern World* (London 2000)

Prichard 2015
Sue Prichard, 'The Cotton Board and Cotton Couture', in Amy de la Haye and Edwina Ehrman (eds), *London Couture 1923–1975: British Luxury* (London 2015), pp. 259–71

Quant 1966
Mary Quant, *Quant by Quant* (London 1966)

Quye and Han 2016
Anita Quye and Jing Han, 'Dye Analysis of Coloured Threads and Black Hair from a Court Mantua in the Victoria and Albert Museum, London Collection', report reference no. CTC 2016.09.001, Centre for Textile Conservation and Technical Art History, University of Glasgow (23 December 2016), pp. 1–14

Quye and Wertz 2017
Anita Quye and Julie Wertz, 'Dye Analysis of a Nineteenth-century Walking Dress Dated to 1885, in the Collection of the Victoria and Albert Museum, London', report reference no. CTC 2016.09.003, Centre for Textile Conservation and Technical Art History, University of Glasgow (1 February 2017), pp. 1–8

Reed 2016
Peter Reed, *Acid Rain and the Rise of the Environmental Chemist in the Nineteenth Century* (London and New York 2016)

Remy, Speelman and Swartz 2016
Nathalie Remy, Eveline Speelman and Steven Swartz, *Style That's Sustainable: A New Fast-fashion Formula*, McKinsey & Company (October 2016), http://www.mckinsey.com/business-functions/sustainability-and-resource-productivity/our-insights/style-thats-sustainable-a-new-fast-fashion-formula (accessed 1 May 2017)

Ribeiro 2005
Aileen Ribeiro, *Fashion and Fiction: Dress in Art and Literature in Stuart England* (New Haven and London 2005)

Richardson 1943
E.P. Richardson, 'Walking Sticks of the Eighteenth Century', *Bulletin of the Detroit Institute of Arts of the City of Detroit* (October 1943), vol. 23, no. 1, pp. 6–8

Riello 2013
Giorgio Riello, *Cotton: The Fabric that Made the Modern World* (Cambridge 2013)

Riello 2014
Giorgio Riello, 'The World of Textiles in Three Spheres: European Woollens, Indian Cottons and Chinese Silks, 1300–1700', in Marie-Louise Nosch, Zhao Feng and Lotika Varadarajan (eds), *Global Textile Encounters* (Oxford 2014), pp. 93–106

Riley 1999
Glenda Riley, *Women and Nature: Saving the Wild West* (Lincoln 1999)

Rockstrom et al. 2009
Johan Rockstrom et al., *Planetary Boundaries* (2009), http://stockholmresilience.org/research/planetary-boundaries/planetary-boundaries/about-the-research/the-nine-planetary-boundaries.html (accessed 13 December 2016)

Rothstein 1961
Nathalie Rothstein, 'The Silk Industry in London, 1702–66', unpublished MA thesis (University of London 1961)

Rothstein 1987
Natalie Rothstein, 'Textiles in the Album', in Natalie Rothstein (ed.), *Barbara Johnson's Album of Fashions and Fabrics* (London 1987), pp. 29–35

Rothstein 1990a
Natalie Rothstein, *Silk Designs of the Eighteenth Century. In the Collection of the Victoria and Albert Museum, London* (London 1990)

Rothstein 1990b
Natalie Rothstein, 'Silk in European and American Trade before 1783. A Commodity of Commerce or a Frivolous Luxury?', *Textiles in Trade*, Proceedings of The Textile Society of America Biennial Symposium, 14–16 September 1990, Washington, http://digitalcommons.unl.edu/cgi/viewcontent.cgi?article=1598&content:tsa.conf (accessed 1 May 2017)

Royle 1856
J. Forbes Royle, 'Indian Fibres, Being a Sequel to Observations "On Indian Fibres Fit for Textile Fabrics, or for Rope and Paper Making"', *Journal of the Royal Society of Arts* (28 November 1856), vol. V, no. 210, http://www.jstor.org/stable/41323627 (accessed 14 June 2017)

Rule 1992
John Rule, *Albion's People: English Society 1714–1815* (London and New York 1992)

Saunders 1995
Gill Saunders, *Picturing Plants: An Analytical History of Plant Illustration* (Berkeley and London 1995)

Savary des Bruslons 1723
Jacques Savary des Bruslons, *Dictionnaire Universel de Commerce* (Paris 1723)

Schwarz 1993
Catherine Schwarz (ed.), *The Chambers Dictionary* (Edinburgh 1993)

Sgard 1982
Jean Sgard, 'L'échelle des revenus', *Dix-huitième siècle* (1982), vol. 14, no. 1, pp. 425–33

Sharpe 1995
Pamela Sharpe, '"Cheapness and Economy": Manufacturing and Retailing Ready-Made Clothing in London and Essex, 1830–1850', *Textile History* (1995), 26(2), pp. 203–13

Shashoua 2008
Yvonne Shashoua, *Conservation of Plastics* (London 2008)

Simon 1996
Herbert Simon, *Sciences of the Artificial* (London 1996)

Skidelsky and Skidelsky 2012
Edward Skidelsky and Robert Skidelsky, *How Much is Enough?: Money and the Good Life* (London 2012)

Smith 1756
George Smith, *The Laboratory, or School of Arts* (London 1756)

Smith and Cothren 1999
C. Wayne Smith and J. Tom Cothren (eds), *Cotton: Origin, History, Technology and Production* (New York 1999)

Snodin and Styles 2001
Michael Snodin and John Styles, *Design and the Decorative Arts; Britain 1500–1900* (London 2001)

Somers 2017
Carry Somers, 'Foreword', *Fashion Revolution: Fashion Transparency Index 2017*, p. 3, https://issuu.com/fashionrevolution/docs/fr_fashiontransparencyindex2017 (accessed 27 May 2017)

Sorge-English 2005
Lynn Sorge-English, '"29 Doz and 11 Best Cutt Bone": The Trade in Whalebone and Stays in Eighteenth-Century London', *Textile History* (May 2005), 36(1), pp. 20–45

Spary 2000
E.C. Spary, *Utopia's Garden: French Natural History from Old Regime to Revolution* (Chicago 2000)

Staniland 2003
Kay Staniland, 'Samuel Pepys and his Wardrobe', *Costume* (2003), no. 37, pp. 41–50

Stemp 2015
Sinty Stemp, 'Postscript: London Couture 1975–2000', in Amy de la Haye and Edwina

Ehrman (eds), *London Couture 1923–1975: British Luxury* (London 2015), pp. 304–9

Stephenson 2013
Wesley Stephenson, *Indian Farmers and Suicide: How Big is the Problem?*, BBC News (23 January 2013), http://www.bbc.co.uk/news/magazine-21077458 (accessed 1 May 2017)

Stevenson 2003
John Stevenson, 'The Countryside, Planning, and Civil Society 1926–1947', in Jose Harris (ed.), *Civil Society in British History: Ideas, Identities, Institutions* (Oxford 2003), pp. 191–8

Stone-Ferrier 1985
Linda A. Stone-Ferrier, *Images of Textiles: The Weave of Seventeenth-Century Dutch Art and Society* (Ann Arbor 1985)

Styles 2007
John Styles, *The Dress of the People: Everyday Fashion in Eighteenth-Century England* (New Haven and London 2007)

Styles 2017
John Styles, 'Fashion and Innovation in Early Modern Europe', in Evelyn Welch (ed.), *Fashioning the Early Modern: Dress, Textiles and Innovation in Europe, 1500–1800* (Oxford 2017), pp. 33–55

Thépaut-Cabasset 2010
Corinne Thépaut-Cabasset, (ed.), *L'Esprit des Modes au Grand Siècle* (Paris 2010)

Thomas 1984
Keith Thomas, *Man and the Natural World. Changing Attitudes in England 1500–1800* (London 1984)

Travis 2004
Anthony S. Travis, 'Perkin, Sir William Henry (1838–1907)', *Oxford Dictionary of National Biography*, Oxford University Press (2004), http://www.oxforddnb.com.ezproxy2.londonlibrary.co.uk/view/article/35477 (accessed 28 August 2017)

Trevelyan 2004
Raleigh Trevelyan, 'Trevelyan, Paulina Jermyn, Lady Trevelyan (1816–1866)', *Oxford Dictionary of National Biography* (2004), http://www.oxforddnb.com/view/article/45577 (accessed 17 August 2016)

Turner 1996
Jane Turner (ed.), *Grove Dictionary of Art* (Oxford, 1996)

Wahnbaeck and Roloff 2017
Caroline Wahnbaeck and Lu Yen Roloff, *After the Binge, the Hangover: Insights into the Minds of Clothing Comsumers*, Greenpeace (2017), http://www.greenpeace.org/international/Global/international/publications/detox/2017/After-the-Binge-the-Hangover.pdf (accessed 1 May 2017)

Walkley 1981
Christina Walkley, *The Ghost in the Looking Glass: The Victorian Seamstress* (London 1981)

Wardle and de Jong 1985
Patricia Wardle and Mary de Jong, *Kant in Mode/Lace in Fashion: 1815–1914* (Amsterdam 1985)

Watt 2003
Judith Watt, *Ossie Clark 1965–74* (London 2003)

Webster 2017
Ben Webster, 'One Billion Will Be Added To World's Population By 2030', *The Times* (22 June 2017), p. 25

Williams 1991
Rosalind H. Williams, *Dream Worlds: Mass Consumption in Late Nineteenth-Century France* (Berkeley 1991)

Wilson (1985) 2011
Elizabeth Wilson, *Adorned in Dreams* (1985) (London 2011)

Wimmler 2017
Jutta Wimmler, *The Sun King's Atlantic: Drugs, Demons and Dyestuffs in the Atlantic World* (Leiden 2017)

Zola (1883) 1998
Émile Zola, *Au Bonheur des Dames* (1883) (Oxford 1998)

GLOSSARY

Band knife – Fabric-cutting machine with a continuous blade that can cut multiple layers of fabric at once.

Banyan – A robe-like garment for men, fashionable in the seventeenth and eighteenth centuries. Worn at home and in informal settings. Also called a nightgown.

Blockchain – A cumulative, chronological data structure that tracks transactions to create a digital record that can be distributed publically through an online network.

Block printing – A method of printing a pattern on cloth using wooden blocks on which the pattern is cut in relief. Colour is applied to the wooden block and then transferred to the cloth by placing the block in place and hitting it with a mallet. Each colour is applied with a different block.

Bobbin lace – Lace made by plaiting or twisting together a number of threads on small bobbins around pins that mark out the design, which is supported on a pillow.

Brocade – A type of weave in which a motif or design is created by adding extra weft threads that run only the width of the design and not the full width of the textile. The term was also used to describe patterned fabric in general in the nineteenth century.

Bustle – A pad or structure worn under, or attached to, the back of a skirt to create volume at the posterior.

Calash – A type of hat or large hood that stands away from the head with a structure supported by stiffeners (such as baleen or cane) and usually fastened with ties at the neck, worn by women during the eighteenth and first half of the nineteenth centuries as protection from the wind and rain.

Calico – A plain-weave, lightweight cotton textile, originally imported from India.

Caraco – A style of woman's jacket worn over a petticoat, which became fashionable in the second half of the eighteenth century. Usually made of cotton or linen.

Cellulose – Carbohydrate substance derived from plants, contained in all vegetable fibres and man-made fibres such as viscose, acetate, cuprammonium and Tencel.

Chenille – A fabric with a fur-like texture, made from special yarn (known as chenille yarn) with pile on all sides.

Cherryderry – A silk and cotton textile with a pattern of woven stripes or checks, first imported from India in the seventeenth century and later imitated in England.

Chiffon – A lightweight, sheer fabric with a dull finish made with tightly twisted yarn.

Cochineal – The red dye (carmine) from the *Dactylopius coccus* insect, which is produced by drying and crushing the female of the species.

Cotton – A vegetable fibre found in the seed pod of the *Gossypium* plant.

Crêpe – A medium or lightweight fabric with a textured surface achieved by using hard twisted yarns, textured yarns, chemical treatment or special weaves.

Drawloom – A type of loom used for weaving figured fabrics, in which cords are looped around each warp thread and lifted according to the pattern.

Eyelet – A small hole through which cord or tape is passed to join parts of a garment.

Fast (dyes) – When the colouring of a textile does not loose vibrancy when washed.

Felting – The process of matting together fibres with the aid of water and/or heat, and agitation or vibration, to form a textile. Most commonly used with wool.

Flax fibre – A vegetable fibre derived from the phloem tissue between the bark and the woody core of the flax plant (*Linum usitatissimum*).

Fulling – A stage of the finishing process in wool manufacture. Woven cloth is felted and compressed through exposure to moisture, heat, friction and pressure of varying degrees depending on the desired finish.

Fustian – A mixed fabric, usually with a linen warp and cotton weft.

Ground – The main structural element of a textile onto which decoration can be applied.

Hank – Yarn or spun fibre in a coiled form. Hanks are made in differing lengths depending on the fibre.

Haute couture – As defined by the *Chambre Syndicale de la Haute Couture*, unique models, designed and made in the atelier of the designer and sold to private clients. Models can be sold to other firms who also acquire the right to reproduce the designs.

Linen – Yarn or textiles made from flax fibre.

Loom – An apparatus for producing woven textiles by interlacing multiple yarns in a cross-wise formation.

Manchester velvet (velveret) – A pile textile made from cotton, with a plain-weave back. See *Velvet*.

Mantua – A trained open gown worn over a matching petticoat and stomacher, fashionable in the seventeeth and eighteenth centuries.

Moiré – A watered effect created by applying pressure to a ribbed fabric in a particular pattern, causing some ribs to flatten and reflect light differently to those not flattened.

Mordant – The substance that acts as a fixing agent when dyeing.

Nappa leather – Chrome-tanned animal leather with a soft and pliable finish, often dyed.

Organzine – Silk yarn made by twisting two or more strands of silk together in the opposite direction to that of which they are individually twisted.

Pelt – The fur-covered skin of an animal.

Pick – A single weft thread.

Plain weave – A basic cloth structure in which the weft travels under one warp yarn then over one warp yarn continuously to achieve an even, balanced weave. Also called 'tabby'.

Resist Dye – The process of colouring a textile in which areas of the cloth are reserved from dyeing by the application of a substance (usually wax) that is subsequently removed. Multicoloured textile can be created by repeating the process several times.

Retting – The process, in linen manufacture, of immersing the flax in water or laying it out in the field when damp to decompose the woody matter surrounding the fibres.

Scouring – The process, in wool manufacture, of either cleaning raw wool to remove dirt and grease, or laundering woven cloth before dyeing or finishing.

Silk – Yarn or textiles made from the continuous protein filament produced by the larvae of various insects, most commonly *Bombyx mori*.

Slub – Clumps of fibre spun (either intentionally or accidentally) into yarn to give an irregular finish.

Spinning – The process of turning short-staple fibres into a continuous thread.

Stays – An undergarment or bodice worn by women, reinforced with stiffeners such as baleen (whalebone), which moulds the figure into the fashionable silhouette.

Thrown silk – Silk yarn produced from multiple strands of reeled silk, which are twisted together to create a stronger or coarser yarn.

Twill – A textile weave in which the weft thread passes over more than one warp thread or vice versa, creating a diagonal pattern in the cloth. The most common is 2/2 twill where the weft yarn passes over two warp ends then under two warp ends continuously.

Velvet – A textile with a pile weave in which the warp is raised in loops above the ground weave. The loops can be cut or left uncut (uncut velvet).

Voided textile – A textile made with yarns of two different fibres in which a pattern is created by cutting away or dissolving (with chemicals) sections of one of the yarns. Also applied to velvets in which a pattern is created by only raising the pile in selected areas.

Walking dress – A dress or bodice and skirt ensemble worn during the day for activities outside the home.

Warp – The collection of continuous threads that make up the length of the cloth, through which the weft thread is passed to make the fabric.

Weft – The crosswise thread that is passed over and under the warp threads from selvedge to selvedge to make cloth.

Wool – Usually refers to fibre or textiles from sheep hair, but can also denote that of goat, alpaca, camel, llama and vicuña.

Woollen – Wool cloth made from yarn of shorter-staple wool that has been 'carded' so that the fibres mingle and sit across each other, creating a fibrous, textured and dull finish.

Worsted – Wool cloth made from yarn of longer-staple wool that has been 'combed' so that the fibres sit in line with one another, creating a smooth, more lustrous and compact finish.

Yarn – The continuous thread or strand of textile fibres, either endless filaments or shorter fibres spun together, that are woven, knitted, crocheted, braided or otherwise utilized to create a textile.

CONTRIBUTORS

Clare Browne
    Senior Curator of Textiles at the V&A
Oriole Cullen
    Curator of Textiles and Fashion at the V&A
Edwina Ehrman
    Senior Exhibition Curator at the V&A
Sarah Glenn
    Senior Textile Conservator at the V&A
Veronica Isaac
    Lecturer, University of Brighton; Assistant Curator in the Theatre and Performance Department at the V&A

Connie Karol Burks
    Assistant Curator of Furniture, Textiles and Fashion at the V&A
Lesley Ellis Miller
    Senior Curator of Textiles and Fashion at the V&A; Professor of Dress and Textile History, University of Glasgow
Dilys Williams
    Director of the Centre for Sustainable Fashion; Professor of Fashion Design for Sustainability, London College of Fashion

ACKNOWLEDGEMENTS

Many colleagues at the V&A and elsewhere have generously contributed to the research, development and realization of this book but I would particularly like to thank Dr Lesley Miller, Senior Curator of Textiles at the V&A, for her support, guidance and pertinent advice. I would also like to acknowledge the important contribution of Connie Karol Burks who as Research Assistant for the project worked tirelessly on both the exhibition and book, writing her own essay, preparing the appendices, managing the image list and providing me with vital back-up as I wrote.

At the V&A thanks are due too to Glenn Benson, Blythe House Manager, for his enthusiasm for the project and his generosity in sharing his horticultural knowledge and contacts; Christopher Wilk, Keeper of the Furniture, Textiles and Fashion Department and his colleagues Clare Browne, Oriole Cullen, Dr Susan North, Suzanne Smith and Sonnet Stanfill, Professor Claire Wilcox; Anna Jackson, Keeper of the Asia Department; Dr Joanna Norman, Acting Head of Research and Professor Bill Sherman, former Head of Collections and Research; Dr Veronica Isaac, who as a Research Assistant contributed to the exhibition's early development and Yona Lesger; Linda Lloyd-Jones, Head of Exhibitions and her colleagues Diana McAndrew and Sophie Parry; Joanne Hackett, Head of Textiles and Fashion Conservation and her colleagues Lara Flecker, Sarah Glenn, Keira Miller, Roisin Morris and Lilia Tisdall; for scientific analysis to Dr Brenda Keneghan, Senior Polymer Scientist, and Dr Lucia Burgio, Senior Scientist (Object Analysis); also to volunteers Elizabeth Ehrman, William de Gregorio, Janice Li, Elizabeth McFadden, April O'Neill and Dani Trew, who ably assisted with research. At the Natural History Museum I am extremely grateful to Julie Harvey, formerly Head of the Centre for Arts and Humanities Research, who encouraged and facilitated my research at the museum, providing me with a desk and introducing me to her colleagues; also to Max Barclay, Paul Martyn Cooper, Alex Fairhead, Hein van Grouw, Dr Blanca Huertas, Dr Charlie Jarvis, Paula Jenkins, Dr Justin Morris, Dr Robert Prys-Jones, Douglas Russell, Richard Sabin, Emily Smith, Jane Smith, Clare Valentine, Zoe Varley and Jo Wilbraham. Thanks are also due to Dr Susan Mossman and Natasha Logan at the Science Museum, and Dr Mark Nesbitt, Curator of the Museum of Economic Botany at Kew.

Fashioned from Nature has also benefited from the advice, expertise and support of staff at the London College of Fashion, University of the Arts London, particularly Professor Frances Corner OBE, Head of the London College of Fashion, Professor Dilys Williams, Director of the Centre for Sustainable Fashion, and Ligaya Salazar, Director of the Fashion Space Gallery; and from Professor Rebecca Earley and Professor Kay Politowicz at Chelsea College of Arts, University of the Arts London, who welcomed me so warmly to their research networks.

I would also like to thank the following people for their help and expertise: Rio Ali, Archivist at Margaret Howell; Anne-Marie Benson; Dr Rebecca Cairns-Wicks, Head of Operations, St. Helena National Trust; Cotton Incorporated; John David, Head of Horticultural Taxonomy at the Royal Horticultural Society; Brent Elliott, Head Librarian at the Lindley Library; Errol Fuller; Charlotte Holzer; Sue Kerry; Dr. Brenda King; Nina Marenzi and Sustainable Angle; Marine Conservation Society (www.mcsuk.org); Dr Ben Marsh; Dr Sonia O'Connor; Professor Alistair O'Neill; Professor Marcia Pointon; Dr Anita Quye; Adam Sizeland, Curator of the Museum of St. Helena; Nicholas Schonberger; Lou Stoppard; Professor John Styles; Luke Windsor; Dr Patricia Zakreski and Frank Zilberkweit; and for generously sharing their collections: Dr Pat Morris, MBE; Joanna Hashagen and Hannah Jackson at the Bowes Museum; Rosemary Harden and Fleur Johnson at the Fashion Museum Bath; Jocelyn Anderson Wood at the Maritime Museum in Hull; Susan Capes at Hull Leisure Ltd; and Alison Bodley and Dr M Faye Prior at York Castle Museum.

Both the exhibition and book have been enriched by garments that have been generously donated to the V&A by fashion companies in Britain and overseas. We are extremely grateful to them and to the fashion houses and private individuals who have lent objects from their archives and collections for display in the exhibition.

The design and production of the book has also involved many people. I would particularly like to thank our editor Kirstin Beattie for her patience and tact; Fred Caws for clearing the copyright on the many images and Richard Davis and Rob Auton in the V&A Photographic Studio. I am grateful too to copy-editor Linda Schofield, book designer Charlotte Heal, and Emma Woodiwiss, Production Manager at the V&A. Finally I would like to thank my fellow authors, Clare Browne, Oriole Cullen, Sarah Glenn, Veronica Isaac, Connie Karol Burks, Lesley Miller and Dilys Williams, and my husband Hugh Ehrman for his understanding and kindness.

PICTURE CREDITS

INDEX

Page numbers in *italic* refer to the illustrations

A

accessories 40–42, 82, 122

acid rain 93, 134

acrylic 124

Adidas 156

advertising 67, 69, 119

Africa 40, 109, 119

Agustin, Lenny *164*

air pollution 50, 71, 88–93, 104, 109, 134

Aire, river 30, 45, 93

Alaïa, Azzedine 133

Alembert, Jean Le Rond d' *50–51*

Alexandra, Princess 65–7

Alix (Madame Grès) *136*, 137, 138, 141

alizarin 79, 98

Amazon 157

aniline dyes 71, 76–9

Animal Product collection (V&A) *12–13*, 14

animals, cruelty to 45, 86, 88, 122, *122*, 134

Anning, Mary 101

Aral Sea 154, 155

Arkwright, Richard 36

Armstrong, John, *Newlands Corner 110*

Asia 28, 36, 40, 72, 115, 134

ASOS 160

Atloff, Jean Georges 76

Attenborough, Sir David 109, 155

Augusta, Princess 21

Aurelian Society 55

Australia 69, 101, 119, 178

Avedon, Richard 119

Avery Dennison 178

Away to Mars 168

B

Bacon, Vincent 55

Baekeland, Dr L.H. 130

Bailey, David 134

Bakelite 130

baleen 36–40, *37*, 95

Ballard, Bettina 143

Bangladesh 165, 175

BASF 79

BBC 109

Beaufort, Mary Somerset, 1st Duchess of 21

beavers 40, *41*, 45

beetles, iridescence 82, *83*, 85

Belle, James Cleveland 116

Bentham, Jeremy 45

Berketex 115

Bernhardt, Sarah 146

Bethnal Green Museum, London 14

Bevan, Edward J. 137

biomaterials 173

birds *81*, 82, *85*, 88, 98, 109, 134, *135*

Black, Sandy 120, *121*

Blame, Judy 160

bleaching *32*, 33, 71

Blumenfeld, Erwin, *Stockings* 130, *131*

Bodichon, Barbara Leigh Smith 76

Boode, Lewis William 82

boots 76, *76*, 133

Bradford *92–3*

Brando, Marlon 119

British Celanese 128

British Cellulose and Chemical Manufacturing Company 137

British Clothing Industry Association (BCIA) 114

British Fashion Council (BFC) 114

British Museum, London 65

British Nylon Spinners 130

British Painted Silk Manufactory 21

brocades 30

Brongniart, Adolphe-Théodore 101

Brontë, Charlotte 104

Brussels 33

Brydson, John 128

Budi, Felicia *164*

Buffon, Georges-Louis Leclerc, Comte de *16*, 17

Bulstrode, Buckinghamshire 21

Burdett-Coutts, Baroness 88

Burton, Montague *112*, 115–16

Busvine *127*, 128

butterflies 21

C

Calder, river 30, 93

Calico Printers Association 130

Callot Soeurs 128

Canada 86, 88

Canton 28, 40

Cardin, Pierre 133

Caribbean 40, 42, 71

Caro, Heinrich 79

Carothers, Wallace 130

cars 109, 134

Cartwright, Edmund 36

casein 128, 130

Castro, Orsola de 163

Celanese 128, 137

Celebes 72

cellophane 137, 141

celluloid 124, 128–30, 137

cellulose 75, 124, 128, 133, 137–41, 155

cellulose acetate 128, 130, *136*, 137, *138–40*, 141

Central America 75, 82

Centre for Sustainable Fashion (CSF) 155, 156, 165–8

Chambre Syndicale de la Couture Parisienne 114

Champot, Auguste *90–91*

Chanel, Gabrielle 'Coco' 116, 130

Chardonnet, Count Louis de 75

Charles, Prince of Wales 112–14

Charlotte, Queen 30, 47

Chelsea College of Arts, London 160

China 21, 28, 30, 40, 45, 72, 155, 157

chintz 30–33

Christian, Mr 21

Christianity 14–17

Clark, Galahad 163

Clark, Ossie 114, 124

climate change 151, 155, 157, 163, 173

coal-tar dyes 14, 76, 79

Cobbe, Frances Power 88

cochineal *15*

Coke, Lady Mary 30

Colcombet 137, 141

collectors 65, 104

Collinson, Joseph 88

Collinson, Peter 55

Colne, river 30

Colour Design and Style Centre 116

Columbia 175

Conran, Sir Terence 116

Conscious Earthwear 160

Cook, Captain James 101

Cooper, Gladys 122

Cording, J.C. 77

corsets 36, *37–9*, 95

Costello, Tony 124

cotton 28

  denim *118*, 119, 133, 163

  growing and harvesting 33, *70*, 160, *178–9*

  as high-fashion fabric 116–19

  in nineteenth century 71, 93

  pollution 93, 155

  printed fabrics 30–36, *34*

  properties 33

  traceability 175–8, *176–7*

  water requirements *154*, 155

Cotton Board 116

Council for the Preservation of Rural England (CPRE) 109

Courrèges, André *132*, 133

court dressmakers 67, 114

Courtaulds 128, 130, 133, 134

couturiers 95, 112, 114, 137–41

Cresta 115

crinolines 79

Cromford, Derbyshire 36

Crompton, Samuel 36

Cross, Charles F. 137

Cunningham, Allan 101
cupra 128
Curtis, William, *Flora Londinensis* 58
Cust, Hon. Mrs Edward 82

D
Dandridge, Joseph 55
Darwin, Charles 17
Davis, Sir George 116
Davison, Isabella 72, *73*
Defra 163
Deng Xiaoping 157
denim *118*, 119, 133, 163
department stores 67, 95
Derwent Valley 36
Design Copyright Act (1839) 69
Diana, Princess of Wales 112–14
Diderot, Denis, *Encyclopédie* 47, 50, *50*, *51*
Dieppe 40
Dior, Christian 112, *140*, 141, *142*, 143, *144*, 146
Dobbs, S.P. 114
Doueillet 67
Douro, Marchioness of 72
Dow Jones Sustainability Index 163
Drecoll 128
dresses
    silk mantua 30, *46*, 47–50, *52–4*
    walking dress *94*, 95–8, *96–7*
dressmakers 27, 67, 95, 114
DuPont 128, 130, 133
Duckworth, Susan 120
dyes
    alizarin 79, 98
    aniline 71, 76–9
    coal-tar 14, 76, 79
    methyl violet *78*
    natural dyes 98
    pollution 45, 155
    silk 50
    synthetic indigo 119
    Turkey red dyeing 79, *79*

E
East India Company 28, 36, 40
eBay 157
Eckersley, Tom, *Help Save Our World* 135
Ehret, Georg Dionysius 21, *24*
elastic 75–6
elephants 45
Elizabeth II, Queen 119
embroidery 55, *57*, 71, 82
employment 155
    slavery 11–14, 71, 155, 156
environmental issues 134, 141, 151–73, 175–8
Environmental Justice Campaign 175–8
ermine 47, 86
Esprit 160
Estethica 163
Eugénie, Empress 82
Eulalia, Princess *74*
Everard, Mrs *48*
Everybody's World 168
Evrything 178

F
fans 42–5, *42–3*, 82, *84–5*
Fashion Group of Great Britain 114
Fashion Revolution 165, 175
Fassett, Kaffe 120
feathers 71, 72, 82, *85*, 88, *90–91*, 98, 146
Fédération du Prêt-à-Porter Féminin 114
felt 40, 98

Ferguson, Esther *117*
ferns 100–105, *101–4*
Ferragamo, Salvatore 171
fibres 28–36
    man-made fibres 108, 116, 124–30
    see also cotton, wool *etc*
Filippa K 168
fireflies 82
First World War 109
Fisher, Eileen 168
flax 9, 28, 33, 45
Flemish lace 33
Fletcher, Dr Kate 173
Flintoft, Joseph and James 104
florilegia (flower books) 55
Le Follet 67
Ford, Thomas 69
Forster, Thomas 72
fossils 101
France
    fashion houses 67, 112
    lace *32*
    linen 33
    man-made fibres 128
    silk industry 21–7, 47, 50
    synthetic fabrics 137–41
Friends of the Earth 134
From Somewhere 168
Fuenmayor, Neliana 165
fur 71, 116
    accessories 40, *41*, 86
    ermine 47, 86
    in nineteenth century 86, *86–7*
    opposition to use of 88, *122*, 134
    pine marten fur 86, *87*
    in twentieth century 122–4, *123*
fustian 36
Futamura 137

G
Galliano, John 143
Garthwaite, Anna Maria 55–8, *58*
Gatty, Margaret, *British Sea-weeds* 65
Gerard, John, *Herball* 55
Germany 33, 79, 116, 128, 134
Gesner, Conrad, *Historia Animalium* 55
Gibb, Bill 120
Girardon, Delphine de 72
Glasgow 71
glass, spun 72, *74*
globalization 157
GMO seeds 160
gold thread 27
Goodone 168
Goodyear, Charles 75
Gore, Al 165
Gould, John 82
Les Grands Magasins du Louvre, Paris 95
Grant and Gask 72
Great Exhibition, London (1851) 14, 72, 77
Greenpeace 134, *164*, 165, 175
Grigsby, Emilie 128
Grose, Lynda 160

H
H&M 168, *169*
Haarlem *32*, 33
Hahn, Nicole 165
Hammesfahr, Hermann 72
Hamnett, Katharine 11, 160, *161*, 165
Hancock, Thomas 75
handbags *124*, *129*, 130

Hargreaves, James 36
Harper's Bazaar 113, 137
Harris, Moses 21
Harrods *86*
Hass, Hans and Lotte 109
hats 40, *41*, 82–6, *87*, 95, 98, *98–9*
Hawkins, Benjamin Waterhouse *15*
Hawkins, Desmond 109
Hello! 114
Hendrix, Jimi 124
Hepworth 116
Here Today Here Tomorrow 156
Hill, Octavia 88
Hoechst dyeworks 79
Holland 32, 33, 128
Hollar, Wenceslaus, *Group of muffs and articles
    of dress* 40, *41*
Hollywood 115
Holroyd, Amy Twigger 157
Hondius, Hendrik, *Nova totius terrarum orbis
    geographica... 22–3*
Honest By 178
Honiton lace 101
Horrockses Fashions *118*, 119
hosiery 130, *131*
The House of Beauty & Culture 160
Howell, Margaret 120, *121*
Hudson, William Henry 88
Hudson's Bay Company 40
Humanitarian League 88
Hummel, John James 79
Hyam & Company 69
Hyatt, John 128

I
ICI 130
Illustrated London News 72, *92–3*, *104–5*
Imperial Federation World Map *15*
Incorporated Society of London Fashion
    Designers 114
Independent 116
India 33–6, 71, 72, 82, *154*, 160
indigo 28, 119
Indonesia 175
insects 82, *83*, *85*
International Exhibition, London (1862) 72, 128
internet shopping 157, 160
IOU Project 168
Ireland 33
iridescence 71, 79–82
Iris Textiles *167*
Isaac, Veronica 82
Italy 30, 47, 112, 116, 119, 128
ivory 40, 42, *42–3*, 45, 128

J
Jaeger 119–20
Jaeger, Dr Gustav 119–20
James, Charles 137, *139*
Japan 88, 112, 116, 120, 128, 157, 160
Jarlgaard, Martine 165, 178
Java 72
jeans *118*, 119, 133, *153*, 155
Jenny 128
Jermyn, Dr George 101
jewel beetles 82, *83*, *85*
jewellery *81*
Jockey Corp 175
Johnson, Barbara 28, *29*
Johnson, Samuel 156
Jones, Stephen 143

K
Kagan, Sasha 120
Karina, Indita *164*
Keith, Linda 124
Kering 165–8
Kew Gardens, London 21, 76, 101
Kilburn, William 58, *60–61*
King, Martin Luther 173
Klein, Calvin 119
knitwear 112, 116, 119–20, *121*
Kroll, William 163

L
labels 175, 178
lace 32, 33, 71, 95, 101, *103*, 126
Lachaume 143
Lancashire 30, 36
Lanvin 128
Laroon, Marcellus, 'Old cloaks, suits and coats' *26*
leather 116, 120–22, *161*
Lebon, Mark 160
Lee, Vernon 88
Leeds 45
Lelong, Lucien 137
Leman, James 55
Lemon, Margaretta 88
Levant 47
Levant Company 28
Levi Strauss & Co. *118*, 119, 153
Lewin, Lucille 160
Libbey Glass Company 72
linen 9, 28, 33, 116, 120
lingerie 128
Linnaean Society 21
Linnaeus, Carl 55
Liverpool 72
Lombe, Sir Thomas 30
London 28
    fashion industry 27, 67, 112, 114
    fur trade 28
    international exhibitions 14, 65, 72, 77, 128
    printed textiles 36
    silk industry 30, 47, 55
London College of Fashion (LCF) 173
London Designer Collections 114
London Fashion Week 114, 163
London Model House Group 114
Louis XIV, King of France 27
Louis XV, King of France 17
Louvre Palace, Paris 55
Lowe-Holder, Michelle 168, *168*
Lycra® 133, *133*
Lynx 134
Lyon silks 21–7, 47, 50, 95

M
McCartney, Linda 134
McCartney, Stella 165, *167*
Macintosh, Charles 71, 75
McQueen, Alexander 143–6, *144–5*, *147*, 157
Macy, Joanna 173
madder 79
Madras 72
magazines 67, 114
makech beetles 82
Malaya 76
man-made fibres 108, 116, 124–34, 155
Manchester 69, 88–93, 130
mantua dresses 30, *46*, 47–50, *52–4*
maps 20, *111*, *162*, 163
Margaret, Princess 119
Marine Conservation Society *135*

Marks & Spencer 115, *162*, 163
Martin, Ellis *111*
Mary, Queen of Scots 55
Mechlin 33
menswear 67, 114, 116
Mercure Galant 27
mercury poisoning 98
metal threads 30, 47, *126*
Methodists 45
methyl violet 78, 79
Mexico 71
Middle East 28, 47, 50
Milan 112
millinery *see* hats
mink 122, 124
Minney, Safia 160
Moffet, Thomas, *Theatrum Insectorum* 55, *56*
moiré silk *80*, 82
monkeys *16*, 17, *123*
Montagu, Elizabeth 47
Mooney, Tara 173
Moore, John 160
Morris, Desmond 109
Mort, Frank 116
Moses, Elias & Son 69
Mosquito *115*
mother-of-pearl 40, 42, 82, *84*
moths, silk 28–30
museums 64, 65
muslin 71, 82, *83*

N
Nash, Joseph, 'Turkey: No. 1' *102*
Nash, Paul 116
National Geographic 146
National Nature Reserves 109
Native Americans 40
Natté, M. & E. 85
Natural History Museum, London 65
Natural History Museum, Oxford 101
Nemeth, Christopher 160
Net-a-Porter 160
New Look 143
New York 112, 119, 128, 175
New York Times 157, *172*, 173
New Zealand 119
newspapers 20–21, 67, 114
Next *115*, 116
Nicoll, H.J. & D. 69
Nielsen UK 175
Nike 156, *158–9*, 168
Noble, George, *View of the Court of St. James's 48*
North America 28, 40, 47, 86, 112, 114
North Pacific Seal Convention (1911) 88
Norway 86
Norwich 21, 27
Nova 124
nylon 130, *132*, 133, *142*

O
Obama, Barack 173
Observer 133
oil 134, *135*
Ordnance Survey *111*
Orsini, Anna 163
Orta, Lucy 157–60, *161*
ostrich feathers 88, 146
Oxfam *162*
Oxford University 101

P
Pagano, Margareta 116

Paisley 71
Pakistan 163
parachute silk 116, *117*, *162*
Paris 27, 65, 115
    couturiers 67, 112, 114
    department stores 95
    Japanese designers 120
    synthetic fabrics 128, 133, 137
Paris Ethical Fashion Show 163
Parkes, Alexander 128
Parkin, Molly 124
Parkinson, Norman *113*
Patagonia 163, *172*, 173
Paterson, H., 'Gathering ferns' *104–5*
patterned textiles 55–8, 65, 95
Paxton, Sir Joseph 65
People for the Ethical Treatment of Animals
    (PETA) 134
People Tree 160
Pepys, Samuel 40
Perkin, William Henry 76, 79
Perspex *129*, 130, *132*, 143
Peru 47
Pfeiffer Brunel 86, *86*
Philippines 72
Phillips, Eliza 88
Philosophical Transactions 21
Pieters, Bruno 165, *166*, 178
PimaCott® 178
Pinault, François-Henri 165
Pine Coffin, Brigadier John 101
pine marten fur 86, *87*
pineapple fibre 71–2, 73, *170*, 173
Planet Money radio show 175, 178
planetary boundaries 151, *152–4*
plastics 124, 128–30, 141
Poiret, Paul *126*, 128
pollution 14, 151, *164*
    air pollution 50, 71, 88–93, 104, 109, 134
    water pollution 45, 50, 88–93, 134, *135*, *154*, 155
polyester 128, 130, 155
Pomet, Pierre, *A Compleat History of Druggs* 58, *59*
Pop Art 130
Portland, Margaret, Duchess of 21
Potosí mines 47
Powis, Lady 30
Primark 165
Principles 116
Pringle 119
printed textiles 36, 55, 58, *60–61*
Provenance 165, 178
Pulse report 175
Puma 156
Punch 88, *89*
PVC 130–33, *132*

Q
Quant, Mary 114, 130–33, *132*
The Queen 65, 114

R
radio 109, 175, 178
Raeburn, Christopher *162*, 163
railways 64, 65
Ramblers Association 109
Ramsay, Allan, *Mrs Everard 48*
Rana Plaza factory collapse 165, 175
Ratty, Sarah 160, *161*
Rauschenberg, Robert 168
rayon 75, *127*, 128, 134, 137
Re-Made in Leeds 168
ready-made clothing 67–9

ready-to-wear 114–16
Rébé 143
Reboux, Caroline *87*
Renaissance 55
repairs 27, 172
reptile skins 116, 122, 124, *124–5*
repurposing 168
resilience 156–7
Restoration 27
'Rhodophane' 141
Ricci, Filippo 163
Ricci, Nina 137
road transport 109
Roberts, Patricia 120
roller-printed textiles *79*
Rose, Stuart 163
Rowan Yarns 120
Royal Botanic Gardens, Kew 21, 76, 101
Royal Commission for Inquiring into the
　　Pollution of Rivers 93
royal fashions 27, 47, 65, 112–14
Royal Society 21, 55
Royal Society for the Prevention of Cruelty to
　　Animals (RSPCA) 88
Royal Society for the Protection of Birds (RSPB)
　　88, 134, 143–6
rubber 71, 75–6, *76*, 128, 133, 137
Ruisdael, Jacob van, *View of Haarlem with
　　Bleaching Grounds 32*, 33
Ruskin, John 88, 101
Russia 40, 47, 71, 86, 88

S
St Helena 101
St James's Palace, London 47, *48*
Saliba, Mayya *170*
Sambourne, Edward Linley, 'A Bird of Prey' *89*
Savile Row, London 67
Schiaparelli, Elsa 128, 137, 141
Schwabe, Louis 72
Scotland 33, 65, 69, 71, 119
Scott, Sir Peter 109
Sea Birds Preservation Act (1869) 88
sealskin 86, *86*, 88
second-hand clothes 27, 67
Second World War 109, 112, 115, 116
Sekers, Agota and Miki 141
Selfridges 168
semi-synthetic fabrics 137–41
sericulture 28–30, 47
sewing machines 67
Shell 109, *110*
shells *138*, 146
Shepherd, Arthur *112*
Shields, Brooke 119
shipping containers 157
shoes 28, 122, 130
shops 67, 69, 95, 114–16
shot silk 82
Sicily 47
Sierra Leone 109
silica 72
silk 25, *31*, 36
　　Lyon silks 21–7, 47, 50, 95
　　mantua dresses 30, *46*, 47–50, *52–4*
　　moiré silk *80*, 82
　　parachute silk 116, *117, 162*
　　silkworms 28–30, *29*, 47, 71
　　shot silk 82
　　Spitalfields industry 30
　　velvet *35*, 36, 95
silver threads 27, 30, 47

Simon, Herbert 156
Singapore 72, 76
slavery 11–14, 71, 155, 156
Sloane, Sir Hans 55
Smedley, John 120
Smith, Frederick William, 'Rhodochiton volubile' *66*
Smith, Sir James Edward 21
Smith, Dr Robert Angus 88–93
snake skin 122, 124, *125*
soap 71
soda ash 71
Somers, Carry 175
South America 50, 71, 72, 75, 82
South-East Asia 40, 134
Space Age 130, 133
Spain 30, 47, 116
Sparkes Hall, Joseph 76
Spitalfields, London 30, 47
spun glass 72, 74
stays 36, *37–9*
steam power 36
Stéphanie, Princess of Belgium 101
stockings 130, *131*
Stoppard, Lou *168*
Storey, Helen 133, *133*
Streat, Sir Raymond 116
suede *125*
sustainability 155–73
Sustainable Apparel Coalition (SAC) 163, 178
Sutherland, Graham 116–19
'sweated' labour 11, 67
Sweden 86
Switzerland 79
synthetic fibres 108, 116, 124–34, 155

T
T-shirts *174*, 175–8, *176–7*
tailoring trade 30, 67
Taiwan 28
The Tatler 114
television 109
Tencel® 133, *133*
Tender Co. 163
Tennant, Charles 71
Terylene 130
Thames, river 36
theatre 67
Thomson, Richard 116
The Times 65
Top Shop 115–16
'tortoiseshell' 40–42
traceability 175–8, *176–7*
transparency 156, 165, 175
transport 109, 134
Treacy, Philip 146
tree ferns *100*, 101
Trevelyan, Paulina Jermyn 101, *103*
Trevelyan, Walter Calverley 101
Tridou, Madame *94*, 95–8, *96–7*
Trump, Donald 151
Turkey 30
Turkey red dyeing 79, *79*
tweed 112, *112*, 120
Twiggy 124

U
United Nations 151, 157, 163
United States of America
　　animal protection laws 88
　　cotton production 71
　　environmental issues 157, 165, 173, 175–8
　　furs 122

man-made fibres 128, 130, 137
　　ready-to-wear 114
upper class 65–7
urea-formaldehyde resins 130
Uzbekistan 175

V
Valenciennes lace 32, 33
Vallet, Pierre, *Le Jardin du Roy Très Chrestien
　　Henri IV 55*
Van Swinderen, Elizabeth Lindsay de Marees 86
Vanderbilt, Gloria 119
Vasudevan, Shibin 156
Veasey, Nick, *38–9, 98*
velvet *35*, 36, 95
Veruschka 124
Victoria, Queen 76, 101
Vilmorin and Andrieu 143
viscose-rayon 75, *127*, 128, 137
Vogue 122, 143
Voltaire, François Marie Arouet de 42
vulcanization, rubber 75

W
Wales 69, 115
walking dress *94*, 95–8, *96–7*
walking sticks 40, 42
Wallace, Alfred Russel 17
Walmart 163
Walters, Hon. Mrs 21
Ward, Dr Nathaniel Bagshaw 101–4
Wardian cases 101–4, *102*
Washington Convention (1975) 134
waste 14, 155, 156, 173
water pollution 45, 50, 88–93, 134, *135, 154*, 155
water supply 151, *153*, 155
waterproof clothing 76
Watson, Emma 6, 7
Watts, George Frederick 88
　　A Dedication 89
weaving, silk 47–50
Weisz, Otto 119
Wellington, Duke of 72
West Africa 40
West Indies 28, 72
Westwood, Vivienne 112
whalebone 36–40, *37*
whaling *44–5*, 45
Whistles 160
Whitney, Eli 71
Wichmann, Joachim, *The Whale Fishery 44–5*
The Wild One (film) 119
Wilkes, Benjamin 21
Williams & Sowerby 72
wool 28, 30, *31*, 36, 71, 93, 116, 119–20, *121*
World Wildlife Fund (WWF) 134, 163
World's Columbian Exposition, Chicago (1893) *74*
worsteds 30
Worth, Charles Frederick 67

Y
York 27
Yorkshire 30, 45, 93
Young, Baroness Lola 156
Youth Hostels Association (YHA) 109

Z
Zappos 157
Zara 157
Zola, Émile, *Au Bonheur des Dames* 95
Zoological Society 65